WHATEVER HAPPENED TO PEGGY SUE?

A Memoir by Buddy Holly's Peggy Sue

PEGGY SUE GERRON
GLENDA CAMERON

2008

Togientertainment inc.
Subsidiary of The Owners Group Inc.

PUBLISHED BY

TogiEntertainment, Inc.   TogiEntertainment, Inc.
56 Expressway Place   602 South Broadway Avenue
5601 NW 72nd   Tyler, TX 75701
Street Suite 342   903-595-4249
Oklahoma City, OK 73132
405-728-5536

Subsidiary of
The Owners Group, Inc.
Tyler, TX

First published by TogiEntertainment, Inc. 11/29/2007
First released by TogiEntertainment, Inc. 3/1/2008

ISBN: 978-0-9800085-1-7 (sc)
ISBN: 978-0-9800085-0-0 (hc)

Printed in the United States of America

This book is printed on acid-free paper.

Acknowledgements

I started keeping a journal about the time I became engaged to Jerry Allison, drummer for The Crickets. He drew me into his world of rock 'n' roll in 1957 when he invited me to The Biggest Show of Stars where I heard my friends, Buddy Holly and The Crickets, sing my namesake song, "Peggy Sue," for the first time. As time went by, I continued making journal entries to give me a sense of security in a world that was moving so fast I didn't feel as though I could keep up. This book is a culmination of those journal entries and my memories of those days. It has been a work of love, long hours, and tears. I want to thank all the precious people whose gift of friendship, advice, and assistance helped make it possible.

Sandra Harper, Al Omernick, John Langford, Tom Reed, Melody Potter, Mark Faulk, Leor Zolman, Shannon Reinert, George Stephenson, Erik Anderson, Kenneth Broad, David and Maryline Bigham, Anne Linville, Larry Welborn, Jerry and Pamela Naylor, Danny Todd, Casey Wiley, Randy Smith, Eddie Weir, Betty Lou Drury, Johnnie von Aspern, Ingrid Kaiter, Travis Holley, Patricia Holley, Roddy Jordan, Dick Cole, Don Kittrell, Tim Rice, Bobby Vee, Chris Rees, Dr. C. J. Schoenrock, Georgiana Veit Hagen, Rita Box Peek, Mike Gruber, Marco Ellman, David Brandon, Gary and Ramona Tollett, Bill and Sharon Griggs, Alex Price Kissire, Carl Bunch, Tommy Allsup, George and Barbara Tomsco, Alan Clark, Frank Blanas, Donna Blanas, Terry Nolan, Stan Lark, Terry and Jan Wilson.

These acknowledgements would not be complete without remembering the ones who have already passed. In memory of rock 'n' roll, they are:

Norman Petty, Vi Petty, Norma Jean Berry, Jimmy Self, Ray Ruff, George Atwood, Robert Linville, Max T. von Aspern, Chuck Thorpe.

Finally, I give my sincere thanks to all the fans all over the world who have asked for my story and who have kept the music and the memories alive.

Contents

CHAPTER ONE

The Lubbock High School Years

*I*t was September 1956, my first week at Lubbock High School, and I was terrified. Members of the football team barreled around corners and vaulted down stairs as if they owned the school. I knew I'd go sprawling across the floor if one of them ever ran into me, and being a dreadfully shy sophomore, I'd be completely mortified as I lay there with books scattered and cancans showing.

I managed to navigate the stairs without incident, and breathed a huge sigh of relief as I walked out the back doorway on my way to the band room—an annex outside the main building, sharing prestige with auto mechanics and woodworking, very close to the garbage incinerator and back alley. Without warning, a young man jerked open one of the school's large entry doors and bolted into the hallway. I hadn't seen him coming and, I guess, he hadn't seen me either because he knocked me totally to the floor, causing my books to scatter everywhere. My worst nightmare had come true. There I sat with my new poodle skirt and cancans up over my knees, completely humiliated.

Making sure to balance the guitar he held in one hand and the amp he had in the other, he rushed to my side and bent over me. "I'm terribly sorry, but I don't have time to pick you up. But, you sure are pretty," he said with a sincere tone in his voice. "Are you hurt?"

"Only my dignity," I replied. As he started walking toward the auditorium, leaving me on the floor trying to gather my books around me, I began to doubt the sincerity of his apology.

A girl, who'd seen the whole thing, came over and asked, "Don't you know who that is?"

"No, I don't know who that is," I said, and at that particular time, I didn't care.

"Wow, that's Buddy Holley!" She sighed, as she drifted off into her own world at the thought of being so near to him.

"That's Buddy Holley?" I'd heard him on the radio but had never seen him. I found out later that day that he'd been invited to participate in a school assembly even though he'd graduated the year before.

Despite my initial embarrassment, high school life began to get better. A few weeks after school started, one of the boys in my band class asked me to go on a double date. I was thrilled. I'd met him when we were in band together at R.W. Matthews Junior High School. At the time, I was a twelve-year-old, seventh-grade, alto-saxophone player; he was a thirteen-year-old, ninth-grade drummer. It'd been crush at first sight for me, and I'd continued to like him and think he was *kinda cute* even after he hurt my feelings one day when he commented that I was a "short, fat little girl."

I was certain about one thing: It was never boring when he was around, especially during band practice. Jerry Allison always found a way to get the band director's attention, and that didn't seem to be too difficult because Director Paul Lovett's forte was also the drums. Not surprisingly, Jerry had been one of his favorite students. Mr. Lovett, who had played and toured professionally in a band before becoming a teacher, encouraged all of us to be more outgoing, personality wise, because he wanted us to enjoy entertaining and not fear the audience. I wasn't so sure Jerry needed any additional encouragement in that area.

After basically ignoring me in junior high, Jerry became quite friendly once I entered high school. He called me a few times just to chat, and our conversations became longer with each successive phone call.

My family only had one phone, and like any teenager, I was a phoneaholic. My mother would become so annoyed when I'd keep the line busy preventing her from making any calls that, sometimes, I had to go over to my friend Wilma's house and use her phone.

One day when I visited Wilma, she was on the phone talking to Jerry. Her mother summoned her to go take care of her little sister, so she handed me the receiver without saying anything to Jerry and whispered,

"He'll think it's me. You talk to him until I get back. He won't know the difference."

I picked up the conversation where he and Wilma had left off. But sometimes, I'd forget that I wasn't Wilma when he'd ask a question, so finally, I had to tell him who I really was. Jerry said, "I thought so."

Later, I learned that Wilma had had a crush on Jerry at that time, but he was only talking to her because he knew we were close friends, and he was seeking her advice on ways to ask me out. When he finally did muster up enough nerve to ask me for a date, I immediately quipped, "Are you sure I'm not too fat?"

"You're not fat anymore," he said.

"Well, *you're* still short," I replied.

That irritated him, but he asked me again if I wanted to double date.

"Who with?" I asked nervously, as this would be my first date ever.

"My best friend and his girlfriend," Jerry said. "We'll go to a movie at the State Theater downtown."

The State was the newest movie theater in Lubbock, and I hadn't been there yet, so thinking it would be great fun, I agreed—but only if my parents approved. I thought they'd be more likely to allow me to go if it was a double date. Quite honestly, I felt the date would go smoother if there were other people along to talk to, and I believed Jerry felt the same way.

As protocol dictated, Jerry came to the door to pick me up. Walking to the car, we heard my mother remind me to be home by eleven. Just as I started to get into the front seat, Jerry's friend let out a loud, rolling, hiccupy laugh. I looked over my shoulder at him and started to giggle. It was Buddy Holley, the guy who'd knocked me over in the hall. Scooting under the steering wheel, Jerry asked," What's so funny? Why are y'all laughing?"

Buddy chuckled. "I've already overwhelmed your Peggy Sue."

"Overwhelmed is right," I said. "He knocked me down in the hallway at school."

We all laughed. Then I was introduced to Echo McGuire, Buddy's date. They had graduated together and had dated on and off throughout high

3

school. After years of attending their children's school functions together, Buddy's and Echo's parents had become close friends.

I thought Echo was cute. She was really short—I thought about 5' at the most. She had dark, curly hair, and a very big smile with amazingly white teeth, in contrast to Buddy's, which had that West Texas brown-fluoride stain on them. I also thought Echo was nicely dressed for the date. She was wearing penny loafers and a shirtwaist dress with a cancan petticoat under the full skirt. She had a small waistline, but the belt that curved down in the back made it look even smaller.

Throughout my sophomore year, Jerry and I went steady off and on, and I got to know his best friend, Buddy Holley, even better. He was so likable that it didn't take long to feel extremely comfortable around him. As a threesome, Jerry, Buddy, and I spent most of our time together just hanging out at my house, listening to records or to Jerry arguing politics with my dad. We also hung out at the Hi-D-Ho, drinking Cokes or a sour lime, and talking—seeing and being seen.

Every important thing that happened to a couple became common knowledge at the Hi-D-Ho drive-in in Lubbock, Texas. The main drive-in was on 19th Street right down from Lubbock High; the Hi-D-Ho Jr. was on College and about 1st Street. The building had plate-glass windows in the front that curved down the sides so we could drive all the way around and see who was there and with whom. We would drive from one Hi-D-Ho location to the other, park, get out of the car, watch the guys kick tires, and talk to our friends. All my girlfriends dragged the drive-in on Saturday night. If we had a date, we did the same thing. Going steady? The Hi-D-Ho was the place to be seen. Having problems? The Hi-D-Ho was the place to work things out. I always wondered how many girls were proposed to at the Hi-D-Ho and how many breakups happened there.

Every now and then, Buddy, Echo, Jerry, and I would double date by going bowling, horseback riding, or out to see a movie. Jerry, a senior, was playing gigs part-time with Buddy and other musicians around town, and although Buddy worked as a tile setter in his oldest brother Larry's tile business when he needed money, he was seriously pursuing his music career, too. As a result, the two of them were always talking about music during our dates. Echo never failed to express her opinions about music either. Her church approved of neither musical instruments as part of the worship service nor dance of any kind because gyrating bodies could lead to impure thoughts or actions. Being a staunch member of the Church of Christ, Echo preferred that the guys did something else. After all, people danced to their music, so they were creating an unwholesome atmosphere. I told her I was sorry she didn't dance because it was really a lot of fun. I said that I loved to dance, but the dances I went to were usually at school, church, or parties at a friend's home, and my parents wouldn't let me attend them unless they were being chaperoned. Of course, I was only a sophomore whereas she had already graduated, so she would look at me like I was just young and pathetically unknowledgeable and get back on her soapbox that Buddy and Jerry should abandon their thoughts of a music career.

Mostly, Jerry and Buddy were playing country western music then—*Grand-Ole-Opry* style—and I didn't really like it. In fact, I once told Jerry that Buddy sang through his nose like a hillbilly.

My favorite music was R&B—Clyde McPhatter, Fats Domino, The Platters, Lloyd Price with his "Lawdy Miss Clawdy," Hank Ballard's "Work With Me Annie" and "Annie Had A Baby," Clarence 'Frogman' Henry's "Ain't Got No Home," and LaVern Baker. My all-time favorite was "Devil or Angel" by The Clovers. I drove Mother crazy with that one.

I was thrilled that Jerry and Buddy liked my R&B records. Of course, I shouldn't have been surprised because Elvis had been to Lubbock in early 1955 and had set everybody on fire with his style. Jerry started borrowing my records so he and Buddy could study the sound.

♬

Jerry and I had our *final* breakup in the summer of '56, not long after he graduated. At school, I'd become known as *Jerry's girl*, so even during the times we weren't going steady, the other boys were hesitant to ask me out. Basically, I was bored going steady with Jerry. He'd hardly ever walked with me between classes because he had a penchant for always wanting to be the first one out of class so he could go behind the band room and smoke. At first, I thought smoking made him look like a rebel, and, maybe, that had been part of the reason why I'd been attracted to him, but now, I used his smoking and the fact that he wouldn't be in high school because he had graduated as reasons to break up with him.

If truth be told, there were even more things that bothered me. Before school had ended, a girl in Jerry's senior class had started running over to me every time she saw me just to step on my white buck shoes, leaving a mark on them. When I told Jerry about her, he just laughed and said, "Oh, yeah. She's a good drinking buddy of mine." I was feeling more like a possession than a girlfriend. I was going steady, but was he?

I decided it was time to break up with Jerry during the band banquet at the end of the year. My friends, who had been given corsages that spanned from their knuckles all the way to their elbows, made jokes about how small Jerry's tiny split-flower wrist corsages always were. I was aware that his mother was the one placing the orders, but that hadn't softened my feelings any, especially since I knew he was playing at clubs on weekends and had the money to buy me really nice corsages like the ones my friends wore. So, when banquet time came around, I was once again embarrassed by my corsage. I know it sounds petty, but this was the last straw. I vowed that would be our last date.

After I gave Jerry back his class ring, I began to receive many social invitations, which quickly boosted my self-image. I was really thrilled when the boy whom I enjoyed dancing with at school parties called and asked me for a date on Saturday night. We went to the movies and then stopped by the Hi-D-Ho for a sour lime. I thought that we had a great time, but the following Monday at school, he hardly talked to me. The whole week went by, and finally, on Friday, he said, "I need to talk to you—and, besides, I want you to sign my yearbook."

"Sure. I'll meet you in the hall where all the windows are right after school," I said. I could hardly wait. I just knew there had to be a reason why he was ignoring me, and now maybe I'd find out.

As soon as the bell rang, I hurried to the hall where he was waiting for me. He smiled and I smiled, and then I asked, "What's been wrong with you all week? You sure haven't been very friendly."

"I need to tell you something," he said, looking around to make sure no one could hear us.

"Okay. Talk to me," I said.

"I need you to promise that you'll not say anything about what I'm going to tell you. I mean it. I don't want to have any more problems about this, and I don't want it all over school," he said.

"Okay, I promise. Now tell me." I was getting impatient with his clandestine attitude.

"After I took you home Saturday night, I was followed all the way home from your house. When I pulled into my driveway, a car stopped, and someone yelled out the window, 'So *you* had a date with Peggy Sue.' It was Jerry Allison, and there were some more boys in the car. I just went into the house, and they left. I think it's better if we don't date."

"Are you sure it was Jerry Allison?" He nodded, and I said, "I can't apologize for Jerry, but I'm terribly embarrassed that happened to you." He signed my yearbook, I signed his, and we said goodbye. As I walked away, I thought, Peggy Sue, you haven't done anything wrong. Why did you feel so embarrassed? But I was just devastated. When I got home, I sobbed to my mother, "Jerry Allison has embarrassed me."

"No, Jerry Allison has embarrassed himself. Now, just forget about it."

I sniveled. "His parents need to be told what he does."

"It's not your place to do that," Mother said.

About that time, Daddy came home from work, and sobbing all over again, I immediately told him about the incident. Naturally, he agreed with my mother. "She's right. Just let it go," he said. "By the way, Lillie, I invited a really nice young man from the base for dinner Saturday afternoon. He's very homesick and very bored. There aren't a lot of social events for the men living on the base. He's Catholic, and he's stationed here to get his pilot's license. He's just a little older than Peggy Sue. And, Peggy Sue, since school's about out, it won't hurt you to take Bill to the Newman Club at church so he can meet some more young people. He's from Florida and hates what he calls the West Texas desert. He can't understand why anybody would want to live here." My father chuckled.

These days, the people of Lubbock looked down on the young men stationed at Reese Air Force Base, who were considered transients and possible predators, especially after what had happened to Joyce White. Approximately a year before I attended Lubbock High, the young local woman was reported missing and finally found buried in a cotton row. The stalks had been put back in the earth to make it look like a normal cotton field. She'd been dating a young officer who was about to become a pilot. They had announced to their parents that they'd be getting married as soon as he finished school. Shortly thereafter, she'd gone missing, which was completely out of character for her, and no one could find her. They questioned the young man and insisted on a lie-detector test; each time, the results came back normal. Finally, after several months had gone by, the young officer confessed and showed the authorities where he had dug her shallow grave in the snow. The reason he had killed her was because she was pregnant, and the military would've immediately dismissed him because of it. After that, it was nearly impossible for a young man from Reese Air Force Base to get acquainted with anybody unless he knew someone who could introduce him.

Anyway, Bill was nice. Mother fixed a great dinner, and we all talked and laughed. At about nine o'clock, Daddy said, "Peggy Sue, you can drive Bill back to the base for me, but you come straight home."

"Oh! Keen! I get to drive on the base?" I asked excitedly.

"Remember all the rules," Daddy warned.

The drive from my house to the base was about fifteen miles of straight road. It was not really dark yet but was getting close. West Texas stays light longer than most places because the land is so flat that there's nothing to block the sun until it falls off the horizon. I drove up to the gates where the MPs were guarding the entrance and slowed down, as Daddy had showed me, in case they wanted me to stop. But they just waved me through, probably because Daddy was a civil engineer in the Federal Civil Service and had all kinds of stickers on his car. Bill guided me to his barracks, stepped out of the car after thanking me for bringing him back, and then asked, "Is it all right if I call you about going to church?"

"Of course. I'd like you to meet some of my friends," I replied, as I reached over and locked the passenger front door. Once again, the MPs just waved me through the gates. I turned on the radio. I could hear Lubbock's deep-throated, sexy-sounding DJ, Misty, on the station, spinning songs for lovers in the night. Humph—'40s music. My sister's music.

Just as I turned off the radio, I noticed a car, practically on my bumper, that seemed to have materialized out of nowhere. I thought it was strange that I hadn't seen it follow me when I left the base because there hadn't been anything on the road to block the view, and there were no other entrances to the road, just desolate farmland. Just about the time I decided it was a Lubbock police car, lights began to flash, warning me to pull over. But, something wasn't right—the lights were on the windows down by the doors instead of on top of the car. I looked at the speedometer to see if I was speeding, knowing that Daddy would not let me drive to the base again if I was, but I wasn't speeding. I pulled over, and to my surprise, it was not a police officer that got out but an MP from the base. The person in the passenger seat stayed in the car. How could I have not seen them when I left? I looked at the officer and asked, "Is something wrong, Sir?"

"No, I just wanted to see who was driving this car," he replied stiffly.

"This is my father's car. Do you want to see my license?" I asked when he didn't say anything else.

"No, that's okay. You can go straight home now," he said robotically.

How did he know where I was going? When I got home, I told Daddy the whole story. I still couldn't figure out how the car had managed to slip up behind me without my knowledge. Daddy looked puzzled and said, "I'll check into it Monday and find out what they were doing."

The subject was not brought up again until a few weeks later when nearly the same eerie thing repeated itself—only this time, I was singled out while driving on one of Lubbock's busiest streets.

I'd been cruising the Hi-D-Ho with some girlfriends and had just dropped off the last passenger. It was about nine o'clock, and I was on my way home for the night. Suddenly, what looked like the same car that had stopped me before was flashing its lights behind me.

"Did I do something wrong? Do you want to see my license?" I asked the MP.

He said, "No, just be careful going home."

A million thoughts raced through my mind as I pulled away from the curb. At first, I mostly focused on how creepy I thought this whole situation was and how strange the MP seemed, but then I began to fume and said out loud, "How *dare* he tell me what to do when I was not even near the base. How can an MP just stop someone on a Lubbock street? Just wait till I get home and tell my father."

Daddy was up when I got home. He listened intently as I told him what had happened. Afraid he would take the car away from me, I ended with, "I was driving on College Avenue, not even near the air base. How can they stop me?"

9

Daddy looked a little uneasy. "I don't know. Maybe they're checking the car because it's registered to me on the base. They're probably wondering who you are and why you're driving the car. All right...all right...we'll talk about it later. I'll try to find out what's going on."

As I left the room, I heard him say, "Lillie, I really don't like this. I don't mind them keeping tabs on me because of my security status, but I don't like it at all when they extend the watch to you or my daughter. Maybe I should just get another car for the two of you to drive."

♫

It looked like summer was going to be really fun. I went swimming every day at Mackenzie Park, and this summer, we were going to take our first vacation ever. We hadn't been able to go anywhere before because my father had been sick since the winter of my third-grade year when we were living in Fort Worth, Texas. The year before, we'd moved there from Roswell, New Mexico.

As a child, I remember a doctor coming to the house to take care of him, and a nurse who lived down the street would come to administer B-12 shots and some other medicine. I didn't know what it was. The long and short of it is that Daddy had been very sick for a long time. I remember the doctor talking about his extremely low blood pressure, and for a while, he couldn't walk alone or even drive a car. Neither he nor my mother would ever discuss his health with me. For that matter, they would never discuss any of the strange events that periodically happened to my family. But now, he appeared to have truly recovered from the mysterious illness. So, he had purchased a used brown and tan Ford, and we were going to drive all the way to Sacramento, California, to visit my only sister, Johnnie. I could hardly wait to see the ocean off of San Francisco Bay. I'd never seen an ocean before.

For the first time ever, Daddy, Mother, and I really had fun together. I drove most of the way to California and all the way back home at the end of our visit. Unfortunately however, things changed for the worse once we got back to Lubbock and school started. I couldn't study due to all the yelling that was going on in the house between my mother and father, and consequently, my grades began to drop. Whatever the problem was between my parents, I was not privy to the cause, but I surmised that my mother was having some medical problems and was easily upset. Anyway, the last place anyone wanted to be was at my house as life there was extremely unpleasant. I stopped inviting my girlfriends over, and finally, Daddy called Johnnie to see if I could live with her. He was concerned that I would lose interest in school and flunk out, and he didn't intend to allow that to happen. For that reason, in December of my junior year, I moved to Sacramento to live with Johnnie and her husband, Von. I finished the spring semester at El Camino High School and then returned home to Lubbock to spend time with Mother and Daddy, as well as attend summer school at Lubbock High. In the fall, I returned to Sacramento to attend Bishop Armstrong Catholic Girls School.

It was beautiful in California, but I truly missed West Texas. I missed my parents and the friends I'd left behind—even Jerry, who had become almost a permanent fixture at my house while we'd been dating. Sure, we'd had our differences, but we'd also grown very close. Even though it'd been nearly a year since I'd seen him, I hadn't stopped thinking about him, and I missed him more than I wanted to admit.

The last time I'd seen Jerry, he and Buddy had come by my house on 1st Street in Lubbock. I'd been sitting barefoot on the front porch, drinking ice tea to cool off from helping Mother clean house. I was filthy dirty from head to toe after stripping the old wax off our hardwood floors. My fingernails were gunky, my knees were black, and I was definitely having a bad-hair day. The last thing I wanted was for *any* boy to see me.

I watched Buddy careen up in his old red Cadillac with Jerry riding shotgun and Don Guess, a local bass player, in the back seat. When they pulled up to the curb, Jerry and Buddy were laughing and cutting up like they always did together. When they saw me on the porch, they became serious.

Jerry and I had broken up for what appeared to be the last time, and I think they were wary about how I would react to seeing him again. When we weren't joking around, having a good time together, Jerry and I were tormenting each other with sarcasm. Buddy had always served as a good buffer for us. But even with him there that day, I didn't get up and walk over to the car. I wasn't angry; I was just embarrassed for them to see me so unkempt and was ashamed that my grimy short-shorts were way too short.

I sat on the porch, while they sat in the car at the curb. For what seemed like an eternity, we just looked at each other, and then Buddy broke the ice. "Hi," he drawled, giving me an arching wave through his open window. His ear-to-ear grin asked, "Can we stop and talk, or are you going to throw something at Jerry?"

I couldn't help but smile. At that moment, Jerry jumped out of the car, already talking before he reached the porch. Jerry was always talking, always entertaining—he was always *on*. Oblivious to my humiliation, he clowned that they were making a record and were on their way up to Amarillo to play at a dance and become famous. Unimpressed, I just looked at him.

"But only if the car holds up," Buddy shouted out the window.

Miserable with worry about how I looked and irritated at Jerry for bringing me to the attention of the entire neighborhood, I was unable to join in the fun or in Jerry's enthusiasm about his potential musical success. Instead, I said something petulant like, "Yeah, sure. Come back when you're rich and famous." I was embarrassed to think that this was something I'd said to him more than once. Not surprisingly, he shot a sarcastic comeback—we always had comebacks for one another.

Changing the subject, I looked over at Buddy, who was still sitting behind the wheel in the Cadillac. "What's wrong with the car?"

He shrugged and smiled. "I don't know; it just keeps using oil."

Buddy was a musician, certainly not a mechanic. My dad had taught me how to take care of cars, so I asked a question that wasn't really a question—I already knew the answer. "Have you had the oil changed lately, Buddy?"

His eyes widened in mock surprise. "You mean I have to change the oil?"

"Yes," I teased back, "and the filter, too." I grinned and just shook my head at Jerry.

We talked a while longer before Buddy said they had to be going. As Jerry jumped back into the Caddy, I waved them on their way, doubting that the car would last until Amarillo, much less until they found stardom.

♫

Chapter Two
"Peggy Sue"

"Jerry called this afternoon," Johnnie announced as soon as I walked in the door.

"Jerry Allison?" I asked, completely surprised.

"Yes. I told him you were at your after-school job—that you were working as a dental-assistant trainee. He said that he wanted to ask you to attend a rock show here in Sacramento on October 18. Mother gave him our number. I invited him and Buddy to spend the weekend at our house while they were here. He said Mother could fill you in on all the details. You need to call her," Johnnie said.

Well, according to Mother, Mrs. Allison had called her a couple of weeks earlier and had asked her permission for me to attend this *Show of Stars* in Sacramento where Jerry and Buddy would be performing. Mrs. Allison hoped Mother would be able to convince the nuns to let me attend and said that *the boys* would get as many complimentary tickets as we needed if the nuns wanted to take some of the other girls, too. Apparently, Mrs. Allison didn't know I was living with my older sister; Jerry must have thought I was boarding in the convent at school. I wasn't sure my mother had understood the request, but she'd always liked Jerry when I dated him, so she and Daddy had given their consent. I didn't understand why the invitation had to go through our mothers, but at that point, I really didn't care either. All that mattered was that she'd said yes and that I'd be able to see my friends again. I'd missed their constant laughter and hearing about their dreams for the future. The more I thought about them, the more I just couldn't wait to see them again.

♫

As usual, I drove fast, with all the windows rolled down. My long, blonde hair blew in the wind, wreaking havoc with my Rosemary Clooney hairdo. But I didn't care. I was rebelling against the fashion of the day, refusing to wear the requisite scarf. After all, I was seventeen and going to my first rock 'n' roll show.

My brother-in-law's little red and white '55 Mercury Monterey hardtop zipped in and out of the freeway traffic as I twirled the radio knob, switching through stations trying to find one playing "That'll Be The Day." Incredible. My friends from Lubbock, Texas, had a hit record—a rock 'n' roll hit at that. I hadn't heard it being played in Sacramento yet, but during our last telephone conversation, Mother had said it was on all the radio stations in Lubbock.

I couldn't find it, but satisfied by knowing I'd be hearing it soon in person, I set the dial to a rock 'n' roll station and settled in for the half-hour drive downtown to the Sacramento Memorial Auditorium. The sun was nestling into the coastal range west of Sacramento as a giant harvest moon began to rise. I lit up a Viceroy—smoking was one of the things I'd learned from attending a Catholic girls school—and thought about this latest turn of events in my life.

Buddy Holly and The Crickets, as Jerry and Buddy were calling themselves now, were on the *Biggest Show of Stars for 1957* bill. Everybody knew that being with the *Show of Stars* meant you'd *made it*. I knew Buddy and Jerry had *made it* because they were sharing this tour with some of the names I'd been spinning on *my* record player forever—some since 1955. The Drifters; Eddie Cochran; Frankie Lymon and the Teenagers; Paul Anka; the Bobbettes; Clyde McPhatter; and two other West Texans, Jimmy Bowen and Buddy Knox of The Rhythm Orchids were just some of the many acts advertised, as different artists would join or leave the tour at each venue.

It was strange to see Buddy *Holly* and The Crickets on the advertisements. When I pointed out the spelling to Mother, she told me the story about how Decca had misspelled Holley, leaving out the *e*; Buddy hadn't corrected the recording company error, and he'd now adopted the spelling as his recording and stage name.

14

Nervously, I lit another cigarette as I drove in the twilight toward the Memorial Auditorium in Old Sacramento, and I didn't know if I was more anxious for them or for me. Thank heaven that this time, I was clean, dressed, and having a great hair day—unlike the last time I'd seen them. Jerry had never seen my hair long, and I hoped he'd like it. I wondered if there had been any changes in him, too.

That splendid orange moon cast a warm glow on Old Sac as the freeway ended and I wound my way through the downtown area to the back of the auditorium where Jerry had said to come. He'd left instructions for me to knock on the backstage door and tell the doorman that I was a guest of The Crickets. I could find only one parking space about a block and a half away, and I had some trouble parallel parking. I kept checking the dashboard clock. It was almost time for the show to start, and I worried that the doorman wouldn't let me in.

After I finally got parked and turned off the ignition, I quickly brushed my hair and checked my lipstick. It was orange sherbet, to match my cashmere skirt and sweater. I stepped out into the cool autumn evening. *Destiny* loomed.

♫

The lights framing the Sacramento Memorial Auditorium were shining through the trees, lighting my path across the parking lot. As I crossed the street, I saw a tall, thin man in the shadows, pacing up and down the sidewalk by the backstage door, obviously waiting for someone. I wondered if it could be Jerry but decided it wasn't because this man was too tall. Then the man started walking toward me, and the closer I got, the faster he walked. It *was* Jerry, and he looked so grown up. I matched his pace, and when he started running toward me, I found myself running toward him. He opened his arms, and I ran right into them. We held onto each other while he hugged me tight and literally swept me off my feet. That was the warmest, safest, most romantic hug I'd ever received.

"I was afraid you weren't going to make it." He sounded relieved as he pulled back to see my face.

For the first time in my life, I had to look up at him. His light-brown hair had always been in ducktails, but now the sides were cut very short, and he had an impish curl combed down onto his forehead. I'd always thought he had the cutest smile I'd ever seen, and in the moonlight, it all but sparkled.

I started to talk, asking him how he'd been, but he interrupted, "We have to hurry, Peggy Sue. I've gotta get backstage and get ready to go on." He held onto my arm as he rushed me into the auditorium, chattering to me all the way inside.

When we got to the side door, a security man joined Jerry, and they took me straight into the theater. The atmosphere was electric. The auditorium was packed up to the balconies, and people were still streaming in. We had to work our way against the crowd to reach the seat Jerry had picked out for me.

"Here it is. It's one of the best in the house—in the center and on the aisle. I'll be back to get you after the show, but that security guard," he said, pointing to the man who had moved to stand several feet away beside one of the large columns that supported the balcony, "will stay close by to make sure you're okay."

I thought it was very sweet of Jerry to be so protective.

"Stay in your seat so I can find you after the show, and don't talk to anybody," he cautioned.

Due to the cacophony of sounds only an auditorium full of excited teenagers can produce, I knew he wouldn't be able to hear my reply, so I just nodded. I was too overwhelmed for words anyway.

"See ya later." His blue eyes twinkled, and he flashed me one of his let-me-entertain-you smiles as he half-danced, half-bounded back down the aisle toward the stage. I'd never seen Jerry look so happy.

I sat on the edge of my seat, looking around at the enthusiastic young people as they settled into their chairs. My heart was beating fast in anticipation of seeing the greatest rock show in my life—well, the first rock show I'd ever seen in my life—but it'd be the greatest, too. After all, it comprised all my favorite singers *and* my best friends.

The house lights dimmed, and a hush swept across the audience—the calm before the storm. The Master of Ceremonies appeared, welcomed us and announced the first act. When the curtain opened to Chuck Berry belting out "Maybellene," pandemonium broke out. Throughout the auditorium, people rose up out of their seats and began dancing where they stood. I'd never seen anything like it before in my life. I was so

16

mesmerized by both the audience and music that I thought I'd surely died and gone to heaven.

After he played his new hit, "Rock 'n' Roll Music," Chuck Berry danced off of the stage and one of my all-time favorites, LaVern Baker, was introduced. The crowd calmed down and just listened to her enchanting voice sing "Jim Dandy" and "Tweedle-Dee." Next was Fats Domino, who gave another phenomenal performance. Everyone, including me, seemed to know every word to his songs. The whole audience sang along with him on "Blueberry Hill."

None of the performers introduced their songs. They didn't have to—the audience already knew them by heart. Furthermore, there was no encore from any of the bands on the *Biggest Show of Stars for 1957*, regardless of how much the audience screamed and gyrated. The entire program was meticulously choreographed. Once an act finished its performance, it left the stage, so the next act could be announced.

Other kids had found these performers only after the white radio stations began playing their records. I'd known their music for years, and they'd become my friends, keeping me company through many lonely, dark nights. I was thrilled to finally see such artists in person; I'd never even seen pictures of them before. I knew they were black only because I'd obtained most of their records from my brother-in-law's friend who serviced the jukeboxes in the black cafes and clubs in Fort Worth and Dallas. In fact, one of the reasons I'd probably not heard The Crickets yet was because I rarely listened to the radio. When I wasn't in school or working, I was spinning the records of R&B artists.

The curtain closed on Fats Domino, and the MC came back onto the stage. "This next group is new," he announced, "but they have taken the charts by storm. All the way from Lubbock, Texas. Ladies and Gentlemen . . . *The Crickets!*"

"That'll Be The Day" blasted from the stage as the curtain reopened. After only a few bars, the audience erupted again. They jumped to their feet and, before long, were literally dancing in the aisles. I was just dying to join them, but I knew I couldn't get up—Jerry had told me to stay in my seat, and the security guard was still standing against the column, looking in my direction. The band was on the right side of the stage, so I didn't really have a clear view of them. I tucked my foot under me to sit a little higher and stretched until I could see.

They'd all changed so much. They looked older and more mature. Gone were the teeny-bopper white socks, Levi's, and T-shirts; they were now professionally attired in matching gray suits. Their onstage rapport, charming magnetism, and the pure bliss they felt from playing for such adoring fans were things I'd never seen in them before. I was so proud that tears started welling up in my eyes.

I recognized Joe B Mauldin playing bass. He hadn't been with Jerry and Buddy when I was around, but we'd been classmates at Lubbock High—in fact, we'd flunked biology together. I didn't recognize the other guitarist with them.

Jerry leaned into his drums. Poised over them in his usual *attack position*, he reminded me of a cat pouncing on his prey, giving it everything he had. Jerry was definitely *on*. I noticed how thin Buddy looked, but I also noticed how polished he seemed as he moved around the stage in front of the band. They were grinning from ear to ear, looking like nobody else had ever had as much fun as they were having right at that moment. I was so busy assessing every aspect of their appearance that it took a while before I could actually listen to the music, but at last, I stopped looking at my friends and started to hear *The Crickets*.

They were electrifying! Buddy's voice no longer had that nasal, hillbilly sound. Even with his quirky little hiccup, it was full and resonant. I'd never heard a group with the drums and guitar so fused. Jerry's pulsing rhythm projected that powerful, distinctive sound of his which I'd learned to recognize over our years in band together. And Buddy's guitar was speaking a language of its own—the language of R&B, with a little western swing thrown in. This was West Texas rock 'n' roll, and the California audience was loving it!

The guys were drawing off the energy of the crowd and off each other. Buddy never stood still. He would swing up to the microphone, lean into it to sing, then rock back on his foot, and spin around to play his guitar to the band before pivoting back to sing to the audience again. He continually looked over his shoulder at Jerry and grinned. Even on stage, they had their usual, mutual-admiration society going. Buddy and Jerry were feeding off each other's guitar and drum licks, looking at one another and laughing when they hit one they liked, as if to say, "Hey, Man, did ya hear *that* one?"

They moved into "Oh Boy." The crowd never stopped cheering and clapping—or dancing. Not one bobby-socked or penny-loafered foot could remain still while The Crickets were playing, including mine. I just couldn't believe that these were *my* friends up there on stage, creating this kind of excitement. Right then, I knew they weren't just going to *make it,* but they were going to *make it BIG!* It was such an incredible feeling to know how far they'd come and how far they were going to go. Buddy and Jerry had worked so hard to get their music out of Lubbock, and now they were taking it to the entire world.

They ended the song, and Buddy stepped up to the microphone with his hand resting on the edge of his guitar. He obviously wanted to say something, but the audience didn't want talk; they wanted more music. But as he began to talk, the crowd became quiet.

"I don't know why they decided to put this record out with just *my* name on it, but I want everybody to know it's *us*...The Crickets." Buddy paused before continuing. "This is a special show tonight, and we're playing this song for a special person."

He glanced over his shoulder at the band and started the countdown, "One, two..."

It was a moment forever frozen in time as I met *Destiny.*

"If you knew Peggy Sue, then you'd know why I'm so blue, oh Peggy, my Peggy Sue-u-u-u..."

No matter that the screaming crowd had absolutely no idea who I was, I suddenly felt as if the whole world was looking at me. At seventeen, my sole objective in social situations was to keep from being noticed. I was so embarrassed, I could have died.

My heart pounded, and my cheeks were on fire. With people all around me bouncing, swaying, and singing my name over and over, I sank down in my seat, covered my face with my hands, and cried out to myself, What have y'all done to me?

It took a few minutes for my heartbeat to return to normal so I could take a deep breath. The crowd was still in total ecstasy when the song ended.

After "Peggy Sue," the curtain came down, the Master of Ceremonies came out and announced intermission, and the lights came back on.

I looked toward the aisle where the security guard was standing and saw Jerry trying to get through the crowd to my seat. He threw out his hand to grab mine, and we meandered against the crowd toward the stage. The backstage lights weren't on yet, so I became immersed in total darkness as soon as I walked through the doorway leading to the backstage area. I was following Jerry's lead, or trying to, when, all of a sudden, this arm reached out, grabbed me, and started to hug me. I was scared out of my wits. Then I heard a familiar voice ask, "Aren't you glad your mother named you after my new hit song?"

"Only in your dreams," I answered Buddy, as I scrambled to get my balance. "I was here first."

The lights came on, revealing Buddy standing in front of me with his head thrown back laughing heartily. When Buddy was completely thrilled, it showed all over his body, and this was one of those times. His smile began to fade and his shoulders gave a slight droop as soon as Jerry said, "We're leaving. I have someone to play the drums while I'm gone this weekend."

Realizing that Buddy had wanted to come with us made me sad, and I quickly said, "You do know that you are invited, don't you?"

"I really appreciate the invitation, and you'll never know how much I would like to leave this bus for a weekend. We can replace Jerry with another drummer, but there is only one Buddy Holly and I have to be here. What do you think about 'Peggy Sue'?" Buddy asked.

"It was so exciting. I loved it. Made me want to dance. And I can't wait to hear it on the radio. I'm so thrilled to be here tonight. Thank you for the invitation. I'm glad that it finally worked out, and you and Jerry are getting to do what you've always wanted to do," came out of my mouth, but all the time, I was thinking, I wish you guys had named it something else.

Jerry said, "We better go. They'll start to line up the acts soon. Hey, Bud, I'll meet you in Stockton Sunday at the auditorium," and started to push us through all the musicians who were taking a smoke break at the backstage door.

"Hey, Jerry, gotta date?" somebody catcalled.

"Hey, Man, this is Peggy Sue," Jerry declared proudly.

As we ran for the car, a couple of girls standing outside the auditorium gawked at Jerry, and one asked, "Are you with the show?"

"I sure am."

"Would you give me your autograph?" she asked.

"No, I don't have a pen or anything to write with. Sorry," Jerry said.

"I do! I do!" cried the girl.

"Give them your autograph, Jerry," I said. "What will it hurt?"

After signing his autograph, he said, "Hurry. Get into the car. I just want you to know that I've asked everybody on the tour if they know where Carmichael, California, is. But nobody's ever heard of it. Let's go so I can see if it's really here."

I laughed. "It's a suburb of Sacramento."

"Are you hungry?" Jerry asked.

"Starving! There's a great pizza parlor on our way home to Carmichael," I told him.

"Sounds great, Peggy Sue," he said as we pulled away from the curb.

Jerry talked all the way to the pizza parlor. Then, as soon as we were seated, he asked, "What do you really think about our new record?"

"I was really, really, really surprised," I replied, raising one eyebrow and smiling. "It's very flattering. Come on, Jerry. Who wrote the song? Buddy just said he did, but on stage, he said The Crickets did." Before he had a chance to answer, the waiter came and we ordered a pizza. "With everything on it but anchovies," I said.

Jerry asked, "What's anchovies?"

"They're little, very salty fish. You don't want any either. Trust me. Okay?" I answered.

He smiled and answered my earlier question. "I wrote the song just for you—well, not exactly. Buddy really wrote the song, but Norman helped with the bridge."

"Norman who?" I asked.

"Norman Petty. His wife's name is Vi. They have a group called The Norman Petty Trio. Ever heard of them?"

I got excited. "Is 'First Kiss' their record?"

"Yes. Have you heard it here in Sacramento?" Jerry asked excitedly.

21

"You bet. They play it all the time. I love the record. Who's the girl singing?"

"That's Vi, and you should hear her play the piano. Have you heard any of our records? Especially 'Peggy Sue'? It's playing all over the world and is climbing the charts," Jerry said, definitely hoping I'd say I had.

"What does that mean? Climbing the charts? And, no, I haven't heard any of your records," I said apologetically.

"They have magazines called *Cash Box* and *Billboard*. They write all about the records and the artists who make them, and they track how many records are sold. They list the Top 100 across the USA. 'That'll Be The Day' has already sold a million records, and we'll be getting our first gold record to hang on our walls. Now 'Peggy Sue' is on the chart, and we are just killin' 'em."

"I'm so thrilled for you and Buddy. I know this is all the two of you have ever wanted." I reached into my purse and pulled out a cigarette. I thought that Jerry was going to faint.

"I didn't ever think I'd see you smoke, especially since you stopped dating me because I was smoking behind the band room," he exclaimed.

"I attend an all-girls school where everybody smokes, including some of the nuns. My mother and father don't know that I smoke, so I'll tell them after I graduate. Besides, you had your T-shirt sleeves rolled up and looked like a thug when you were in Lubbock High," I teased. "Tell me more about this gold-record hit you have. I loved it when you guys came out playing that song tonight."

Jerry said, "Well, you know, Buddy and I got the idea from watching John Wayne in the movie 'The Searchers.' I swear, Peggy Sue, if he said, 'That'll Be The Day,' once, he said it a hundred times in that movie."

"Oh," I said. "I haven't seen it."

"After Buddy and I'd seen the movie, we were sitting in my bedroom, and we just started to write this song, and we wrote it in a few minutes. Then we started to rehearse it. Buddy didn't have much luck with it with Decca. They wouldn't let him do it rock 'n' roll. So, we went to Clovis to record it. I mean we had it down, and there were no changes needed. We even had the vocal backup practiced."

Jerry talked all the way home about Norman; Vi; recording at the Norman Petty Studio; Clovis, New Mexico, where the studio was located;

his plans for the future; the tour they were on; and the tours they had already scheduled. It seemed to me that they were really on their way to stardom. We were almost to my sister's house when I asked, "How are Buddy and Echo doing? Do they keep in touch?"

"They certainly do not," Jerry exclaimed.

"Oh, I'm sorry," I said.

"Echo's getting married. I think to a Church of Christ minister. You do remember how she hated our music, don't you?" Jerry asked and laughed.

"I guess she won't have to worry about it anymore if she's getting married." As I pulled into the driveway, I continued, "Is there anything you would like to do tomorrow since you have a few days off?"

Jerry just smiled. "Whatever you want to do."

I laughed. "By the way, how tall are you now?"

"I'm exactly six feet tall, and if my face would clear up, I think I'd look pretty good," he teased. Then he added, "I've had the Asian flu. In fact, the whole bus has had it."

"Well, we're home. Come in and meet my family. I have a new baby niece. Her name is Kim Ruth. Do you remember my sister and brother-in-law, Johnnie and Von?"

"Yes, I do, and the records he got for you in Fort Worth off the jukeboxes."

"That's the one," I said.

Jerry was easy to talk to. In fact, all anyone had to do was just be an attentive listener; he could take care of all the talking if the situation was right. We got Jerry settled on the sofa sleeper downstairs, and I excused myself and went upstairs to bed. It was nice seeing Jerry and Buddy. I guess I was more homesick than I'd thought.

♫

CHAPTER THREE
Carmichael, California 1957

*J*erry and I had a light breakfast around noon and then went to ask my brother-in-law, who was practicing golf in the front yard, if we could borrow the car so I could take Jerry sightseeing.

"Sure, Peg, but be careful with Jerry. I'd hate to have to pay him for his hands," Von joked.

"No problem," Jerry said. "My hands are so broken and ugly—I've already broken them twice."

"You're kidding," I said, astounded, wondering if his hands ever bothered him when he was playing his drums.

"No, I was playing golf and got mad when I missed my shot, so I hit a tree with my club. Well, the club wrapped around the tree and hit across these fingers," Jerry said, pointing to his hand, "and broke them. Another time, I got them caught in my mother's Mixmaster. I wanted to see what would happen if I stuck my fingers in the beaters. She told me it would break them, but I stuck them in anyway. Sure enough, she was right."

I drove Jerry around Carmichael, showing him all its tourist attractions and my favorite haunts. Although it was Saturday, the doors to my high school, Bishop Armstrong, were open, so I took him inside. Jerry thought it was pretty funny that there were no boys in our school. The boys' school was next door, and a garden of bright red roses separated the two contemporary-looking buildings. Our hallways opened to the outside allowing us to see into the boys' classrooms when we changed classes; however, their doors opened to the opposite side of the building so they couldn't see into ours. It was taboo for them to look out their windows when we changed classes.

Two of my favorite teachers were in the office, so I took Jerry inside and introduced him. I was instantly amused by his deportment. Sister Manuela O.S.M., the vice principal, and Sister Mary Celestine S.M., the principal, were attired in their official habits. It was probably the first time Jerry had been face to face with nuns, and I believe, it was the only time I'd ever seen him at a loss for words. He didn't know whether to bow or what! But, coming from a Baptist background and having a mother who was a teacher, he was extremely polite and behaved himself quite well.

"This school is beautiful," Jerry commented as we went out the door.

I agreed. With all the ivy and plants growing everywhere, it looked more like a greenhouse. "I'm lucky that I got to go to school here my senior year," I said, and then I added, "I think it's time for a Coke. I want you to see Rick's, my Hi-D-Ho in Carmichael. You'll laugh. It's only one small building with no carhops. You have to go to the window and order, but I'll say one thing for them, they have the best hamburgers I've ever tasted."

It was such a beautiful California day that, after leaving Rick's, we took the ten-minute drive up the Fair Oaks Curve to the American River where we could sit on the rocks or wade in the water.

"Come on, Jerry, let's walk down by the river," I said.

Dark-green oak boughs draped toward the river rock and fallen oak trunks rested on the river's edge, creating perfect spots to sit and take in the serene view. The only sound was the babbling water running downstream from the Sierras. Astounded by the scenery, Jerry breathed, "Isn't it beautiful?"

"Wouldn't you love to have something like this in Lubbock?" I asked.

"Yeah. With this kind of weather to go with it." He started skipping rocks on top of the water. One...two...three...like a little boy, tense, as if something was on his mind. Finally, he said, "Peggy Sue, I need to have a serious talk with you."

"Okay. Talk."

"I know you've met a guy out here. I heard he even came to Lubbock to see you last summer. Are you still dating him?" he asked, continuing to look toward the water.

"No," I replied. "He joined the Air Force."

"Oh? What's he going to be? An officer?" he asked sarcastically.

"He's on the Air Force swim team. In fact, he even set a record, and there was a write-up about him in the newspaper."

"Does he come from money?" Jerry asked.

I started to laugh. "It depends on what you call money. His dad's a contractor of sorts. He owns all the Roto-Rooter franchises in Northern California. Their home is a lot bigger than the one I grew up in. Plus, they have a ski boat, trailer, swimming pool, and lots of other goodies. There are four boys in the family. The three who are old enough to drive have their own cars, and there's a gasoline pump on the grounds for all the company vehicles, so the boys don't have to pay for their gas. Yes, I'd say they live a very comfortable life."

Jerry gave me a serious look and asked, "Are you going to marry him?"

"No, I'm not," I replied matter-of-factly.

"Why not?"

"Because his whole family's Mormon, and mine's Catholic. When our parents thought we might get married, our mothers talked and cried about it until I just couldn't stand it any longer, so we broke up. My mother thought it would be just awful to marry a Mormon. She wants me to be married in the Catholic Church in order for the wedding to be blessed. For that to happen, he would have had to become Catholic or agree that our children would be raised Catholic. His mother wanted him to get married in the Temple and live a strong Mormon family life. There was no compromise—just tears and yelling. After we broke up, he joined the Air Force because he'd always wanted to be a pilot. As for me, I still have to graduate from high school, and then I'll decide what I'm going to do with my life. So, no, I'm not going to marry him. I'm going home when school's out."

"I'm glad you realized it wouldn't work out. You're from two different backgrounds," Jerry said.

"Yes, I know. That's what everybody kept telling me."

"Did you love him?" Jerry asked.

"I don't think I know what love is. I thought I knew what it was, but I know now that I don't. Is love having things in common like dancing, swimming, and music? Is it having fun whether you're doing something or just sitting around together? If *that's* love, well, I guess I did love him."

"Swimming and dancing do not constitute a marriage," Jerry announced huffily.

"I didn't say it did, and I don't want to talk about it anymore!"

As I started to get up, Jerry put his hand on my shoulder and, in a soothing voice, he said, "Hey, don't be mad. I'm trying to ask you something."

"It seems to me like all you've been doing is asking me questions," I shot back.

"I want you to marry me when you graduate from school," he said.

"You what?" I exclaimed.

I gasped when he got down on his knee, took my hand, and said, "I love you. I want to marry you. Will you marry me?"

"Jerry, I don't...know...why...Why would you want to marry *me*? You could marry any girl in the whole world that you wanted to," I stammered.

"Well, I don't know about that, but I *do* know that I want you," he said. "You don't understand. I wrote the song for you." Then he quickly added, "Buddy and I did," and continued speaking rapidly. "We knew if it was a hit, you'd hear it and you'd know it was us and maybe you wouldn't ever forget us. I had to do something to make you understand. You're the nice Lubbock girl who comes from a nice family. You're the only girl who can be my wife and the only one I would want to have my children. I can afford to take care of you the way you should be taken care of. I know I've never been in the Country Club, but I can learn; and if I can't, Peggy Sue, I can surely buy you one all your own."

"Don't be silly," I broke in. "That's not important, Jerry. You and I have only one thing in common and that's music."

"That's not true. Our families are similar in both background and income. And we're both from Lubbock."

"Yes, I know. But you don't dance, you don't swim because it gives you an earache, you're up all night and sleep all day, and worse than that, you travel all the time. Plus, I'm still Catholic and you're still hard-shell Baptist—or at least your family is."

"Being Baptist is not a problem. I promise we'll get married in the Catholic Church. I'll handle my parents," he said.

"Speaking of parents, I've never even met yours, Jerry."

"My mother knows how I feel; I've already told her. She just wants me to have whatever makes me happy. She already knows the family you're from; she approves. Please say yes. Besides, when I travel, you'll come with me."

"I don't know what to say." My head was swimming from his questions and marriage proposal.

"Say *yes*. You *have* to marry me. You just don't understand how important you are to me. I won't accept no. I've dreamed about you since I was in high school, and I couldn't stand to let anybody else have you."

"Jerry, I'm not sure how I feel about you. I can't marry you if I don't love you."

"Yes, you can. I love you enough that you'll get over that feeling. I promise you will. Say *yes*," he begged.

"You still want me to say yes even though I've just told you I'm not sure I love you?"

"Yes, I do. I know it's the right thing to do. I'm older than you and more mature."

"You're only one year older than me," I reminded him.

"I know, but I've already been around the world twice in mileage, and you're still a little girl. Buddy's been my best friend since the seventh grade, and I couldn't even stand to let you marry *him*. I'd give Buddy anything of mine, but I couldn't let you marry him. *Please say yes*."

"What if my feelings don't change after we're married?"

"They will. It's only natural that you'd feel that way now. It's because.... Well, you never have had a.... Well, that type of relationship with anybody. You know what I mean?" he said, stammering for words.

"Not exactly," I said.

"Peggy, have you ever gone to bed with anybody?" he asked.

"Well, what do you think?" I shot back at him.

"I know you haven't. But, that's precisely what I'm talking about. Your feelings will change after we're married. Now say *yes*."

"Since we're on the subject, have *you* ever slept with anybody, Jerry?"

"Not anybody that counted," he replied callously.

"That's pretty cold. What happened? It just didn't work out?" I asked.

"We didn't have anything in common," he replied bluntly.

"Well, all right. I'll say yes, but I may change my mind before this summer, and if I do, you have to accept that." I must admit that, at times, my logic didn't always make sense even to me, but at that moment, my main purpose was to put an end to the conversation without hurting Jerry's feelings or upsetting him. Besides, maybe I *could* grow to love him before summer—I already thought he was a great friend. But if not, I'd already told him I might change my mind.

"You won't change your mind. I'll see to that. I'll be back for your graduation with your folks this summer, and I'll bring your engagement ring. I know they won't say anything if we wait until you graduate to become engaged. I've already talked to your mom and dad. They said I could come for graduation."

"You talk to my mother a lot, don't you?" I asked, wondering what *that* was all about.

"Yep. And by the way, we're booked until Christmas," Jerry informed me.

"Does that mean that I won't be seeing you until then?" I wondered how I was supposed to learn to love him if he was never around.

"That's right. But, I'll be sending you my itinerary, and we can write to each other, okay?"

I looked into his pleading eyes and replied, "Okay."

♫

The following day, Johnnie, Von, and I took Jerry to Stockton for his next show. The freeway traffic leaving Sacramento was horrendous, and he missed his performance because we weren't able to get him to the auditorium on time. I was terribly embarrassed. I asked, "Will you be in trouble for missing the rock show?"

He laughed. "Peggy, I think with a busload of musicians like we have, one white drummer ain't no big thing to replace."

29

As we drove up to the backstage door where the buses were parked, we saw a concerned Buddy pacing the pavement. He came running over to Jerry and said, "God! You missed the show, and I thought you were going to miss the bus too! Hurry up, Jerry. We don't want them coloreds gettin' mad at us. I don't feel like ridin' in the back of the bus again. Every time I do, the fumes make me sick."

There had been no wave, no jovial laugh, and no smile when Buddy saw us. This was *not* the way I was used to seeing him behave. Clearly, life on the tour bus had taken a toll on him.

Jerry had told me about some of the problems the four Crickets had encountered on the tour. There was no set show. Acts came and went depending on their availability and the location. On this particular leg of the tour, The Crickets was the only white band riding the bus, which meant that Jerry, Buddy, Joe B, and Niki Sullivan had to become part of the black entertainers' world.

A busload of blacks couldn't stop in a white neighborhood to eat at a white restaurant or stay at a white hotel, and the black part of town hadn't treated the white Crickets much better. Restaurants had refused to seat them, and hotels had refused to allow them to spend the night. If they could, they'd catch a ride to the white side of town, but if they couldn't, they had to sleep on the bus and rely on their fellow musicians to bring them food. Sometimes, the black headliners had pretended The Crickets were their white valets just to get them into a hotel.

When The Crickets first joined the tour, the other acts had teased them for being a one-record hit, but now that "Peggy Sue" was climbing the charts, the teasing had become less frequent. Also, it had made the black entertainers less resentful toward sharing the marquee with four little white boys from Lubbock, Texas.

Jerry's stories about the racial problems they'd encountered made me remember the day my mother had taken me with her to the second floor of Sears & Roebuck to pay our bill. I'd stood there looking at the water fountains standing side by side. One was labeled *Colored*; the other was labeled *White*. Wondering if it was really true that if you drank out of the *Colored* fountain you would die, I'd walked over and taken a quick swallow. The water was cool and clear—just like the water from the *White* fountain.

And, I didn't fall down dead. I'd turned and looked at my mother to see if she'd been watching me. Of course, she'd been.

Once we were outside, I'd proudly proclaimed, "I didn't die."

She'd replied, "Of course you didn't, but you could have gotten me in trouble."

"It's against the law?" I'd asked.

"Yes," she'd replied.

That had been enough for me. I'd never pushed that envelope again. But, I'd always wondered why people had to make such a big fuss about the color of someone's skin.

While Jerry got his suitcase out of the trunk, Buddy kept anxiously watching the bus load. He looked like he was ready to bolt back toward it at any moment. Finally, he turned to me and said, almost pathetically, "I sure hope next time *I* get to go to Carmichael." I looked into his cheerless, brown eyes and knew that he was homesick, too.

Jerry grabbed his suitcase and, without even giving his new fiancée a hug or kiss, yelled, "I'll call you from a hotel," as he and Buddy ran toward the bus.

I felt sorry for them. This was not the way it was supposed to be if you were a star. However, I admired them for making the best of a world they knew nothing about. After all, they had *made it*. And this was show business.

♫

CHAPTER FOUR
Christmas 1957

*C*hristmas 1957 was extra special for my family. My brand-new niece, little Miss Kim, would meet her grandparents for the first time. My sister had packed every blanket she owned in case we needed to keep the six-month-old baby warm. The weather could fluctuate radically in the twenty-two hours it would take to drive straight through from Sacramento to Lubbock. After we'd packed the car three times and gone over Von's checklist again, we were on our way.

The 1955 red and white Mercury was my brother-in-law's second baby, and he'd gone over every detail of the car. It had been greased, lubed, waxed—everything a man could do to prepare it for the trip and to project the image that this was *his* car.

Von, a Tech sergeant stationed at McClellan Air Force Base, helped keep America safe in the duck-and-tuck '50s, and the military spilled over into his personal life, making him a stickler for detail. His motto was a place for everything and everything in its place. I still thought he was incredibly cool, though, because he liked to assemble model airplanes, play golf, and dance—he and my sister had even won a jitterbug contest once. Furthermore, Von had played trombone in the Air Force Band. He was very kind to me—and a much better cook than my sister.

We'd been on the road about two hours when Johnnie said, "Don't forget, Von, we have to stop and warm the baby's bottles."

"Yes, Johnnie," Von exclaimed.

"Do we get to eat, too?" I asked.

"Yes, Peggy Sue," he answered jovially.

We drove all day and were making pretty good time. I was bored and slept on and off the entire day. Around ten o'clock, Von said, "Peg, wake up and drive a while for me, would ya?"

"Sure. I'd love to."

He slowed down and pulled over. I noticed that we were in the middle of nowhere. I got out of the car, ran over to the driver's side, and scooted in saying, "It's freezing out here. Where are we, Von?" through my chattering teeth.

"We left Albuquerque some time ago. I can't keep my eyes open. Just stay on this highway, and we'll be fine."

I'd been driving for about an hour when a bright, bluish-white light flashed from the sky down onto the road ahead. Uh oh, I thought. We're going to have a thunderstorm. But, how can that be? It's the wrong time of year for a thunderstorm in New Mexico; it's too cold. As close as the flash had been, the subsequent boom should have been deafening, but there was no sound. I didn't have time to assess the situation because the next thing I knew, the car was dying. Von woke up and immediately roared, "You ran out of gas? Turn the stirring wheel! Don't let it die on the highway!"

I screamed, "We're not out of gas unless there's something wrong with your gas gauge! There's no power! There's nothing lit up on the dashboard!"

"Don't let it die! We'll freeze out here!" Von screamed back.

"I don't have any control over it! It's dying all by itself," I yelled as I started to coast toward the right to get off the highway.

Von bellowed again, "Don't pull over! Keep trying to start the car!"

"I said there's no power! If we don't pull over, we'll be in the middle of the road where someone can hit us."

By this time, Johnnie was screaming from the back seat, "Von, quit your screaming!"

Immediately, Von became quiet. Just as the car coasted off the two-lane highway, he took a deep breath and, in his take-charge military voice, said, "Cover up good with all the blankets. Keep the baby under them so she doesn't have to breathe the cold air. I'm going to find a tow truck. Do *not* open the car doors for anyone but me or the highway patrol."

He put on his heavy flight jacket, and I watched him as he walked away—hatless, hunkered down into his jacket, his shoulders slightly bending over against the wind, and his hands in his pockets. He looked so cold. I could barely see him in the distance when an old pickup passed us and then stopped beside him on the highway. I watched as he got in. They gave him a lift to the next town, and in about forty-five minutes, he returned with a tow truck. By that point, we had gotten really cold. It took the rest of the night to tow the car to a garage in Vaughn, New Mexico, and wait for a mechanic, but by the time the sun was up, it had been fixed.

"What was wrong with it, Von?" I asked.

Von looked at the mechanic, who was wiping his hands on an old red rag as he walked out of the garage, and asked him, "Yeah, what exactly was wrong with the car?"

After a moment of silence, the mechanic muttered, "It sure is strange that a new battery would've been drained like that."

"Yeah, I'll see if I can get a refund when I get to Lubbock," an irritated Von replied.

I wondered if the bluish-white light I had seen flash from the sky had anything to do with the battery being drained. After all, the car had died almost immediately after that. Hum. Maybe I had just witnessed one of those secret New Mexico desert tests that the newspapers always reported on.

We arrived at my parents' home in Lubbock around suppertime. As I walked up to the door, I could smell the fried chicken, mashed potatoes, gravy, green beans, and homemade bread. Immediately, Mother started ooing and gooing over the baby, while Daddy looked at little Kim and said, "Yep, it's a baby girl." Grandpa, who was from Alsace-Lorraine, France, was absolutely thrilled because she looked French to him. Indeed, I was home, and I was so glad.

Jerry was waiting for me in the kitchen. He didn't stay long though, and as I walked him to the car, he told me he would pick me up the following day so I could meet his family. He said, "Don't worry, Peg. I've already asked your mother. She said it'd be all right because I won't be here for Christmas."

"What? I thought you were going to have Christmas off," I said.

"I was, but we got booked in New York. We're doing *Alan Freed's Christmas Jubilee Show* at the Paramount Theater. It's headlined by Fats Domino, Jerry Lee Lewis, and the Everly Brothers. Then we're going to appear on the *Arthur Murray Dance Party*. We just couldn't say no, even if it was Christmas," Jerry explained.

"For something as important as that, I wouldn't want you to either," I said.

He kissed me very lightly, and we said good night.

♫

Because I had to wear a uniform to school, my wardrobe choices were extremely limited. I was excited about meeting Jerry's parents but also apprehensive about making the right first impression. I asked Mother what I should wear, and she suggested my straight, black wool skirt with the two kick pleats and pockets on front, a white pullover sweater, my black and white oxfords, and my white Donnie Boone angora socks—quite the style for California.

"What if they don't like me? What's his mother like?" I asked apprehensively.

"She's very nice...a typical mother of boys...you'll like her. Just give her a chance. Try to forget she's a teacher," Mother said, knowing I *loathed* schoolteachers. She continued telling me what she knew about the family. For a while, it sounded like Jerry was an only child, but my mother added, "He has an older brother who lives in Odessa."

As I walked into the kitchen, Grandpa, lingering over his morning coffee, said, "Well, don't you look nice today? Where are you going?"

"Jerry's picking me up in a few minutes. I'm going to spend the day with his parents."

"Tell him I listen to them on the radio all the time. Their music's really good and really clean."

"Grandpa! *You* listen to rock 'n' roll music?" I gasped, never thinking of my octogenarian grandpa as being so cool. My uncle Paul, his only son, and Paul's wife, Peggy, whom I was named after and who played the drums, had a country swing band that played dances in West Texas every time they got a chance. Occasionally, they played at the Cotton Club on the Slaton Highway. In his younger days, Grandpa had loved to go dancing there, so I'd just surmised that swing was the only kind of music he liked.

"Yes. I always listen to Jerry and Buddy's music. It's a good clean sound like country western, and the new beat is really good. You can understand the stories to the songs. Be sure you tell 'em now."

"Thanks, Grandpa. I'll tell them." After I kissed him goodbye and told him how much I loved him, I was on my way.

I was nervous when I walked into Jerry's house. The first person I met was his dad, James Delbert—Buddy—or JD, depending on who was talking to him. He was the biggest man I'd ever been near. He must have stood 6'3" or more; and if he'd chanted, "Fee, fie, fo, fum," I would've run! But instead, he flashed a beautiful smile that lit up one of the kindest faces I think I'd ever seen, and I was immediately at ease. I was amazed at the family resemblance between him and his first cousin Dan Blocker, the TV star who'd suddenly been showing up in cowboy shows within the last year. Mr. Allison had a great personality—he loved to talk, and he laughed a lot. One of his traits was to break into a verse or two of some really old folk-type song whenever he heard something in a conversation that cued it in his head. I asked him where he had learned those tunes and, in turn, he told me a little about Jerry's family history.

Mr. Allison said that his dad had sung such songs and that the Allisons were from Hill County in Texas. Louise's family, the Fergusons, came from the part of Texas he referred to as the river bottoms, and then he laughed and said that, actually, the two families had only lived a few miles from one another.

After he and Louise married and had two boys, they moved to Lubbock. He went to work for the Texas Highway Department, and Louise taught school. She was a teacher in East Texas until she was fired for being pregnant. She'd always wanted to be a special-education teacher, so when she came to Lubbock, she worked her way through one degree, attending college part-time, and she was in the process of finishing a second one. To help her out, Mr. Allison raised the two boys, worked full-time, and handled all the household chores.

Although I had only been with them for an hour, I could tell that, even at their ages, they were still deeply in love with each other and very proud of Jerry—although he hadn't chosen the type of career they'd anticipated for him. They'd thought Jerry would grow up to be a commercial artist, or something like that, and that his brother Jamey, named James Delbert after his father, would be a teacher, or at least both of them would have jobs that required college degrees. But, as fate would have it, both boys quit college.

After dinner, Jerry brought out a big cardboard box with *Pilot* on the side and said it was my Christmas present. I was uncomfortable opening it since I didn't have a gift for him. What a great gift—a brand new Pilot record player. It was the latest style and had an automatic changer that held ten 45s at a time.

"Thank you, Jerry, but you shouldn't have," I said.

"Now you have a new record player to play your records on." Jerry beamed. I began looking in the box. Puzzled, he asked, "What are you looking for?"

"Cricket records."

"I'll get you some," Jerry said, turning red when he realized that I didn't have any of their records. He began to explain that Pilot Manufacturing Company had sent three free record players to Norman Petty for the Crickets.

Of course, I thought he had purchased this gift especially for me, so when I heard the explanation, the split-flower corsage image flashed through my mind, and I said, "Well, I feel funny keeping it if it was meant for you."

"No, it's for you. I want you to have it," he exclaimed, and began putting the record player back into the box so I could take it home. "Peggy Sue, we're leaving for New York tomorrow. Your mother said you could ride to Amarillo with us if you want to."

"Sure," I said.

♬

The next morning, Jerry and his parents picked me up. We had to drive to Amarillo—about a hundred miles north of Lubbock—because there weren't any direct flights from Lubbock to New York. Seeing Mr. and Mrs. Allison in dress clothes made me feel like we were going to church, but I knew that was standard airport attire. In West Texas, people went to the airport simply to have something to do. Most of the time, women wore high heels with their dresses and sported fashionable, little white gloves just to go watch complete strangers get on and off the airplanes. All dressed up as they were, I thought the Allisons were a very handsome couple, and I could tell that they thought Jerry Ivan, if not perfect, was pretty close to it on this day.

Jerry drove and I sat in the front with him. I noticed how nice he looked in his white dress shirt and brown-tweed sport jacket. He was no longer wearing Levi's; rather, he was wearing dress pants like my Dad wore, with no pleats in the front. The way they fit, they showed off Jerry's long legs. He was so much taller and filled out that he didn't look like the same boy I'd dated in high school. Then it hit me—he no longer was a boy; he'd become a man.

Jerry was cruising down the highway with one hand on the steering wheel and the other on the radio dial, twirling it back and forth, trying to find a rock station he thought might play their records, especially "Peggy Sue." He was never still. When his fingers were off the dial, he would be keeping time to the music of whatever song was playing by beating the dashboard with his hand like it was a drum. Finally, we heard the last part of "That'll Be The Day," but it was the only Crickets song we found.

"Why aren't they playing 'Peggy Sue'?" I asked.

"Well, they're playing it somewhere, or it wouldn't be going up on those magazine charts," Jerry said.

We pulled up in front of the airport, and Jerry and his dad began to unload all the luggage and instruments. Leaning against a fence, Buddy began singing "Peggy Sue." I laughed and so did he.

"Thought you were going to miss the damn plane, Man," Buddy joked.

"You know better than that," Jerry shot back. "Hey, I took insurance out on all our instruments and suitcases in case they lose something. At least we won't have to part with the bread to buy more." Opening a small notebook, he continued, "And, being the organizer that I am, I made a checklist so we can be sure everything gets loaded."

"Yep. You're really organized. It's a good thing; somebody needs to be. Peggy Sue, wanna go with us?" Buddy asked.

I laughed. "I wish I could, but I don't think my parents would understand."

38

Buddy said, "Come over here. I want you to meet my parents."

Mr. and Mrs. Holley were charming. Mrs. Holley said, "Oh, I'm so glad to meet you, young lady, and you look just like I thought you would. Please, call me Ella. You know, my hair used to be blonde just like yours."

Mr. Holley, a tall man, probably 6'2" or so, with dark hair that was graying at the temples, spoke up, "And that's why I married you. Because of that and your blue eyes."

Then I met Mrs. Mulcahy, Joe B's mom, who was also a very nice-looking woman, and I said hi to Joe's sister, Larue, who had been a cheerleader at Lubbock High.

Joe B had been popular in school, too. He was a great dancer and friendly to everyone. He was a little guy, and when I saw him on stage at the *Show of Stars* in Sacramento, the standup bass had looked even larger than it was because of his size. I'd always thought he was cute, and sporting a fresh-cut blonde flattop, the fashion haircut of the day, he looked exceptionally charming today.

Niki Sullivan, who was actually one of Buddy's cousins, wouldn't be traveling on this trip. When they returned to Lubbock from their last tour, Niki quit the group. According to Jerry, he'd told them he was just tired of traveling and of the harsh schedule they had to follow. So, now, The Crickets would be performing as a trio instead of a foursome.

Buddy was dancing around, teasing, and having an all-around good time until they had to board. Jerry gave me a hug and said he would call me from New York. Buddy and Joe B were standing near enough to hear our conversation and mockingly chimed, "We'll call you, too." Jerry gave them a pursed-lip look that silently communicated, *Real cute guys.*

As they started up the steps to the airplane, their coats thrown over their shoulders, Buddy turned and yelled, "Come on, Peggy Sue. It's not too late." He could see me laughing, and he waved to me just as he went inside. I could see Jerry sitting next to a window waving to everyone. The excitement built for all of us as the airplane took off down the runway with everybody waving. It seemed like all Jerry and I ever did was say goodbye to one another. I looked around at the crowd. I'd met almost everybody; however, there where people I hadn't been introduced to, and I had no idea who they were or why they were there. I wondered if some of them were just spectators.

Mr. and Mrs. Allison started toward the car to drive back to Lubbock. This time, I rode in the back seat. Mrs. Allison talked all the way home, making the ride that much faster. I was still a little intimidated by her being a teacher. I felt I *had* to make a good impression on her, so to make conversation, I asked what Mr. Holley did for a living. Mrs. Allison said, "Oh, he works a lot for his son, Larry, who's a tile contractor. I think money has been a real problem for the family, and since Buddy has done so well, I'm sure, from what he's said, that he's made them a little more financially secure."

"Do you mean he helps his mother and father so they don't have to work so hard?" I asked.

"Not just them, but his grandmother, too," she said.

"I think that's really wonderful. All the boys that I know that age are not even aware of what responsibility is." Already apprised of the situation but wanting to keep the conversation going, I asked, "By the way, what happened to Buddy's girlfriend?"

"Do you mean Echo McGuire?" Mrs. Allison asked, as she turned in her seat to face me.

"Yes," I said.

"They broke up. Her parents sent her away to college."

"Is Buddy upset?"

"Jerry said he wasn't. I believe their lives are too different to ever make a go of it. Music means too much to Buddy to have to stop playing because of a girl and her family."

By now, we were in front of my house, and I invited them in to visit with my parents. Mrs. Allison declined, saying she knew my folks wanted to visit with my sister and me while they had us home for the holidays. They would stop by another time.

"I'll be leaving for California right after the New Year, but I'll probably see you this summer. Thank you for taking me along to the airport. It was very nice meeting both of you," I said.

"Oh, I'll see you before you leave. I think it'd be nice if we could have a cake and coffee date. That way, just you and I could get to know each other better," Mrs. Allison said.

"Yes, that would be very nice. Thank you."

As soon as I walked into the house, everybody started asking questions. "Did you get him on the airplane?" Mother asked.

"Of course, Mother, and I met Mr. and Mrs. Holley, too."

"The phone has been ringing off the hook. I think these boys have gone crazy," Mother said. "Everybody you have ever known has called, and the rest want dates."

"Oh, Mama."

"I'm serious. I told them to call back tomorrow," she said.

"Well, I don't want any dates."

She said, "Dr. Strauss' little boy called. He wants you to go out to a Christmas dance, and I've known his father all his life..."

"Mother," I said, interrupting her, "I've only dated him once, and that was for a square dance. He's a nice boy, but he never talks; and besides that, if I put on my high heels, I'm taller than he is."

"That short, young man is a senior at Texas Tech and is going to be a doctor just like his father and grandfather. He'll take over their practice when he graduates," she said.

"I'm sorry, Mother. Doctor or not, he's still too short. Besides, I think Jerry and I are getting married," I said.

"When?" I could tell Mother was exasperated.

"I don't know yet. Certainly after I graduate."

"Well, you can say that again," Daddy declared. "I've made arrangements for you to go to nursing school at the Catholic hospital in Amarillo. You've been accepted, and you need the education."

"Can we talk about this after I graduate *high school*?" I asked.

My dad gave me a serious look and said, "You're going to be eighteen then, and I can't force you, but please think about it. I'd never tell any of my kids who to marry, but..."

"You're right, John," Mother interrupted. You're the one who has to decide who you're going to sleep with, and once you give your word that means forever." Mother was adamant. "We've never had a divorce in this family, and we're not going to start with you! You have no idea what your life is going to be like married to a musician."

"I thought you liked Jerry," I exclaimed.

"I do, but that doesn't change a thing," Mother replied.

"Well, Mother, you've already got me married and divorced all in forty-five minutes," I said.

"Just think it over, Peggy Sue," Daddy said.

"Yes, Daddy. I promise. Mary wants me to go to Texas Tech. She wants me to join the band sorority."

Mother smiled. "Well, that's a good idea, and you can live right here at home."

"No, it's not a good idea. I don't want to go to college and belong to a sorority. Sororities are just a bunch of bull, and all the girls in them come from the same mold. Mary and a lot of others are my friends, and that's fine for them, but not for me. If I went to college, it would be a waste of time and Daddy's money, and you know I'd never graduate. There's no point in going unless I'm going to graduate."

"Have you ever thought about what you want to do?" Daddy asked.

"Yes, I want to go to New York with Buddy and Jerry and find a job. I want to act and dance. Would you let me go to New York?" I begged.

"No, we won't and that's that. No, not alone in New York. You've been raised a decent girl and would never make it alone in New York. I want you to get that out of your mind. It's not safe. If you won't go to college, then it's RN school for you," Mother said.

I gave a very audible sigh and then said, "Thanks, Mother. I'm going to bed. The Tech band sorority invited me out tomorrow night. Is that all right?"

Mother rolled her eyes at my insolence, and I left to go make my bed down in the living room before she could respond. I was exhausted. I wondered just how old I had to be before I could make a decision about my own life. Being seventeen, I thought I was fairly mature, and I felt that I had the right to make my own decisions. Man. No one else seemed to think so, though.

♫

The next day, we finished Christmas shopping and began getting things ready for Christmas Day. Around seven o'clock, Mary picked me up, and we went to her friend Beth's house to meet a couple of other girls who were in the same sorority. Beth's house must have been the largest one in Lubbock—the driveway was at least a mile long. She was watching for us from the upstairs window and opened the door as soon as we stepped onto the porch.

"Hi, Peggy Sue. We've only met once, but I feel like I really know you; I've heard so much about you." She started to laugh. "How does it feel to be famous?"

"I beg your pardon," I said.

"The song, you know," Beth said.

"Oh, you mean 'Peggy Sue.' I think it's great that they're doing so well with their music. What do you think about their sound?" I asked.

"Hell, I think it's just great. It's set Lubbock on its ear. We only had Jerry in Tech for about a month. If I could play and write music like he does, I wouldn't waste my time in college either. It's too bad that the music professor wouldn't acknowledge what talent and great ability Jerry had so he could contribute more in class. That way, we could all have learned something different. I bet some day the whole college will be talking about their music as an art contribution."

"I hope you're right," I replied.

"Let's go, everybody," Mary shouted.

"Where are we going?" I asked.

"Well, I've got the booze and the mix. Where should we go to talk and drink? Do you have any ideas, Peggy?" one of the other girls asked.

"My dad is building a new house down the street. Why don't we go over there and have a housewarming. It's not finished, but we can take a candle, and nobody will find us," I suggested.

Mary spoke up. "Great idea, Peggy, but your mother would sure be mad if she knew."

I laughed. "Well, they always tell me if I'm going to drink to do it at home."

We drove over to the house with everybody talking at once. Inside, we huddled in a circle, lit the candle, made sure everybody had something to drink, and began the housewarming.

"The reason we're having this meeting tonight is because we want you in our sorority, and we felt that if we got to you first, you would want to belong to ours," Mary said.

"That's very flattering. Why me?" I asked.

"For a lot of reasons," Beth said, "but, most of all because we like you, and it would be a feather in our cap to have you."

"Why? Because you feel that I'm different? It's because of the record, isn't it?" I asked.

"But you have to admit the record isn't hurting your popularity any," Mary replied.

We talked the whole thing over for hours...and drank...and drank...and drank some more. By midnight, I barely knew my way home—and I was sitting in it. (Well, it was *going to be* my new home.)

"We'd better get something to eat or you're going to get sick, Peggy, and I can't take you home in this condition or your mother will kill me," Mary said.

We drove to the Hi-D-Ho for a sandwich and glass of milk. "Well, are you going to give us your answer?" one of the girls asked.

"Not tonight. I don't know if I'll even go to college, but if I do, I'll let you know. Fair enough?" I replied.

"Fair enough," echoed across the car from one girl to the other.

"You better take me home now," I said quietly, as my stomach began to churn.

"I'm on my way," Mary slurred, and ten minutes later, we were in front of my house. I knew Mother would be up talking to my sister, and here I stood not even able to focus on the front door. Well, here goes, I thought. I'll give it the old American try.

"What's wrong with you, Peggy Sue?" Mother asked.

"I think I ate something that made me sick, Mother. I just had a sandwich, but I think I'm going to throw up."

Unfortunately, we only had one bathroom, and it was in the middle of the house. I made it there and shut the door, thinking to myself that if I could just throw up I'd be all right. And I was right. I managed to get rid of everything in my stomach and turned to sit down, but when I did, I fell off the toilet and landed right on my butt. Of course, everyone heard this commotion. I woke up not only my father but also my brother in law. In seconds, they were both in the bathroom with me.

"What happened?" Daddy asked, his voice filled with compassion. "Are you hurt?"

"I went out and drank too much. Mother will kill me. Please, Daddy. Don't tell her," I pleaded.

Daddy laughed.

"It's not funny, Daddy."

By that time, everyone had joined us in the bathroom—nothing like having a family meeting in the john.

"Lillie, help your daughter get her gown on," Daddy said.

"Is she hurt, John. Should I call a doctor?" Mother asked.

"No, Lillie, I can take care of the diagnosis," he said.

Unable to get up off the floor by myself, I looked up at Daddy with a prayer in my eyes pleading, *Please don't tell Mother.*

"Her main problem is that she's *my* daughter. The other is she's seventeen. I think she's learned something tonight," Daddy said.

Oh, thank you, Daddy, I thought. He's not going to tell.

"What are you talking about, John?" Mother asked.

"Your baby is drunk," he replied.

"Thanks, Daddy. I needed that," I whimpered, my head aching from all the chatter.

"Peggy Sue! You've been drinking?" Mother screamed.

Oh, God, I pleaded, and then I said, "Yes, Mother, I have, and I may die from it the way I feel."

Mother helped me with my gown, and Daddy took me to bed. Johnnie and Von were staying in my room, and I was sleeping on the hide-a-bed in the living room. Mother and Johnnie chose this moment to come into the living room to talk to me. Not now, I thought. Not now. Not when I'm dying.

"I told you if you want to have a drink, you can do it in your own home. Did you go out to the Cotton Club? Did anyone see you in this condition?" Mother asked.

"No, Mother. I didn't go to the Cotton Club, and the only ones that saw me were the girls I was with. Besides, I *was* home. We went over to the new house and sat on the floor with a candle. Please, Mother, wait until tomorrow. I'll be better then, and we can discuss it further."

Well, Mother would not let it lie. She kept fussing and carrying on for what seemed like forever.

"Lillie, will you stop it? She'll be all right by tomorrow. You act like you've never seen anyone under the influence before," Daddy yelled from the bedroom.

"Not my daughter, John. Not my daughter," Mother yelled back.

I'd just laid my head down and was making a real attempt to stop the bed from spinning when the phone rang. Mother rushed over to answer it so it wouldn't disturb the baby. My sister asked, "Who'd be calling at this hour? I hope nobody in the family's had an accident."

"Pleeease, just let me sleep," I muttered. "I'm not up to this."

"Yes, she is, but I think she's asleep. Let me check. Peggy Sue, it's long distance for you. Can you talk to Jerry, or are you too sick?"

"I'm not sick, Mother. I'm drunk."

"Well, for heaven's sakes. You don't want Jerry to know that, do you?"

"Mother, quit trying to protect me. Give me the phone. I can talk. Hi ya, Jerry. What're ya doing? Tell me what time it is in New York."

"It's 2:30 here. We went over to Coral Records today. Guess what? 'Peggy Sue' has sold one million records!"

"How do they know that?" I asked, forcing myself to speak clearly.

"Because of the record orders they have, and they're pressing more. They wanted to put your picture on the record sleeve, but I wouldn't let them."

"Why not?"

"Because! I don't want any boys to have your picture in their bedrooms. You're going to be my wife. They suggested having a picture of a model, but Buddy told them no. He told them that there's only one Peggy Sue, and he wouldn't have a false one. 'Besides,' Buddy told them, 'she's not brunette; she's a natural blonde.' Then he told them to forget their advertising ideas, so they did. I told Buddy that we're getting married when you get out of school."

"Was he upset?"

"No. Well, just a little at first. I told him that nothing would change between us. He said he knew that, and he thinks you're just great, but he said if I'm getting married, so is he. That way, we can all travel together. He didn't think you'd want to travel with us unless there was another girl along. What's wrong with you, Peggy Sue? Are you sick?"

"Uhhhh, yeah. I'm not quite feeling myself, but I'm quite sure that I'll be better tomorrow. Jerry, I don't understand. Is Buddy going with somebody I don't know about?"

"No, he's not going with anyone that he'd marry. Well, I mean anyone he'd take home to Mother," Jerry said.

"How can he just get married then, especially if he doesn't have a serious girlfriend?" I asked.

"Well, I hope he's just talking. We're leaving for another tour, the *America's Greatest Teenage Recording Stars*, just after the New Year. That'll give me time to talk him out of his crazy marriage idea. I'd better go now. Did I wake your pop?"

"No, and you'd better not call him that. He doesn't like to be called *pop*," I said.

"I love you, Peggy Sue, and wish you were here."

"I wish I were there, too," I exclaimed.

"Can't you talk?" Jerry asked.

"No, Jerry, not without the whole world hearing me," I said.

"I'll call you again when you get to Sacramento," Jerry said. "Are you going out New Year's Eve?"

"I don't know what the family will be doing that night. If we do, I probably won't be out too late," I answered.

"Well, have fun. By the way, the shows are really crazy. There's a balcony right out on the second floor. No matter who walks out there, the crowd just screams and yells. Phil Everly stuck his hands out the window and the crowd went wild. They don't have any idea who anyone is. They just assume you're a star or you wouldn't be on the second floor. I'd better get off the phone now, Peggy Sue. I'm going to have to write another hit record just to pay for this phone bill."

"Good night, Jerry. Talk to you soon," I said, as I lay back on my pillow, trying to visualize the million people who'd bought the record. I wished I could thank each and every one of them personally for accepting Buddy Holly and the Crickets.

♫

CHAPTER FIVE
Pomp and Circumstance

*S*hortly after returning to Sacramento, I received Jerry's new itinerary stating that The Crickets would be playing on the Everly Brothers Tour for about twenty-four days. Wow! How neat! The Everly Brothers were *too* groovy!

Our writing ritual started up again. I had to send my letters to the venues on the schedule at least a week in advance, or Jerry wouldn't get them. I was looking over my calendar to see where I needed to send my next letter when he called to tell me they were traveling all the way to Australia. They would stop in Hawaii to perform a show on the way there, and again, on the way back. Norman would be traveling with them, and maybe, since Vi wouldn't be there, they would have a little freedom. "You know," he said excitedly, "just the guys."

The tour was scheduled to last until approximately February 9, and because he didn't know how long it would take a letter to reach Australia or how much it would cost, Jerry told me not to send him any more. He would try to send cards when he could and would call me when he got back to the States.

Quite honestly, I was glad to finally have a break from writing. Between school, my journal, and letters to Jerry, my hand was becoming quite numb. Sometimes, instead of writing across the page, I would write diagonally so it would look different—that is until Jerry complained that he was getting a stiff neck from reading them and that all the guys were teasing him, saying, "Oh, you got another letter from Peggy Sue. We can tell by the way you're bending your neck to read it." So much for creativity.

Oh, those picture postcards! They were beautiful. Here I was stuck in school studying math, English, business machines, and religion while Buddy Holly and The Crickets were out having the time of their lives. On one card, Jerry wrote that they were traveling with the number-one recording artist in Australia, Johnny O'Keefe, and that they were all crazy about his record, "Wild One," especially Buddy.

As usual, before they arrived home, their next tour was already in the making, and this time, it was a long itinerary. On February 20, they were booked for *The Big Gold Record Stars*, or as I called it, the Florida tour. Once the Florida tour ended on February 25, they had to pack for, and organize, their trip to London. They were scheduled to be in London by March 1 for two shows at the Trocadero, Elephant and Castle. This time, both Norman and Vi would be traveling with them. After a twenty-five-day tour in England, they would begin the *Alan Freed Big Beat Show* in New York City on March 28. I wondered if high school would ever end for me.

♪

"England calling Peggy Sue—person to person."

"Yes, this is she." Eager anticipation ran through my body. "Jerry, is that you?" I shouted.

"It's me. It's me. I love you," Jerry exclaimed.

It was the first time I'd really heard excitement in Jerry's voice when he said those words. Maybe he really *did* love me. However, as soon as he continued, I realized his high spirits were not the result of his missing me, but rather, of the adrenaline rush left over from the shows.

Talking so fast that he was running out of breath, Jerry said, "Peggy Sue, you just would not believe it. The crowds are enormous, and they just sit there without making a sound and really listen to us play. For the first time, audiences have really wanted to hear *just us*. Our first show just about scared us to death. We walked out on stage, everybody clapped, and then they sat down, totally silent. Buddy looked at me, winked his eye, and said, 'If they start throwing things, run fast.' As soon as the first song ended, the audience started to applaud, scream, and yell for more. We started breathing again and then started to laugh. We finally had a show we really felt good about. God! You can't imagine what a feeling that is! Buddy and I want to stay here for the rest of our lives, and guess what? We finally have decent living conditions for the first time ever. At the hotel here, all you have to do is put your shoes out in the hallway at night, and they pick them up and shine them and return them before you even get up. Breakfast in bed! We've never been treated like this before. Buddy and I share a room most of the time. It's great because we're writing and talking all the time..."

"Is Joe B having to stay by himself?" I interrupted.

"He likes it that way," Jerry said.

"Don't y'all forget about him," I joked.

"No problem. Joe B just likes to do his thing, but Norman and Vi are about to drive Buddy and me crazy. They plan every day for us to go sightseeing. Buddy and I are plotting to get out together alone so we can see the London we want to see. You know, the clubs. Norman is so straight you can't get him to let his hair down. At least he hasn't tucked Buddy's napkin in under his chin at the dinner table like he did in Australia."

"What?" I asked.

"Yeah, we were all sitting there at dinner about to eat our spaghetti, and Norman got up and tucked Buddy's napkin in under his chin so he wouldn't get anything on him. I guess being the front man means no spaghetti stains on your clothes, but it sure embarrassed Buddy. Really though, it's super the way Norman takes care of things. We've gone from chitlin tours to royalty! I don't think I'll ever go back on a bus again...not after this. Norman and I got into a little disagreement on the plane."

"What about?" I asked.

"He came over and sat down by Buddy and me. He looked at Buddy and said, 'Well, who are we going to get to play drums after Jerry gets married?' and Buddy looked at me and said, 'Well, who are we going to get to manage us since Norman's already married?' We both started to laugh. Norman didn't think that was so funny.

"Then Norman said, 'Let's talk about Peggy Sue since I've never met her.' I asked, 'What do you want to know?' and he said, 'Do you think she's going to let you travel after you're married?' I told him, 'Yep. I sure do.' Then he wanted to know what religion you were. You have to understand, Peg. That sort of thing is very important to Norman. I just looked at him and said, 'I know you're not going to like this, but she's Catholic,' and then he said, 'Your mother won't stand for that.' I told him my mother doesn't have a choice, and for that matter, neither does he and that everyone in the world isn't Baptist. They're just all trying to get to the same place, so what difference does it make? By that time, Buddy spoke up and told Norman that we weren't going to discuss the matter any more."

"Well, if he keeps that up, he's just going to upset Buddy," I said.

"No, I don't think so, because I said, 'Now he doesn't really think we need him to pick out our wives does he?' and Buddy said, 'No, he just doesn't want the group to get married. He thinks that'll hurt the image.' Norman just thinks he must make all the decisions for us. I think it's an age-difference thing. I have to go now. I'll call you after we get back to the States. I'll sure be glad when you're out of school."

"Be careful, and tell Buddy and Joe B 'hi' for me," I said as I hung up the phone.

♫

It was already May and only a few more weeks of school remained. As I snuggled into my bed, I wished I could just travel forward in time to graduation day and skip all the rest, especially the mandatory Senior Prom. At Bishop Armstrong, you had to attend the prom, or you couldn't graduate. I marveled at how they expected girls to get dates at an all-girls school. Besides, I was engaged. I wondered how Jerry would feel about me going with someone else. But, if I had to go, maybe my friend, Theresa, could set me up on a blind date. Graduation day was scheduled for June 4, and I couldn't wait to be through with high school.

As I drifted off to sleep, I wondered how lucky I really was. The record had sold over a million copies, but I couldn't even get a date for the Senior Prom. Oh, well, like Scarlett O'Hara, I'd worry about that tomorrow.

♫

When I got home from school the next day, a short letter and another long itinerary from Jerry awaited me. It looked like he'd be taking another bus tour after all. Well, I thought, the show must go on.

At midnight, right on the dot, the telephone rang, and I answered by asking, "How long have you been home?"

51

"How did you know it was me calling?" Jerry asked.

"You're the only one I know who calls at this hour," I replied.

"I guess I woke you up," he said apologetically.

"That's all right. Is everything okay?"

"Yep, we're all fine. I talked to your mom today. She hopes you're still graduating."

"Funny. Funny. What's new with Buddy and Joe B?" I asked.

Well, we got off the plane in Dallas, bought three motorcycles and rode them home to Lubbock."

"You did what?" I asked.

"You heard me," he said.

"I didn't know any of you even knew how to ride a motorcycle."

"We didn't really. Buddy's been on his cousin's before, but we learned on the way home. Buddy fell once and I burned my leg."

"Jerry, did Norman know what you guys were doing?"

"No, he would've had a fit. We got paid in cash for a show in New York, so we took the money and bought 'em. I felt just like James Dean. It even rained on us and, boy, was it cold. Did you know that it's three-hundred miles from Dallas to Lubbock?"

I laughed. "I don't think the world is ready for you and Buddy."

"It never has been, and it would be too much of a shock to get approval now," he said jovially.

"I got your itinerary. I thought you weren't going to take a bus tour any more."

"Well, we need to make the money while we can. We've decided to take a car after this road tour is over. I love you, and I'll call again soon."

"I love you, too, Jerry, and please be careful on the bikes."

I wrote to Jerry twice a week. Via the United States Postal Service, we discussed crystal, pottery, china, and silver; but discussing such things was as far as we got. We never seemed to be able to agree on anything.

Meanwhile, my friend Theresa fixed me up with a date for the Senior Prom. I was *so* thankful that I didn't have to take my brother-in-law. That would've been too embarrassing. I told Jerry about the dance so he understood that it was a mandatory affair. I didn't want him accusing me of being disloyal during our long-distance relationship.

Prom night wasn't so bad after all. Richard was a nice boy, but he was very polished. We had a great time because he was a good dancer and I did *love to dance*. Plus, now I could graduate. Little did I know that there would be one more hurdle awaiting me.

♫

Two days prior to the actual graduation ceremony, we had a full-dress rehearsal. Everything seemed to be just fine until one of the nuns walked up to me and said, "Well, *you* just may not graduate."

Dumbfounded, I gave her a blank look. "Excuse me?"

"I thought you knew better. Now you may not graduate. Your skirt is *too tight*."

After all the years of trying to be accepted by school systems and never quite feeling like I fit in, this was just too much. Keep me from graduating *now*—after complying with all the rules and regulations, regardless of how inane they usually seemed? With Mother, Dad, and Jerry already on their way to California to attend my graduation ceremony? No way!

I tightened my lips and said defiantly, "My *mother* sent me this skirt to wear."

She walked off, visibly miffed, but didn't say anything else. I felt a little guilty for talking that way to a nun, who probably was just stressed because she had a million things to do.

I knew my graduation dress would pass inspection. It was definitely not too tight. It was fitted at the waist and then flared out gracefully, but not too much. My grandpa had bought it for me for a graduation gift. It was a white cotton princess style, soft like a handkerchief, with cap sleeves and smocking down the bodice. Eight tiny rows of peek-a-boo lace went all the way to the hem. It was lovely, and if it had gone to the floor, it would've made a great gown for a formal wedding.

♫

Johnnie was frantically cleaning house, cooking, and fussing. I was lost in my own thoughts as I changed the sheets on the beds. On one hand, I couldn't think of anything better in life than to be Jerry's wife and travel with the group, but on the other hand, I kept thinking something was missing—maybe *that special feeling*, but I didn't know what I was supposed to be feeling. If real love meant having *that feeling*, I sure hoped I wouldn't miss it.

Eighteen. The magic age. Why does most of the adult population think that when a person turns eighteen, she's ready for the world? That it's time for her to leave the nest and go to college or get married? Who made that rule? I wondered if seeing Jerry again would put everything back into perspective and help me find the answers to some of my questions.

I didn't have long to wait. Their car drove up into the driveway, and we all ran out to meet them. Everybody was talking at once. Johnnie was proudly showing off how much Little Kim had grown, and Mother was so busy talking and playing with the baby that she didn't have time for the rest of us. Daddy said it had been the most entertaining trip he'd ever had. Jerry started to laugh. "I drove most of the way. Your dad gets a little nervous when I drive with one hand and play the dashboard drums with the other."

"I do think it makes the trip a little more fun, don't you, Lillie?" Dad asked.

"What did you say, John?" Mother said, completely captivated by Little Kim.

"Nothing, Lillie. Peggy Sue, I think I know why Jerry wants to get married." Jerry turned beet red. "When we stopped for the night, he wanted to sleep in the same room with us. He doesn't like sleeping alone," Daddy said.

As we walked into the house, Daddy asked me if I was really going to get my diploma.

"Well, that's what they tell me," I said.

"And you didn't even have to burn down the school. I'm really proud of you for sticking it out. This is the biggest day in my life. Both my daughters have graduated from high school—and me, I didn't finish the eighth grade."

"You never really gave us a choice either, did you, Daddy?"

"That's right. When do you graduate?" he asked.

"Tomorrow night," I said proudly.

Everyone started talking at once, catching up on months' worth of gossip and news. Jerry and I went out onto the patio where we could be alone. I asked him, "Did you really buy me an engagement ring?"

"Yes, I did. One just like you ordered."

"What do you mean?" I asked, puzzled.

"One very large carat and not a single flaw in it. I had a hell of a time finding a good diamond. I want to wait until the right time to give it to you so it'll be romantic."

"Can I see it? Does your mother know you bought it?" I asked.

"Are you kidding? She helped me pick it out," he exclaimed.

"How about Norman? Is he taking it any better?" I asked apprehensively.

"It's hard to tell who he's the most upset with, Buddy or me."

"What has Buddy done?"

"He's determined to get married, too," Jerry said.

"I didn't know he was going with anybody. Who is she? Do I know her?" I asked.

"You won't believe it when I tell you. Buddy and I have talked endlessly about this. He's determined to get married. There's a girl in Lubbock he could marry, but everyone knows her reputation; he likes this girl he's seen in New York, too, and nobody in Lubbock knows her. He feels his mother will more readily accept the girl from New York."

"But, Jerry, are you saying he hasn't even dated her? I asked in amazement.

"That's what I'm saying. This woman is a receptionist at Peer-Southern Music where her aunt is the head of the Latin division, and I guess he thinks they would have something in common."

"Woman?" I snapped. "How old is she?"

"I don't know, but she's older than Buddy. Come on. Let's not talk about them any more. Here, look at this," he said as he pulled a velvet box from his pocket and opened it. Inside was the largest diamond I'd ever seen. It was set in white gold and stood all alone. "The jeweler called it...uhhh..."

"A solitaire," I said breathlessly.

"Do you like it?" he asked nervously.

"It's beautiful," I exclaimed.

"Well, I just want you to know I'm the kind of guy who won't say keep the diamond even if we don't get married," he joked.

I laughed. "Okay, Jerry. I'm not the type of girl to give the ring back either. I guess that makes us an even match."

Romanticism gave way to impulse, and Jerry took out the ring and slid it on my finger. I was stunned. I couldn't believe this was happening *now*. He put his arms around me, and as he kissed me, I could tell by his tenderness that he cared for me very much.

"What are you thinking, Peg? You have a funny look on your face. Don't you like the ring?" Jerry asked, breaking my thoughts.

"It's beautiful, Jerry. I-I don't know what to say." I kept thinking to myself, This is moving too fast...I don't really know you...Where's the feeling I'm being swept off my feet? Is this all you feel when you're in love? There must be more. I know...I'll wear the ring until I get back to Lubbock, and then I'll explain to him why we can't get married so soon. I'm just not ready, not ready at all.

We walked back into the house and showed my family what we'd done. Mother said she'd already seen the ring. Jerry had shown it to her right after he bought it. My brother-in-law poured champagne, and my family toasted us before we sat down to dinner.

Mother asked, "What's happening tomorrow?"

"I want to go shopping," I said quickly, remembering I needed to buy a new dress for the after-graduation dance and parties.

♫

The next morning, Jerry said, "Peggy, I want to buy you something for your graduation. What would you like?"

"How about a new dress?" I asked.

"You can have any dress in town you want," he exclaimed.

We shopped for hours. I tried on dress after dress, hats, and shoes. Jerry was having a good time giving his opinion on the color, style, and fit. Not only did we *look* young, but we *acted* young and carefree. In one store, I did a soft-shoe number for the clerks when they wouldn't wait on us as quickly as we'd expected them to.

Jerry laughed. "How long have you been dancing in department stores, Peggy?"

"Well, I don't know, but it works really well when you want their attention. And, it's a lot better than having a temper tantrum," I replied.

Jerry laughed again and said, "I guess I'm going to have my hands full just keeping up with you."

Finally, I found a beautiful dress at Joseph Magnin's that fit perfectly. It was a soft yellow organza with a full skirt and cancan that bounced as I walked.

"We'd better get home. You have to get ready to accept that piece of paper your dad wants so badly," Jerry said.

As we walked into the house, everyone bombarded us with questions. They all wanted to know where we'd been all day and asked if we knew that we had to leave shortly for the ceremony, and therefore, needed to get ready. I pulled the dress from the box to show everyone. Daddy turned white and then managed a little smile as he gently took me aside to talk to me.

"What's wrong, Daddy?" I asked.

"I just want you to know I'm not going to ruin it for you because you're graduating tonight," he said.

What do you mean?" I asked, wondering what could possibly be wrong.

"You can wear the dress tonight, but I don't like the idea of a man buying you clothes," he said.

"Why?"

"Because men don't pay for your clothes unless you're married to them," he replied seriously. "It's not respectful."

Jerry had walked over to us and overheard the conversation. Daddy turned to him and said, "Jerry, I know that you didn't mean this to be anything more than a gift for Peggy Sue, but she's been raised to be a lady, and as old fashioned as that may sound, you're not to wear the dress again until the two of you are married."

"Mr. Gerron, the dress was her idea," Jerry said. "I wanted to buy her a graduation gift. I would've bought her anything she asked for. There was no other intention, Sir."

"I'm sure that's true, Jerry, but you have to understand the old Southern manners we old Southern people have." Daddy laughed and the tension was quickly relieved.

Jerry and I dressed for the occasion, and we left for the same Sacramento Memorial Auditorium where I had heard Jerry and Buddy play "Peggy Sue" for the first time, except today, it had taken on all the pomp and grandeur of a Catholic ceremony. The Bishop was seated in the middle of the stage, and we genuflected and kissed his ring as we received our diplomas. Eva stood in line in front of me. I didn't know her very well, but she'd always managed to smile and say hello whenever we passed in the halls at school. I'd been a little surprised the first time I saw her at Bishop Armstrong because I'd never had a black schoolmate before. Daddy had raised us not to be prejudiced, but we still had to abide by Texas rules, which dictated separate schools for blacks and whites.

After graduation, I handed Daddy that all-important piece of paper. It was one of the very few times I'd ever seen him with tears in his eyes.

"You've made me a very proud man today, Peggy Sue," Daddy said. "I wanted to be a doctor like my father, but when he was killed in that buggy accident on his way to take care of a patient, I had to quit school and work to help support the family. Now all we have to do is get you into college, right?"

"Oh, Daddy, I just got out of high school, and you're ready to start me in college. Could I at least go to the dance tonight first?" I asked.

He laughed. "I gave you and your sister the best gift I could—making sure you'd both know how to read," he said as he gave me an approving hug. I felt that I had finally accomplished something that had made both my parents proud. Graduating from a Catholic school had always been Mother's dream. The only way she would've been happier was if I had become a nun, but alas, she resigned herself to the fact that I was engaged.

Jerry and I left for a chain of champagne parties and the graduation dance. As we got into the car, I could sense something was on his mind because his mood had changed. Every time there was a new experience where he was unsure of himself, he had a tendency to get quiet. I was concerned that he was overwhelmed by the number of parties we'd be attending and the fact that he wouldn't know anyone there.

"Listen," I said. "If you don't want to go to the dance, we don't have to, but I have to go to the parties. All my friends are expecting me, and since I'll be leaving for Texas soon, I have to say my goodbyes."

"No, that's all right. I want to go and meet your friends. We didn't have anything like this in Lubbock when I graduated. Just remember, I'm a country boy. Can I ask you a question though?" he said.

"Sure."

"Why did you kiss that ring after that black girl did?"

I started to laugh. I thought for sure he was joking, but the look on his face made me wonder whether he was making a racial comment or really asking about why we kissed the ring. I decided on the former. I looked him straight in the eye and exclaimed, "You've got to be kidding!"

"Well, I am, sort of. Didn't you think about it when you did it?" he asked.

"Oh, sure. The Bishop should've been wearing two rings on his hand like the water fountains in Lubbock. One for the *Whites* and one for the *Coloreds*."

"Right. I see your point now. I was just joking anyway."

We sat in silence on our way to the first party. I kept thinking no one could be that shallow or prejudiced, could they? Especially Jerry since he had been living in such close proximity with blacks during the bus tours. Finally, I broke the silence. "Jerry, I've been raised to believe that you can't judge a man by his color. You judge him for himself."

"I was raised in Texas, too. Remember?" he said.

"My dad would've killed me if I hadn't been more liberal than that," I explained.

"I just meant that's something you wouldn't see at a graduation in Lubbock, Texas, now is it? Blacks and whites together at graduation and acting like it's completely normal? Let's not talk about it anymore, okay, Peg?"

By that time, we were at the first party. My friends were delighted to meet Jerry, since he was all they'd heard me talk about for a year. One thing about Jerry, when he was on center stage, he came alive—laughing, singing, playing the drums. However, at social events, he acted intimidated—definitely out of his element. He was very quiet—almost withdrawn. We partied all night, but I wasn't sure he was really enjoying himself. At least, I thought, he was making the effort. We got home about four o'clock the next morning. When I awoke, I noticed that Mother had already packed everything for our trip back to Lubbock—Daddy and Jerry had to get back to their schedules. We said our goodbyes, and before long, my parents, Jerry, and I were on our way home.

CHAPTER SIX
Summer 1958

After taking Jerry home, we drove to the new house Daddy had built on 16th Street. I hadn't seen it since the night the Texas Tech sorority sisters and I had sat on the bare concrete floor drinking ourselves miserably ill. I had tried to picture what my new home would look like, but my mind's eye had not even come close to envisioning how beautiful it was with its dark-red brick, brown shutters and trim, and brown wrought iron stretching from the porch to the roof.

This looks nothing like where we lived in the Arnett Benson addition, I thought. All the homes there were small and wood-framed. Some were well kept with tidy yards, but others were in bad shape.

"Well, well, the Gerrons have certainly stepped up in the world," I said appreciatively.

Mother laughed. Daddy was so proud his buttons were about to pop.

"You know, Peg," he said, "I watched every inch of this brick house being built. It's just what I always wanted. Come inside."

I wondered if this was the same tone of voice he had used when he showed off his babies for the first time.

"See this entry hall?" he said. "See these doors? Look at the way they close. You can shut the living room off for privacy."

"Mother, when did you buy all the new furniture?"

"While you were gone," she teased. "Your room is at the end of the hall because Daddy wants you back there so you'll be protected."

"From what?" I asked in a soft, puzzled tone, a half smile on my lips.

"Who knows," she replied, grinning and rolling her eyes.

We both began to giggle, as we frequently did when the subject of Daddy's militaristic, overprotective nature toward me came up.

I had the most beautiful bedroom I'd ever seen. A modern, whitish-gray bedroom suite, complete with a bookcase headboard and a six-drawer dresser with a big mirror on top of it, replaced my mismatched furniture from Arnett Benson. Knowing me as she did, Mother had placed my Pilot record player right beside the bed.

Graduation presents were everywhere. Some of them were from people I knew; others were from people known only to my parents. Wow, I thought, this is better than Christmas! They're all for me! After I opened two or three, my enthusiasm waned, however, because they all seemed to be the same thing. I bet I had ten traveling irons.

My parents had bought me all kinds of Samsonite luggage. They knew I'd need it since I'd be traveling with Jerry soon.

♫

It seemed as though I couldn't make a climate change without getting strep throat. By evening, my throat was killing me, and my skin burned hot with fever. Finally, by Friday, I felt like I just might survive. I managed to get dressed and even comb my hair, and then I lumbered into the kitchen.

The way Mother was looking out the window, I assumed she was watching for the mailman, and I asked in a weakened voice, "Isn't it too early for the mail to come?"

"He usually comes early," she replied offhandedly. "But, I'm watching those cars parked out front with all the boys in them."

"Oh, is it anybody I know?" I asked, my voice suddenly becoming livelier and my step taking on a springy, buoyant movement.

"Get away from the window. It's no one you know," she said sharply, turning to put herself between the window and me as if she had to protect me from some evil lurking outside.

"What are they doing?" I persisted, trying to look around her. Now I absolutely had to know.

"They're just sitting there watching the house," she said as she turned to look out the window again.

"Do they want something?" I asked.

"I don't know. I don't want you to go out alone today," she said tensely. Then in a quieter tone, she turned toward me and added, "It makes me nervous."

"Mother, don't be silly. They aren't looking at our house. What would be the point?"

About that time, I got a glimpse of the mailman coming across the street and said, "I'll get the mail."

"No, I'll get it," Mother replied authoritatively.

"I said I would, Mother. Now stop acting that way. I'm not a child."

I opened the door, stepped out onto the porch, and glanced toward the cars. The boys in them yelled, "Peggy Sue!" and waved. I waved back, and they sped off. I didn't recognize any of them. How strange, I thought.

Sporting a big smile, the postman handed me the mail and asked, "You're John's baby daughter Peggy Sue, aren't you? Been in California at school, huh?"

"That's right."

"Well, welcome home, Peggy Sue."

"Thank you," I said as I wondered why, all of a sudden, everyone in Lubbock was beginning to act like they knew me, especially since I'd been gone so long. No one in California had seemed to care who I was, except my classmates, my sister, and my brother-in-law.

I handed the mail to Mother, and we sat down to breakfast. She fumbled through it as she began to nibble on a piece of toast. One of the letters caught her eye. She put down her toast and, with a curious look on her face, began to examine the envelope more closely.

"Who's it from, Mother?"

She didn't even seem to hear me as she began to open and read it. All of a sudden, she turned pale, gasped, wadded the letter tightly into her fist, and stared at me in horror.

My fork fell right out of my hand and rattled in my plate. "What is it, Mother? Tell me."

"It's a filthy letter concerning you, and you don't need to read it," she exclaimed.

63

Reaching out for it, I said firmly, "I'm not a baby. Let me see the letter."

She immediately snatched her hand away, and putting the letter and its envelope into her apron pocket, she said, "No, I'll let your father read it, and then we'll discuss it tonight after dinner."

Well, now I'd have to wait until later to find out what was in that wonderful piece of literature. It must have been good. But, knowing Mother as I did, if she'd seen so much as the word *sex* in it, she would've been shocked, and Daddy would have had to assume his patriarchal duties.

We spent the rest of the meal in silence.

As we began to clear the table, I said, "Jerry's coming over to pick me up in a little while. I'm going to spend the day with him. The group's getting ready to go on another tour, and they're buying a station wagon for the dance band they're trying to put together. If you need me, I'll be at the Allisons' house."

"Don't go anywhere alone. Stay with Jerry," Mother insisted. "Or else come home. I still feel a little nervous about that letter. If you're not going to be home for dinner, call me."

"Yes, Mother."

♫

As Jerry and I pulled into the Allisons' driveway, Buddy and Joe B came roaring up on their motorcycles.

"You guys look like a bunch of hoods," I said. "Does your mother really let you ride that thing, Buddy?"

He laughed. "My mother isn't impressed with it, but my dad loves to ride it." Turning to Jerry, he said, "We have to find another guitar player for the dance band. Who do you think we should get?"

Jerry thought for a moment and then replied, "The only one I know is Curtis, and he's into country."

"Do you think he can play rock?" Buddy asked.

"I think he'll try, and he doesn't have a gig right now," Jerry said.

"Invite him over so we can talk to him." Then, turning to me, Buddy said playfully, "Let me see your left hand, Peggy Sue. I got to see that diamond when Jerry picked it out for you. I was with him."

I stuck out my hand, and Buddy laughed. Sounding just like Little Richard, he threw his head back and yelled," Well al-l-l-l right!"

"I heard you're getting married, too, Buddy," I said.

"Yeah, that's what I hear, too," he replied, his eyes flashing with devilment.

"When do I get to meet her?" I asked.

"Soon, Peggy Sue, very soon. I have to go. See you cats later tonight, maybe."

"What're y'all going to do?" I asked.

"I don't know about Jerry or Joe B, but I'm going out with the boys tonight," Buddy said, his eyes sparkling.

I just shook my head and started toward the kitchen door, but I stopped dead in my tracks when I heard Jerry say, "I know where you're going. You're going over to see that girl we were talking about earlier, huh?"

I glanced back over my shoulder. Buddy's face was blood red.

"Look, Jerry. She's leaving town. I helped her out of a bind, and she's grateful. That's all."

He glanced in my direction to see if I had overheard, and I promptly quipped, "Who did you help?"

"Boy, you could hear a pin drop, couldn't you, Peggy Sue?" He shot me his sulky Marlon Brando look, revved his motorcycle, and rode away with Joe B following right behind him.

I laughed. "Is he going out with that girl, Jerry?"

Jerry didn't answer until he came up beside me, and then in a quiet voice he confided, "He's been out with her, but so has everyone else in town."

"What favor did he do for her?"

"He gave her some money so she could move out of town. She's pregnant," he whispered.

I continued to press him. "Why would he give her money? Is it his baby?"

"No, but everybody would think that just like you did. She went out a lot. The dad could be any one of a hundred boys here in Lubbock. The biggest problem is that I really think Buddy loves her. She may love him, too. I don't know. She knows he can't marry her. Remember I told you about the girl with the bad reputation from Lubbock. That's who Buddy was talking about."

"But if he loves her, why doesn't he just marry her?"

The situation seemed simple to me.

"He can't take her home to his mother, Peggy. Everyone knows what she is, and you have to understand the way Buddy's mother thinks. Buddy can do no wrong. To his parents, Buddy and I are perfect examples of good sons. When he gets drunk, his mother thinks he has the flu. My mother at least knows me better than that."

Don't we all, I thought to myself. Don't we all.

♫

After dinner with Jerry's parents, we helped clean the kitchen and then drove to the Hi-D-Ho to see who was hanging out there. I noticed a guy waving in our direction as soon as we parked. Jerry immediately leaned out the window and waved for him to come over to the car. I noted a little wobble in his gait as he approached.

"Hi ya, Jerry, how've ya been? Well, I'm fine. How 'bout you?" he slurred. "What are ya doin'? We're gonna get something to eat." He hiccupped as he said, "Waylon's inside," and pointed in the direction of the Hi-D-Ho.

Acting very formal, Jerry said, "Sonny, this is Peggy Sue, my fiancée; and, Peggy Sue, this is Sonny Curtis."

Sonny leaned in the window and said, "Oh. I hear your record on the radio all the time. Well. Pretty, pretty, pretty, Peggy Sue; and you mos' certainly are. Jerry, you found yourself a real winner."

I started to chuckle. He was smashed.

Smiling, he asked, "How's it feel to be a record?"

I smarted back, "I don't know. I've never been a record, but if I turn into one, I'll let you know."

"No. No. I mean how's it feel to have a hit record named after ya?" he persisted, his breath reeking of alcohol fumes.

"It's very flattering, thank you."

"It doesn't do you justice," he remarked as he lowered his voice to be sincere. "Well, Peggy Suuuuuuuuuuuue, since I've made an ass of myself, I think I'll go in and have something to eat with good ole Waylon."

66

Jerry said, "Sonny, I wanna talk to you tomorrow. When you get up, come over. Will ya?"

"Sure," he said, as he reeled away from the car.

We left the Hi-D-Ho and drove around for a while looking for Buddy but didn't find him.

Jerry said, "It's about eleven o'clock, so I'd better take you home."

"What are you going to do after you drop me off?" I asked.

"Oh, I'm going to a party."

"I'll go with you," I exclaimed excitedly.

"No, not to this party. Everyone is going to be rip-roaring drunk. It's an older couple giving it. The wife thinks she's a songwriter. I promised to drop by and listen to what she's written. I really don't want to go. The last time I went over there, she got so drunk she started to strip. Her husband had to put her to bed. I'll pick you up in the morning around ten o'clock."

"Okay, I'll be ready."

♪

I hadn't been able to get the mysterious letter Mother, or rather *I*, had gotten in the mail out of my mind all day. I didn't say anything to Jerry about it because I didn't have a clue what Mother and Daddy would tell me. When I saw them sitting in the kitchen waiting for me to come home, I knew it was serious.

"Sit down, Honey. I think we should talk about this," Daddy said, looking down at the wrinkled letter he was holding in his hand. "You, of course, know Jerry better than we do, but I think you should know that somebody...we don't know who...we can't tell by the letter...has challenged Jerry and Buddy's friendship."

At first I couldn't figure out what he was getting at, but then, by the way both of my parents were looking at each other, it hit me. "Are you saying that they're queer?"

"No, *we* don't think that. But that's what the letter indicates," Daddy said, trying to be sensitive. "It also says they have pictures."

"Well, that's a lie," I yelled.

"We know. We think it's a lie, too. We think you should tell Jerry and his family. When people start to become famous, other people become jealous."

"Lord, I thought you were going to tell me he'd gotten a girl pregnant. *That* I would've believed." I laughed, relieved that the letter was so ridiculous. I had worried about that silly thing all day. I felt as though a weight had been lifted off my chest, and I breathed a sigh of relief.

Daddy got up and threw the letter into the trash with the rest of the garbage.

♫

The next morning, I was completely dressed and waiting for Jerry at ten o'clock. Eleven o'clock, no Jerry; twelve o'clock, no Jerry; finally, at one o'clock, Jerry rang the doorbell.

"Where have you been? Or, did I misunderstand the time?" I scolded.

"I'm sorry. I just couldn't get up this morning, and I have a hangover."

"What time did you get home?"

"Around four."

"It must have been a good party. Did she strip?"

"No, she behaved herself. I'm going to be tied up today. We have to get the dance band ready, and then we're going over to Clovis."

Annoyed, I said, "Well, I'll just stay home."

"No, I'll bring you home when we get ready to go," Jerry insisted, as he took my arm and led me to the car.

A couple of cars were parked in front of his house when we arrived.

"Who's here?" I asked.

"Just the guys. Come on."

Sonny Curtis, sitting on the sofa, was tuning a guitar, and Joe B was on the floor plucking on his bass. I found a footstool and sat down. About that time, Buddy, who always seemed the focal point as soon as he entered a room, came bursting through the kitchen door, saying, "Hi, everybody. Let's get started. Sonny, can you play 'Brown-Eyed Handsome Man' for me?"

"Okay, you got it." Sonny started to play.

After maybe a verse of the song, Buddy said, "No, not that way. I want you to play it rock. Try it again."

Buddy started keeping time by patting the wall with his hand, and Sonny began playing.

"Stop. That's still not right. Let's do it again. One...two..." he said as he began counting the beat and Sonny started over.

Suddenly, Buddy rushed across the room and grabbed the guitar from Sonny's hands. I was terrified. I'd never seen this intolerant side of Buddy before, and I couldn't imagine what he'd do next.

"Hey, Man!" Sonny shouted, shocked by Buddy's behavior.

Completely out of character for him, Buddy yelled, "Don't play it that way again! Can't you hear what you're doing to that song? This is the way you should play it," Buddy said as he demonstrated the sound he heard in his soul. "Can you hear the difference now?" he asked Sonny.

"Yeah, Man. I can hear it when you play it."

"But can *you* play it that way?" Buddy challenged.

"Man, I sure wish I could. It's hard for me to hear what you hear, but I'm going to learn if it kills me."

Everybody in the room let out a simultaneous breath of relief when Buddy, who started to relax and managed a small smile, said, "Let's go to Clovis and put the dance band together." Then he looked over at me and asked, "Are you coming with us, Peggy Sue?"

"No. Sorry. I can't. I'll see all of you when you get back."

As Jerry drove me home, he said, "We're going over to Clovis again on Sunday. Ask your parents if you can go with me."

We said our goodbyes, and once again, I was left standing by the curb, waving after him.

♫

CHAPTER SEVEN
Clovis, New Mexico

$\mathcal{S}$unday finally rolled around and Jerry, Joe B, and I were going over to Clovis, New Mexico, to meet Norman Petty and his family. Lord, I was nervous. It took me two hours to dress—about twice as long as it would take to get to Clovis the way Jerry drove. Jerry and Joe B picked me up early, and as we were leaving, Daddy said, "Be sure you have her home before midnight."

"No problem, Mr. Gerron," Jerry replied.

It was a ninety-mile trip from Lubbock to Clovis, and the boys talked all the way about Norman, Vi, his secretary Norma Jean, and Norman's parents, who lived with them. After describing them, Jerry and Joe B warned me that Norman and Vi weren't a typical Clovis couple.

"Yeah, Man. Norman's really cool," said Joe B. "I like the way they dress."

Jerry said, "Yeah, they shop in New York and Europe for clothes."

According to Jerry and Joe B, Vi's pride and joy, besides her plants, was a little black and tan Chihuahua named Speedy. "You won't believe how Vi treats him," Jerry said, shaking his head from side to side in wonderment.

Norman's life was music, but Vi's was performing. His instrument of choice was the organ; hers was the piano. Vi had gotten a classical music degree in Oklahoma City, while Norman's talent came naturally—he had never studied music and could neither read nor write lead sheets. Norman would try to teach Vi how to play by ear, and she would try to teach him how to write music. They worked well together, and she would often transpose his ideas into written notes so others would know what he wanted.

Norman had perfect pitch in tuning which, in the boys' opinion, actually led to a really strange idiosyncrasy: Every clock had to be set to the precise second, and if the alarm or chime on it wasn't in key, he got rid of it. They talked about how good the recording equipment, which he had bought with the help of General Harper from the United States Air Force, was and said Norman was an absolute genius with it. General Harper's daughter, Jo, took care of Norman's publishing office in New York.

Jerry laughed. "I've just got to tell you this story. We were overdubbing 'Think it Over' with the Roses. They'll probably be there today. Their names are Robert Linville, David Bigham, and Ray Rush. Anyway, Norman decided we needed to put some piano in it, so he said, 'Robert, go out and tell Vi I need her to come in and play the piano, please.'

"Robert said, 'Yes, Sir,' and he went out into the courtyard where Vi was planting some plants and said, 'Norman would like for you to come in and play the piano,' and then he walked back into the studio.

"Well, she didn't come in. So, in a few minutes, Norman said, 'Robert, go back and tell Vi to come in.'

"Robert said, 'Yes, Sir,' and gave the message to Vi again.

"'Yeah, okay,' she said and kept right on planting her plants.

"In a few minutes, Norman opened up the door and yelled, 'Violet Ann!'

"She threw down her little spade, stormed in with her hands all covered with mud, sat down at the piano, and pounded those notes out with the power of a man hitting a punching bag.

"We were all saying *uh-oh* to ourselves," Jerry chuckled, "but, you know, that's what made the sound on that record. If she hadn't been so mad, 'Think it Over' might not have done so well on the charts."

I could tell Jerry and Joe B really liked Norman as a person, as well as a musician and producer. He was like a parent figure to them, and they respected him for that as much as for his musical ability and production skills.

By the time we reached the Clovis city limits, I was really in awe of the Pettys. I had already felt anxious about meeting them because they were *stars* to me. They were the ones who had recorded my favorite song,

"First Kiss." True, The Crickets were stars in their own right and you'd think being in the presence of anyone else's *stardom* wouldn't bother me after being around them, but it wasn't the same. The Crickets were my friends. The Pettys—that was different!

The closer we got to the studio on 7th Street, the more nervous I became. I'd never been in a studio before. What if they didn't like me?

On the left side of the street, I spotted a building with a "Norman Petty Studios" sign. Cars were parked everywhere. Jerry drove around the block and up into the drive that led toward the back. We walked around the covered-patio area toward the front of the building where Norman met us halfway.

He was a very handsome man, just under six feet tall. His beautiful brown eyes flashed, and with an unending smile he said, "So you're the young girl we've been hearing so much about for a year. Nice to meet you, Peggy Sue. Let me show you around the studio." Instantly, I was at ease.

There were so many people, I could hardly move—it looked and sounded like a family reunion. Norman took the time to introduce me to some of the guests. There were Ma and Pa, who were Norman's parents; Carol and Bob Montgomery, who had partnered with Buddy on "The Sunday Party" on radio station KDAV in Lubbock; and Robert Linville, David Bigham, and Ray Rush, who were the Roses Jerry had told me about. Also, there was a man there, about the same age as Norman, who was really dressed up. He had on a white dress shirt and tie with a nice, light-brown suit and great dress loafers. Norman took me over to him and said, "I would like for you to meet my good friend, Jimmy Self. He's in radio."

"So you're the real Peggy Sue. It's a pleasure to meet you," Jimmy said.

"Thank you," I said quietly.

Norman took me into his office and began my grand excursion into the world of recording. Through the double-paned window to his left, he showed me where the guys set up in the studio and then tried to explain how he recorded. He told me where the mics were and explained how the sound came into the office. I listened intently, but I didn't really understand all the details he was giving me. It was impressive though.

Norman had me sit down in his chair behind the board and then turned on "Peggy Sue" so I could hear what it sounded like from his chair. All I could say was, "Wow!" It was as though by sitting in that chair, I could envision the whole process. I could feel the *power* of the song. The only thing I could compare this moment to was hearing my song for the very first time at the *Show of Stars*.

Next, Norman took me into the actual studio, but there were so many people there that I really didn't get to see much of it. There was something said about the walls being curved like vertical waves to keep the sound from bouncing, but then I was pushed by the crowd into a narrow hall, with Norman and Jerry following, and couldn't hear the rest of the explanation.

Vi, who stood about 5'5" and had really short, red-blonde hair, was in the kitchen cooking with Norma Jean. As Norman introduced me, Vi kept right on cooking and said, "Pull up a chair and we can talk while I fix dinner for everyone."

Like Joe B had said, she was dressed "really cool" in a cute, dressy pantsuit and big, chef-style apron.

Norma Jean stood only about 5'2." She wore penny loafers, bobby socks, and a neatly tucked-in, New Mexican turquoise shirt with no frills. She had two rings of keys attached to her belt on her Levi's. However, these weren't just average key rings—they were the largest rings with the most keys I had ever seen. I couldn't help but comment, "You sure have a lot of keys."

"Yes. I have them with me at all times," she said. "They're to Norman's business."

There were no airs about either one of these women. They were totally comfortable with themselves and had a camaraderie with each other which let me know immediately that they were more like sisters than boss and employee. Vi was more dramatic—just like I had pictured her. Norma Jean was tailored. One looked like an artist; the other looked like a business professional.

"What are you cooking?" I asked.

"Cheese blintzes," said Vi. "Ever had one?"

"No, but they look delicious." I had heard about crepes before but had never seen anybody make one. "Is that a crepe you're making?"

Vi nodded her head and said, "And then after you brown the crepe, you fill it with this cottage-cheese mixture, fold it like an enchilada, and brown it on both sides. Then we serve them with sour cream, fruit, and jam."

"They really smell good."

Vi stopped and looked me over. "Well, you sure are a pretty girl, and I love that dress you have on."

I stammered, "Oh. Thank you."

"Now let me see that diamond ring I've heard so much about," she said as she winked at me.

I stuck my hand out, and she smiled a beautiful ear-to-ear smile that made me happy just looking at her.

"I have to tell you, Mrs. Petty, they were playing your record, 'First Kiss,' in Sacramento. It was one of my favorites."

Vi, breaking into an even brighter smile, said, "Oh, my goodness, please call me Vi. My real name is Violet Ann, so Norman calls me Vi unless he's mad, and Buddy calls me 'Pansy.' I can tell you and I are going to be great friends." Then she immediately began yelling, "Norman! Norman! Come here! Peggy Sue says they're playing 'First Kiss' in Sacramento!"

She looked like she was ready to pack her suitcase and go perform. The guys had told me she had hopes that some day Norman would make her a star, too—just like he had them. She had really caught me off guard when she yelled for Norman—so much so that I jumped. But I got to see first hand just how passionate she was about her music.

"They're really playing 'First Kiss' in Sacramento?" Norman asked me.

"Yes, Sir. I heard it every day when I got out of school and was going home."

"Are they playing 'Peggy Sue' on the radio, too?"

"No, Sir. They're not."

"Oh, okay," he said matter-of-factly, and just like that, he turned around and walked off.

Vi's faded smile let me know that she was disappointed in his reaction to the news I had given.

She turned to me and said, "You know, my career was just starting when Buddy came to Norman to record, and he stopped what we were doing to work with him once 'That'll Be The Day' became a hit. His plan was to work with Buddy, and then we'd start recording and touring again. Now recording others takes up all his time, and the Norman Petty Trio is indefinitely on the back burner. But," she said, as she opened the refrigerator door, "I have to say, he's really happy with what he's doing."

As I gazed around her kitchen, I couldn't believe that anyone could be that meticulous. I had never seen a kitchen organized in such detail. She noticed me staring and said, "I believe a place for everything and everything in its place."

We had been there about an hour when the phone rang. As soon as Norman heard the voice on the line, his face burst into an enormous smile. He hung up and said, "Buddy's here, and he needs someone to pick him up at the airport."

The star had arrived. Several people chimed, "I'll do it," but Jerry and Joe B were already going out the door saying, "We'll go git 'im."

By the time they got back, the food was ready. Buddy came in, starving.

"What were you doing at the airport?" I asked.

"I flew myself over," he confessed proudly.

"You did what?" I couldn't believe what he had just said.

"I'm getting my pilot's license. Small plane. Wanna go flying?"

"No thanks. I hate small planes. They're dangerous, and they make me want to throw up."

"They're not dangerous, Peggy Sue. If the engine goes out, you can land one just like a glider."

Far from convinced, I said, "I think you'd be a whole lot better off if you give up that hobby."

"No way," he exclaimed. "I like it. I'd fly on a kite if I could find one big enough to sit on."

"Buddy, you're crazy," I said sharply.

"I know," he said, with his eyes sparkling and a boyish grin on his face. Looking over at Norman, he said seriously, "Norman, let's record tonight."

"Okay," Norman said. "Do you have something in mind?"

Buddy grinned. "I always have something in mind."

I wished I hadn't come. I didn't want to be the reason they couldn't record. "Jerry, don't forget I have to be home before midnight," I said.

75

"Norman!" Buddy yelled. "You call Mr. Gerron and tell him you'll be responsible for Peggy Sue's virtues, and we can all stay the night."

As Norman reached for the phone, I said, "I don't think that'll help. My dad doesn't know you, Norman. Maybe you should let me talk to him."

"No, no," Norman answered in his take-charge tone. "I'll take care of it."

I knew Daddy wouldn't hold still for me to spend the night in Clovis, New Mexico. I couldn't hear my dad's part of the conversation, but I could see Norman was very irritated. He couldn't believe that my father wouldn't take his word. I could tell that not many people said no to Norman.

Buddy screwed his face into a joking pout. "Just go home and don't stay for Buddy Holly's session. Do you know how many girls would like to be in your shoes?" he teased.

"No, but probably a lot. I'm sorry, Buddy, but the next session you have, I promise to be there if I'm invited."

He started to grin that infectious grin and said, "You definitely are invited and, besides, you're Buddy Holly's Peggy Sue. I'll have Joe B take you home while Jerry and I work on these songs. It won't take Joe B long to learn his part."

"Nope. I brought her, and I'll take her home. We'll just have to do it when I get back," Jerry said.

"I'm sorry, Jerry. I really wanted to stay. You know Daddy. He's quite overprotective, and he's never met Norman before."

"No problem. I had no idea that Buddy was going to fly in. I think he just got in the mood to record because we're all here."

The trip back to Lubbock was much quieter. The guys seemed to be mentally focusing on the recording task ahead. Well, Jerry seemed to be anyway. Joe B was quiet so much of the time that I could never really tell what was going on in his mind.

As Jerry pulled up to the drive, he said, "I'll call you when I get back to Lubbock. Man. Time's running out. We have to leave on that road tour, and we're still not organized."

♪

CHAPTER EIGHT
Commitment Woes

It was two days later before Jerry called me from Lubbock.

"Did you get something good on the session?" I asked.

"Yeah, we're putting together an album."

"Jerry, I have to see you so we can talk before you leave on this tour."

He hesitated a moment. "Sounds serious. Is it?"

"Well, a little. Can you come over?" I asked.

"I'll be there in a few minutes."

It was time for me to tell him that marriage wasn't coming anytime soon because I'd decided to enroll in nursing school in Amarillo. My dad had made it clear how important my attending college was to him. As thrilled as he had been about my high school graduation, he was even more ecstatic about the idea of me getting a higher education. Besides, I just couldn't see marriage in the near future. Jerry was always too busy to plan anything but the next tour, and I didn't want to spend day after day sitting at home with my mother, waiting for Jerry to call. I was satisfied with my decision; the hard part would be breaking it to Jerry.

Jerry had a very concerned look on his face. The first thing he said when he saw me was, "What's on your mind? Are you going to give me the ring back?"

"Well, it's not quite that bad, but I've decided to go to school in Amarillo this September."

"Just like that? Without discussing it with me? I won't hear of it. We're getting married," he said sternly, his face hardened.

"Jerry, your mother is no closer to accepting a Catholic wedding now than she was a year ago and..."

"Buddy wants to have a double wedding," Jerry interrupted.

"What? When? Where?" I stammered.

"In his church, I suppose," Jerry answered.

"No. I can't do that and you know it."

Was he never going to understand that I *had* to be married in a Catholic church for my church to acknowledge my wedding? Throwing Buddy and his Baptist church into the equation didn't change a thing.

In a softer tone, Jerry confessed his true thoughts. "If I let you go to school, you'll end up not marrying me."

"How can you know that?"

He immediately stormed, "I don't want you to be a nurse! I won't have it! I don't want you emptying bedpans and handling men!"

"You're crazy. There's more to medicine than that," I snapped, totally frustrated with his attitude.

"I know, but I won't let you go to school. If you were the best nurse in the world, it wouldn't matter. After we're married, you won't be able to work because I'm up all night and I sleep all day. When would I see you? It just won't work. You don't have to work. All you have to do is be Mrs. Jerry I. Allison. I don't think that's too much to ask of you."

"Well, I'll have to think about it," I conceded, realizing he wasn't going to listen to my reasoning today.

"Promise you won't make a decision until I get back from this tour," Jerry begged.

"Okay, but we have to come to an understanding. I can't just hang around while you're on the road. I have to have something to do," I replied.

"Buddy and I have plans. If you want work, the four of us will plan it out."

"What do you mean *the four of us*?" I asked.

"Buddy, Marla, you, and me."

"What do *they* have to do with it? I don't even know *Maria*, much less know if I have anything in common with her."

As much as I had determined not to let him dissuade me from my decision, this turn of events was actually intriguing me. I knew he was winning me over, but I couldn't seem to stop it.

"Let's just go out tonight and have some fun," he said, seeming to sense that the fight had gone out of me.

"You're on," I sighed, relieved that this confrontation was over.

After our date, Jerry suggested that we go over to his house to visit with his folks.

"Sounds good, unless you're expecting some more musicians to drop in," I said.

"No, not that I know of," he replied. "Do you know how to play 42 with dominoes?" I shook my head. "Well then, I'll teach you. We play it at the house all the time. I love to play games more than anything else I can think of."

I smiled playfully and said, "I hope you're a good loser."

"Nope," he replied with just a little too much honesty in his voice. "I don't like to lose at anything."

The smile faded from my lips as I said, "I'd better keep that in mind."

♫

"Jerry, is that you?" Louise Allison called out as we came into her house through the kitchen door. She was sitting on the sofa in the living room. "Well, hi, Peggy Sue. How are you? Buddy just dropped by to see you, Jerry. I told him that the two of you were out for the evening and I didn't know when you would be in."

"Did he say what he wanted, Mom?" Jerry asked.

"No, he just had a funny story to tell you."

We could hardly get to the living room for all the musical instruments strewn everywhere. How could Jerry's mom live the way she did? It was impossible to sit in the small living room, and if you tried, you'd fall over a bass, drums, or large amps.

"I bet you're really glad when the boys leave for a tour. It's probably the only time you get to use your living room," I commented.

His mother laughed and replied, "I'm the one who bought the old piano when I was pregnant with Jerry. In fact, I was taking piano lessons. I'm sure that's why he turned out to be a musician."

Jerry and his mother both laughed at that story—I bet it wasn't for the first time either.

She continued, "Jerry was the type of child that, when he wanted a pencil or paintbrush, he wanted it right then; so consequently, we got used to everything being left out. The only one it seems to bother is Buddy," she said, calling Jerry's dad by his nickname. "He's the housekeeper around here."

"That's right, Mom. It wouldn't do him any good to try to make you do it; housekeeping and cooking have never been your thing."

"I can't help it if your father cooks better than me. You certainly are going to have your hands full trying to keep house for him, Peggy Sue. Jerry, have you packed for the tour yet?"

"Nope."

"Well, I think you better get started now instead of waiting until the last minute like you usually do."

"Okay, Mom. Come on, Peggy. Help me pack."

Jerry's bedroom was even dirtier and more cluttered. There was about an inch of sand covering everything. He had a New Orleans city-limits sign hanging over his dresser and what looked like twenty thousand other mementos tossed around everywhere. There were clothes all over the floor, but mostly under his bed.

"I believe that's the first time I've seen a closet under a bed," I teased.

"If you think that's bad, you ought to see my mother's bedroom. Pop really gets mad at her. She'll wear everything she has, and then she'll just throw it down instead of hanging it up or putting it in the hamper. Then when she runs out of clean clothes, instead of cleaning her bedroom, she goes shopping."

"You're kidding," I said.

"No, they've fought more over her bed and hiding clothes under it than anything else. Pop refuses to pick her clothes up off the floor."

I grinned. "I hope you don't think I'm going to pick up your clothes off the floor."

"That's what good wives do best," Jerry said.

You want to bet? I thought to myself. I have no intention of being your maid.

When we got back to my house, I asked, "Do you want to come in and say goodbye to my folks?"

"Sure."

Jerry opened the car door for me, and as soon as I got out, he put his arms around me and said, "You know I love you. Please don't think about going to school any more. I never think about anybody but you. You don't realize how important you are to me. Don't forget our song."

"How can I forget? That's all they play on the radio," I teased.

"Lucky to be you, huh?"

Mom and Dad were watching the news. They broke into smiles when we walked in.

"I came to say goodbye for a while," Jerry stated.

"Are you going to be on the road again?" my dad asked.

Yep. Guess I better make money while I can."

"You're absolutely right, young man." Daddy shook his head approvingly. "The older you get, the harder it is to make it."

"I hear that, Mr. Gerron. If Buddy and I work it just right, we'll have it taken care of."

"Do you plan to entertain the rest of your life?" Daddy asked him.

"We plan to open our own publishing company, and if we're lucky, we can take on just the good jobs."

"It sounds to me that you boys have thought it through."

"Buddy and I have tried to think of all the angles," Jerry said very seriously.

"Just one more question. Do you know how to run a publishing company?"

"We're learning every day, Mr. Gerron. I have to go now." Jerry suddenly seemed anxious to leave. Maybe Daddy's questions were becoming too personal. "See you when I get back. Remember, Peggy, you're engaged to *me*."

"I think *I* can remember. Do you think *you* can?" I joked.

Again, we said our goodbyes, and he left.

♫

81

CHAPTER NINE
Goodbye, Grandpa

*M*other was head of the lingerie department at Dunlap's, one of Lubbock's most prestigious stores. She was in the kitchen, about to leave for work, when I heard her call, "Peggy Sue, can you hear me?"

"Yes, Mother, I can hear you."

"I've made a big pot of vegetable beef soup like PaPa likes it. If Nettie isn't here by noon to have lunch with him, will you make sure he gets served his meal on time?"

Nettie was Mother's older sister.

"Not only will I serve Grandpa lunch, but I'll eat with him. Jerry's gone. Remember?"

"Oh, that's right. I have to go to work or I'll be late."

"Don't worry, Mother. Grandpa'll be fine. I'll be home all day with him."

I didn't have to call Grandpa to lunch. He was at the table as soon as the soup started to heat.

"What smells so good, Peggy?" he inquired.

"It's Mama's vegetable beef soup, Grandpa. She made it just for you."

I set the crackers and the iced tea on the table, filled up the bowls, and gave him a dinner napkin. He truly enjoyed his lunch, and I did too.

"You're awfully quiet, Grandpa. Are you okay?" I asked.

"I feel fine except my stomach kind of burns. I'm going to leave you with the dishes and go take a nap."

"That'll be fine. Enjoy your nap."

I had just finished in the kitchen and had sat down in the family room for a minute when, all of a sudden, I heard an enormous sound like a gigantic sigh or gasp coming from Grandpa's room. I ran down the hall and knocked on his door. It was family policy not to enter someone's room without being invited, so I shouted through the door, "Grandpa, are you okay? Can I come in?"

No answer.

"Grandpa!" I screamed. "Let me come in!"

No sound.

I took a deep breath and said, "Grandpa, I'm coming in!"

He was just lying there, not breathing. There was no movement at all. I walked closer to his bed and picked up his hand. There was no response. I tried to gain my composure enough to check his pulse. When I couldn't find one, I panicked. I shook him and yelled in his face, "Grandpa, please say something!" When nothing happened, I ran to the phone to call Aunt Nettie. I knew the number by memory, but I had to run it through my brain several times before I could get my shaking fingers to dial the right numbers.

"Aunt Nettie, this is Peggy Sue. You need to come to our house. I think Grandpa's dead."

"That can't be true!" she shouted and hung the phone up.

I then called the priest of our parish and, finally, made the dreaded call to my mother.

"I'm so sorry, Mother," I stammered, trying to hold back the sobs. "I think Grandpa's dead. He won't say anything."

"Is anyone with you?" she asked.

"No, but I've called the priest. Is there anything else I should do?"

"No, Sweetheart. I'm on my way home to you."

By the time Mother arrived, Aunt Lucy and I were already saying rosary in the hallway, and Aunt Nettie was with the priest who was administering last rights to Grandpa.

The only person who blamed me for Grandpa dying during my watch was me. I couldn't get the thought that there must have been something else I could've done to save him out of my head. It didn't help that family and friends who dropped in to give their condolences gave me pitying glances when they found out I'd been alone with him when he died.

The whole next week was taken up with the funeral. Everyday the house seemed to accommodate greater numbers of family and people I didn't even know. It seemed we were feeding half of Lubbock. I could absolutely picture the walls bulging out until they split open and people exploded out in every direction. I moped around the house wishing the whole thing could just be over.

My only real consolation came from being around my dad. I was so frustrated with all the commotion going on and my raw feelings that I finally said to him, "Daddy, you know, some of these people only come at mealtime."

"I know, Honey." He looked me in the eye and chuckled.

I don't know why but somehow just the way he looked at me and said that made me feel that everything was going to be all right for the first time in what seemed like a long time. My tense muscles relaxed, and I gave him the only true smile I'd given anyone all week.

♫

CHAPTER TEN
Cricket Attack

*I*t was another week or two before Jerry and Buddy were home from the tour. From the way it sounded over the phone, Jerry must have called as soon as he walked in the door. He was probably wondering about the status of our relationship since he'd been gone for so long.

"We just got in. We're unpacking. Can you come over?" he asked.

"Sure," I answered.

Just as I was about to knock on the screen door, I heard Joe B say, "You know, you guys, if you're going to get married, so am I."

"Who to?" Buddy asked. "We didn't even know you were going steady."

"I haven't picked her out yet," Joe B said. "Maybe I'll meet her soon."

"You can't just pick out a wife like that," Jerry scoffed.

"Yes, I can," Joe B declared. "I don't know how to do it any other way."

"That's the way I did it, Jerry," Buddy said.

They all broke into laughter. I did too.

"You guys are crazy, just plain crazy," Jerry rebutted.

Buddy came back with, "You can say that because you got the only Peggy Sue."

"I've known her since the seventh grade," Jerry huffed. You guys haven't even been paying attention to anybody, much less get to know 'em."

I decided this was the perfect opportunity to knock and called innocently, "Anybody home?"

"Yeah, come in. We're just about through unpacking," Jerry said cheerfully.

"Well, how was the tour?" I inquired.

Jerry exclaimed, "Man, you should have seen Buddy."

"What happened?" I asked, expecting to hear about something really groovy that had occurred during one of the shows. All three of them looked at each other. Their eyes began to twinkle, and grins were spreading all over the room. "Well?" I prodded.

Jerry began. "Well, it was our last show, and we had just finished packing the car. I ran back in to see if we had left anything."

"Yeah," Buddy said, "you know how Jerry is. He spends good driving time looking for a cord that got packed first. So I yelled, 'Get in the car! Joe B and I are waiting,' and then I put the car in reverse to back away from the building."

"Yeah," Jerry interrupted. "And then he said, 'Damn. There's a car behind us.' He rolled the window down and said, politely of course..." They all three giggled. Jerry continued, "He said, 'Hey Man, please move,' and this gruff voice answered, 'You're not going anywhere, pretty boys. You guys think you're really smart just because you can turn the girls on. These girls here in this town are ours, and we don't like what we saw in there tonight. We're going to put a stop to this right here and now. Do the world a favor and get rid of all of you.'"

"Yeah," Buddy said, his eyes gleaming with excitement, "and then the car started pulling up closer to us like they were going to push us into the back of the club, and Jerry..."

"Yeah, I hung my head out the window and screamed, 'Move that fucking car, Man!' And they said, 'What did you say? Step out and say it to us.' And then, Buddy reached for his gun, and he flung open the door and stepped in front of their car and aimed straight for the driver. He yelled, 'You son of a bitch! I'm givin' you five seconds to move that fucking car, and then I'm going to start shootin' right into your windshield! You got that?'"

Jerry stood in the middle of the floor holding an imaginary gun in his outstretched hand.

And then, also holding imaginary weapons, Buddy assumed a stance and said, "Yeah. And then Jerry and Joe B jumped out of the car with their drumsticks and a car jack in their hands ready to back me up."

Jerry finished the story. "And they threw their car into reverse, peeled out, and we never saw them again."

They were so pleased with themselves that they were strutting all around the room like banty roosters ready to take on whatever was set before them. I was too stunned to join in their revelry, and I guess it was written all over my face because when Buddy looked at me he stopped dead in his tracks and with a puzzled look asked, "What?"

In a shocked voice, I said softly, "You carry a gun?" I'd never even thought about them having a gun.

Buddy said matter-of-factly, "Yeah, for protection. 'Cause they pay us in cash from the sales at the door."

As my brain absorbed that thought, I said absently, "Oh, yeah, that makes sense."

At that moment I realized there was more to touring than just playing music, having fun, and getting from one show to the next. Rock 'n' roll could have its dark side too.

♫

CHAPTER ELEVEN
The Plan

The vicious cycle of unpacking, rehearsals, recording, laundry, and packing to leave again didn't allow much time for a relationship; when Jerry and I were together, someone else was usually around. We seldom had an opportunity to sit down and talk seriously about anything. So, Jerry left again without either one of us saying a word about a wedding. Maybe it just wasn't a priority right now. I think we both thought we'd get married *one day*, but perhaps we hadn't made time to talk about it because, deep down, neither of us felt we were ready to take that step.

But usually, life pushes us on, whether we're ready or not. We both felt a big change coming—soon. My life was at a crossroads. I was no longer in high school, and in just a few weeks, I would either leave for Amarillo or choose another path for my future. Either way, both our lives would change forever. These were big decisions for me. I asked Mother to meet me for lunch at a restaurant near her workplace so we could talk about my future.

We sat in Furr's Cafeteria for most of Mother's lunch hour just listening to the piano player across the room and making small talk. I was nervous and had a hard time broaching the subject. Finally, I laid my fork down, folded my napkin, and said, "Mother, I've been wanting to talk to you about my wedding plans. I don't think anyone is ready for a formal wedding, especially not after Grandpa's death."

"Now, Peggy. Your grandfather would not want you to feel that way. But, that's not the real problem, is it?"

"No, but I don't know what to do," I confided quietly.

"I take it that you and Jerry *do* want to get married."

I hesitated. "Well, eventually."

"Peggy, it's not proper to be engaged longer than a year. You do know that, don't you?"

Mother always followed the proper etiquette.

"Yes, I know." My eyes locked with hers as I continued to describe my problem. "But, I don't think Jerry's any closer to becoming Catholic than he ever was. You know we can't get married in the Church unless he agrees that our children will be raised Catholic, and Louise won't hear of that."

"She knew you were Catholic before you got engaged. Remember, you chose to be Catholic and, for you, being Catholic is a way of life. I don't think you'll be happy if you marry outside the Church. Think it over very carefully before you decide," she suggested.

Oh, if she only knew how long I had been mulling the whole wedding scenario over in my head, trying to make it work for everyone. Why couldn't she just *tell* me what to do?

Mother paid for lunch, and as we exited, she said, "Come to Dunlap's with me. I want to show you something I've put aside for you."

She took me to the hat department where one of the clerks pulled out an adorable, white-linen hat with a nose veil.

"Oh, thank you, Mother. I love it," I cried, examining every inch of it as I turned it over and over in my hands.

After the clerk put it in a hatbox and handed it to me, Mother stated, "I think, maybe, what you've been trying to tell me is that it's more Louise Allison's comfort level than Jerry's. Actually, it's neither. It's what's right for you. You're the one who has to decide whether you want a marriage that's blessed by your Church or one that's binding only in the eyes of the law. You have to decide, too, whether you want a big wedding or a small one. No one should make the choice for you. But, remember, you can't change it later, and if you make the wrong decision, you'll be unhappy with it for the rest of your life."

I thought about my mother's words as I drove home. What she said was true. There was no way to make everyone happy in this situation. I needed to decide what I could live with. A small wedding wouldn't be bad. Of course, Buddy wouldn't like that, but then he'd never asked me what

I wanted either. I guess the main question I had to answer was whether I really loved Jerry enough to marry him and be his wife "till death do you part," and honestly, I didn't know.

I was in the kitchen when Mother came home from work. She looked around pensively and sighed. "I guess Daddy and I shouldn't have built this big house. PaPa's gone, and now you're practically gone. What were we thinking?"

"Daddy fulfilled his dream," I answered. "That's worth it."

That night, I lay in bed listening to records—my form of meditation—as I tried to make a decision about my future. How could there be so many differences in religion when it came to marriage? All the churches claimed to worship the same God. Why, then, couldn't they have the same rules? I brooded over my dilemma for hours. Finally, I decided not to make a decision on this night, and I turned off my Pilot and fell asleep.

♬

Early the next morning, Jerry phoned, saying excitedly, "Peggy Sue, I'm home. Hurry and get dressed. I'm coming over to get you. Let's go get a Coke. I have to tell you something."

"Okay. Give me forty-five minutes," I said sleepily and reached for my clock to see what time it was.

I got out of bed, brushed my teeth, and dressed. The doorbell was ringing by the time I finished brushing my hair.

"You really don't waste any time, do you, Jerry?"

"No, come on," he said, grabbing my wrist and stepping back on the porch. "We're going to get our blood test today. There's a three-day waiting period, and then we can get married after that."

I yanked my hand free. My heart felt as if it were about to explode. Almost immediately, I said, "No, we can't. Not that fast."

"Why not?" he asked.

I thought to myself, uhhh, and then slightly stammering, I replied, "B-Because it takes more than three days to plan a wedding."

"What wedding?" he asked, his eyes twinkling, knowing he had caught me totally off guard. "We'll elope. Why can't we just drive to Honey Grove, Texas? I have an uncle there who's a Methodist minister, and he can marry us in his house. No more arguing Baptist or Catholic. After we're

90

married, you can still plan a Catholic wedding, and we can renew our vows in your church. That'll give my parents time to accept it. Then both our parents will be happy."

Closing my eyes and shaking my head, I said, "You don't understand. You can't just do it like that. There are Church rules. If we get married this way, we really won't be married in the eyes of the Church—or in the eyes of my parents."

"Please do it my way. I promise it'll work out right," he pleaded.

"My parents will be so hurt if we run off," I countered.

"I know they will at first, but they'll accept it."

The night before, I hadn't been able to make a decision, but now, the answer jumped out of my mouth unsolicited. "I want to wait until I finish nursing school, Jerry."

"No!" he yelled. "I won't hear of it! I've made up my mind! Now let's go get our blood test."

The set of his jaw and the look in his eye told me full well that I was *not* going to change his mind with words, and I really didn't know what he'd do if I absolutely refused to go. I quickly reasoned that getting the blood test didn't mean we had to get married in three days. Rather, three days would allow me a little time to figure out my next step. I grabbed my purse and locked the door.

As I got into the car, Jerry started fussing at me. "You act like you don't even wanna get married," he accused.

"It's not that. It's just that everything has been plodding along with no plans being made, and now you're in such a rush. I had no clue you were expecting to get married so soon."

Fifteen minutes later, we were at Taylor Clinic on University Avenue getting our blood test.

"Now, in three days, we can buy the license at the courthouse," he announced triumphantly.

"Wait just a minute. I want to be sure that I understand your plan. You're telling me there will be no one at this wedding except us and your uncle?"

I wanted a promise from him, and that's exactly the look he gave me when he responded. He looked deep into my eyes with a tenderness that seemed to come from the bottom of his heart. His softened voice said,

"And my aunt. This is what I thought. If my parents aren't there...and your parents aren't there...and we're not married by either of our churches... then they can't say either family's taking preference."

Something in my solar plexus seemed to warn me that this plan wouldn't work the way he said it would. I repeated, "You mean we'll go alone and tell our parents later?"

"After we're married, I thought maybe we'd drive to Dallas for a few days and call our families from there. I know this will work. They'll be disappointed, but they'll get over it faster."

Mother had said I needed to do what was right for me and not let anyone else make the decision. I didn't have a passion for nursing. That was Daddy's dream for me, not mine. I simply hadn't wanted to disappoint him.

I looked Jerry in the eyes and said, "I think I might agree with that. It would stop the Baptist/Catholic feud."

♫

The day we were to purchase our marriage license, Jerry came by to pick me up but had to go back to his house because he had forgotten his birth certificate. We were going to take them to prove we were of legal age to get married. He looked all over the house, and even asked his mother where she thought it might be. I heard him say, "No, Mother!" and then he stormed, "I can never find anything in this house!"

His mother followed him out of the room saying, "I know you're eloping, but what would it hurt for me to go with you to get your marriage license?"

"No, Mom, you can't go with us."

"Well, what if they don't believe you're over eighteen?" Mrs. Allison asked.

Knowing he wasn't going to win that argument without the certificate, he finally gave in, and she accompanied us to the courthouse. The plan was already beginning to fall apart.

After taking Mrs. Allison home, I said, "All right, Jerry. Your mom knows we're getting married. Now, are your parents coming to the wedding? Because they aren't supposed to be there, and if they are, then

I want my parents at my wedding, so the whole plan is off. Now, are your parents coming? Is she going to tell my mother?"

"No, Peggy Sue," he reassured me. "They won't be at the wedding. It will be just as we planned. You'll see."

♫

Jerry made arrangements with his uncle, and it was decided we would be married on the evening of Tuesday, July 22.

On July 21, after my parents went to work, I packed all ten pieces of my new Samsonite luggage and planned what I was going to wear for the ceremony. I decided on the white graduation dress Grandpa had bought me. It made me feel Grandpa would be close to me, at least in spirit, on such an important day. I would also wear the new hat Mother had bought me, my white pumps, and my long, white gloves. It wasn't a very fancy ensemble, but it was certainly nice.

I composed a letter to Mother and Daddy explaining that Jerry and I were eloping and we'd call them when we got to Dallas. I told them Jerry's parents wouldn't be at the wedding either and, by doing things this way, we would solve the dilemma about what church to get married in. I ended the letter by writing, "I love you both with all my heart. Your loving daughter." I would leave it in the middle of the kitchen table so they'd see it as soon as they came home.

♫

CHAPTER TWELVE
The Wedding

*I*t was early evening when we arrived in Honey Grove. I barely had time to notice anything about my surroundings before Jerry's aunt whisked me off to get dressed for the ceremony. What's the matter, I thought. Does she think I'll bolt?

As she closed the bedroom door behind me, all the air went with her. My lungs hurt so badly, I thought I was having a heart attack. I knew, at the very least, I was going to suffocate.

My heart told me getting married like this was wrong. Jerry could wait. I had to get out. I ran to the window, looking for a place to escape. I was able to open it, but there was a hedge that was too thick for me to get through. There was no way out except through the front door, and I couldn't escape that way without creating a scene that would lead to a battle I couldn't win against Jerry and his family.

My parents had raised me to behave properly at all times. I'd come this far, and there was no backing out now. I took some slow, deep breaths and started changing my clothes, resigning myself to the fact that, in a few minutes, I would be Mrs. Jerry I. Allison.

Everything's going to be all right. Breathe, Peggy Sue, I told myself. Don't worry; you're not going to die. It's just anxiety. Remember, you can't please everybody.

I heard the front door open and wondered who it was. Jerry had finished dressing, and I could hear him in the living room, visiting with his relatives.

Someone knocked on my door and asked to come in. That voice...It couldn't be. I cautiously opened the door. There stood Jerry's mother. My mouth fell open, and my heart just sank.

"What are *you* doing here?" I asked angrily. "I thought we decided no parents at the wedding. Jerry assured me you wouldn't come."

"I know, but I couldn't stay away," she said, trying to sound pathetic. Then, twisting my words, she said, "Just because your parents wouldn't come is no reason for us to miss the wedding."

"I didn't *ask* my parents to come. I thought the reason for doing it this way was so neither of our parents would be here," I exclaimed.

"That's *my* baby getting married tonight," she quipped in an uppity tone.

My temper flared. "Yes, and *I am my mother's baby*!"

I was so angry that I felt sick to my stomach. I knew my parents would never understand why the Allisons were permitted to attend the wedding and they weren't. This would be a hurt so deep that it would cause a rift between the two families. Already, my parents believed that the "Allisons" acted as though they were better than the "Gerrons."

In my heart, I knew things would never be right between Louise Allison and me, either. I could forgive her, but I would never trust her again.

At this point, I wasn't even sure that I could trust Jerry. He had promised me repeatedly that his parents wouldn't be at the wedding, but he had broken his promise on a day when everything about our future was based on vows.

I'd compromised everything—my family, my church, my credibility. Jerry and his parents were happy. They had the type of wedding they wanted. Why hadn't he made sure that my parents wouldn't be hurt? It seemed like everything that could go wrong for me had.

Mrs. Allison stared at me and asked, in a slightly sarcastic tone, "Aren't you ready yet?"

Outwardly, I was ready; but inwardly, I was sick, and I was upset on what was supposed to be the happiest day of my life.

I answered, "Yes, I guess I've done the best I can with what I have."

She laughed and cheerfully announced that the bride was ready.

As I walked out of the bedroom and down the hall to the living room, I kept saying quietly to myself, This is it, Peggy Sue. You've really done it this time.

Jerry and I were positioned by the dining room table, which held a beautiful, fresh-cut summer bouquet. As soon as I saw it, the image of a tiny, split-flower wrist corsage flashed through my mind, and I knew that it wasn't Jerry who had ordered the flowers because they never seemed important to him.

Jerry's uncle stood before us, and the ceremony began. It was short and simple. For me, it was just something to get through—certainly not the ceremony of a young girl's dreams. If the pictures Mrs. Allison was snapping didn't show me smiling, it wasn't because I had new-wife jitters. Rather, it was because I was standing there with a broken heart.

After the ceremony, there were no refreshments and no wedding cake. As soon as the picture-taking had ceased, everyone started throwing rice, and we left for our honeymoon.

♫

Halfway between Honey Grove and Dallas, the brand-new, black and gold '58 Chevy Impala Jerry had bought broke down, leaving us stranded on the side of the road, with only the light of a quickly fading sun on the horizon and a rising crescent moon behind us. I wasn't totally surprised when the Chevy died because I'd noticed that it even sat crooked and wondered if it was a lemon. When I'd asked Jerry why it seemed warped, he'd replied that maybe it had something to do with the car's power suspension. I wondered why he had bought that car. Good thing he was a musician and not a mechanic. He'd never make a living as a mechanic. Even *I* could tell *that* wasn't the only problem the car had.

We'd been on the side of the road for at least forty-five minutes with Jerry poking around under the hood when a car pulled up behind us and stopped. A couple of men got out, and as they came near my open door, one asked if there was anything they could do to help.

I said, "Yes, the car just stopped working."

Jerry slammed the hood down, flew around to the side of the car where we were talking, and said, "I think I have everything under control, but thank you just the same for stopping."

One of the men told Jerry he was a mechanic and could probably lend a hand.

Speaking a little faster than normal, Jerry replied, "No thanks. I fixed it. Thanks again."

Jerry got into the car, and smiled and waved as the two men drove away. Then, with clenched jaws and pursed lips, he turned toward me and angrily accused, "What are you trying to do? Get us both killed?"

"What are you talking about Jerry? I don't understand," I said, amazed that he'd immediately gone from being completely in control and confident to throwing a temper tantrum.

"Peggy, you don't talk to just anybody when you're stranded and alone, especially at night and when you don't know them," he lectured.

"I'm sorry. I thought you needed help," I replied.

"Look, Peg. I'm responsible for you now. Don't you understand that?" he asked.

So, I thought, now that I'm Mrs. Jerry I. Allison, is he going to treat me like a china doll encased in glass? I said, "I guess, but they looked like they only wanted to help."

"Well, they didn't come back, so I guess it's okay."

He got out of the car, slammed the door and told me to lock both doors. "Don't open the door unless I tell you to."

He opened the hood again and started to work on the car. Suddenly, the lights came on, and he yelled, "Start the car!" It came to life again, and he ran around to the door.

"Is it all right to open the door for you, Jerry?" I smarted off to him.

He smiled, got into the car, and said, "I think we can make it to Dallas. Should've bought that Cadillac."

"I wish you had, too," I exclaimed.

As we drove into Dallas, anxiety gripped me again. I was suddenly very tired and very scared, and I just wanted to go home. What had I done? Getting married was a horrible mistake, and I couldn't take it back.

I felt like we'd driven all the way across Dallas before Jerry finally stopped at a hotel. As we were registering, the desk clerk looked at the bellman and said, "Make sure this couple has luggage when you go to the car."

Jerry and I looked at each other and broke into laughter. Jerry choked out, "Are eleven pieces of luggage enough?"

It was the first time I had laughed on this Tuesday, July 22, 1958, my wedding day.

♫

CHAPTER THIRTEEN

Mr. and Mrs. Jerry I. Allison

The next morning, all I could think about was what I had done to my mother and father. Around noon, I said, "I have to call my parents, Jerry. They're probably worried out of their minds by now."

He picked up the phone and started dialing, but instead of calling my parents, he called Buddy to tell him what we had done.

After a rather short conversation, Jerry said, "Yes, she's right here. Why? Okay. Okay. You can talk to her."

Jerry handed me the phone.

"Hi, Buddy," I said meekly.

He sang a couple of bars of "Peggy Sue" and then asked, as if in disbelief, "Did you really, really marry him?"

"Yes I did," I admitted.

"Well, tell me how it feels to be married."

"I'm not sure I know," I said. I couldn't just blurt out that I thought I'd made the biggest mistake of my life.

"Now listen to me. I don't want y'all to do anything about a honeymoon. I want you to come straight back to Lubbock, and we'll plan *our* honeymoon. Where do you want to go?"

I could hear the excitement rising in his voice as he mentally began planning a double honeymoon.

"Well," I said, a little more relaxed, "I want to go someplace where it's warm and where there's water and a beach."

"I'll make reservations for Acapulco. We may not have had a double wedding, but we're going to take our honeymoons together. Don't do anything to celebrate, you hear?"

"Are you kidding? Come on, Buddy. You're not just teasing, are you?"

He sounded sincere, but I wanted to know if he was *really* intending to do this. I wasn't up for another disappointment.

"No way. I think we should have the best honeymoon that money can buy. Hell, we can afford it." He laughed. "Maria won't be here for a few more weeks, but we'll be married right fast, and then we'll all leave for Mexico. Now don't do anything. I want your honeymoon to be the same as mine," he warned playfully.

I started to get excited. Finally! Something to look forward to! I laughed and said teasingly, "I don't think you have to worry about that."

Suddenly sounding more serious, Buddy asked, "What do you mean?"

"Oh, nothing. Don't let anything happen to the reservations until I get back to Lubbock. See you in a few days."

As soon as I thought my parents would be home from work, I called them. My mother wouldn't talk to me, but my father did.

"Did you find my letter? Is Mother really upset?" I asked sheepishly.

"Yes, we did. We tried calling Mr. and Mrs. Allison all day to tell them you had eloped, but no one answered, so we know that they went with you. So, yes, your mother's upset," Daddy said solemnly.

"I'm so sorry, Daddy. Jerry promised me that they wouldn't be there. I didn't know they were coming until they showed up," I said apologetically, almost in tears.

"It's all right, Sugar. She'll get over the shock. I hope you know what you're doing," he said, his voice full of concern.

"I don't, but I'm a big girl now," I replied.

"Yes, but remember, you make your bed hard, you'll have to sleep in it."

"I know, Daddy, but it's too late now. I'm already committed. I have to see it through."

"I love you, Sugar. Don't ever forget that. And I'm always here if you need me. Now let me talk to my new son-in-law." I handed the phone to

Jerry, and Daddy continued, "Listen to me. You married her and took her off. If you decide you don't want her, you'd better make damn sure you bring her home so I can take care of her."

"You don't have to worry about that, Mr. Gerron. I'll take good care of her if she'll let me," Jerry answered.

While they were talking, I decided to take a hot bath, hoping it would relax me. As I soaked, the water seemed to cure much of the homesickness I felt.

Pounding on the door, Jerry asked, "What are you doing in there, drowning?"

"No, I'm getting out."

"Hurry up. I'll take you out to dinner and then to a movie."

"That sounds like fun," I said.

Jerry had been in a somber mood most of the day, but now that it was growing later, and he had already drunk six Olympia's in a bottle, his mood was beginning to lighten. He was definitely a night person. We dressed for dinner and then went looking for a restaurant.

"You like Chinese food, Peggy?" he asked.

"Love it," I replied, although every time I ate it, I got sick to my stomach.

Jerry was in such a good mood that I didn't want to spoil it and risk starting another argument. Maybe, I thought, we'd just gotten off to a bad start.

I ate the food as best I could, but he guessed it wasn't my forte.

"I'm sorry. If you'd told me you didn't like Chinese food, we could've gone somewhere else," he said.

"No, don't be silly. It was fine. It was a terrific meal. I loved it," I lied.

As we got up to leave, Jerry ran into two old friends.

"How in the world are you?" Jerry asked personably.

"Just fine. In fact, we're a lot better since we got out of the pen," one of the men replied with a slight chuckle. Agreeing, the other man smiled and shook his head.

His remark made all my blood drain down to my feet.

"That's great, Man. I bet you're glad to be out. Hey, we're just on our way to see a movie, and we're going to be late. See you guys later," Jerry said.

"Hang loose," one of the men said.

As soon as I thought we were out of earshot, I whispered, "Did he say what I think he said?"

"Yes," Jerry replied, looking straight ahead as if we weren't even talking.

"Why didn't you introduce me to them?"

"Because you don't need to know people like that."

"But you know them."

"Yeah, and so do you. You just didn't recognize them. They went to R.W. Matthews with both of us," Jerry informed me.

"Oh," I said in surprise. "What did they go to prison for?"

"Who knows with guys like that! But I'll tell you one thing—I'd rather have them for friends than enemies," he said as he shook his head.

"You know, Jerry, you frighten me. I think I know you so well, and then I wonder if I know you at all. It's like flipping a coin," I informed him.

"I didn't want them to know who you were," he admitted.

"Why?"

"Cuz you're safer that way."

"What do you mean?"

"Never mind. Let's just go in and watch a movie."

Again, another subject was dropped.

After the movie, we walked back to the hotel without saying a word to each other. Just as we got to the hotel door, Jerry broke the silence.

"It's not too late. I'm going to order some more beer iced-down. You need to go to the drugstore and buy some things."

"I have everything I need," I replied.

"No, you don't," Jerry said slowly.

"What do I need?" I asked innocently.

"Don't be stupid," he grumbled.

"Well, I hate to continue being a constant disappointment to you, but you better tell me what I don't have," I snapped.

"You know...feminine things. A douche bag for starters. You know we can't have children right away."

Astounded, I said, "I'm sorry, Jerry. I refuse to go in there and buy something like that. I just can't."

"Everybody uses them. Don't be ridiculous."

His face was turning red again, and his jaws were clinched. I said to myself, I think I just started another argument.

"If I'm supposed to have one of these, you're going to have to go buy it for me," I said.

By this time, we were in our room.

"Very well!" he shouted as he left, slamming the door behind him.

If he's mad now, I thought, wait until I tell him I don't know how to use it. Surely, it comes with directions.

I watched TV until he returned about forty-five minutes later with all sorts of things.

"Here! Use it," he exclaimed as he slammed his purchase down beside me.

I opened the box, took it out, and began looking for the instructions.

"What are you looking for?" Jerry asked.

"The instructions."

"Haven't you ever used one before?" he asked in amazement.

"Oh, sure. All the time. It was required for Catholic school. A new one every year. We used them between classes," I quipped. "I don't think you understand me, and I sure as hell don't understand you. I was taught that lovemaking is as natural as breathing. You aren't supposed to use anything."

Jerry looked at me and frowned.

"Okay, okay," I said. "I'll try to use it. Does that make you feel better?"

He managed a small smile, and then he said, "We're leaving in the morning. We're only a few miles from my grandparents' home in Hill County. I'd like to visit them for a while."

"That sounds nice. I'd like to meet them."

It was late. Time for bed. Well, I thought, another silent night. And it was.

♫

103

The next day, we packed for Hill County.

"What's their house like?" I asked.

"It's a big, old farm house. You'll love Ma-Ma," Jerry said, happily.

We had just gotten out of town and were on the freeway when Jerry started yawning.

"Look," I said, "why don't you pull over and I'll drive."

"Good idea. Take it nice and easy, and stay on the freeway."

"Don't worry. I can handle it. Go to sleep."

It was the first time Jerry had let me touch his new car. He fell asleep right away, and I turned on the radio to listen for any of our records being played. I felt very comfortable behind the wheel. In no time, I was sailing down the road. The car handled beautifully, and I was really enjoying myself, until I glanced in the rearview mirror and noticed a red light flashing behind me. I slowed down and pulled over. As luck would have it, Jerry woke up.

"What happened?" he asked.

"This police officer seems to have a problem," I answered flippantly.

"May I see your license?" the officer asked.

I pulled it out and handed it to him.

"Young lady, do you realize you were going ninety miles an hour?"

"No, I didn't," I replied, as he started in with a long lecture. I sat there and listened for quite a while, and then I said impatiently, "Are you going to give me a ticket? If you are, I wish you'd hurry up so we can be on our way."

The officer narrowed his eyes and started writing. I glanced over at Jerry, thinking he would appreciate my handling the problem and getting us back on the road; but as soon as I saw his face, I knew I had blown it. Oh, boy, I thought. Now he's going to kill me. The officer handed me the ticket.

Very politely, Jerry said, "Thank you, Officer. I'll see to it she doesn't drive any more."

Jerry yelled at me all the way to his grandparents' house. He told me over and over, "You don't get smart with a cop. You probably wouldn't have gotten a ticket if you'd been nice."

"I'm sorry. I promise it won't happen again. Now, can we drop the subject?" I asked, my arms folded over my chest and my face turned toward the window.

"No, not until I'm ready," he snarled.

He bitched right up to the driveway *and* while he was opening the car door.

By the time I stepped out of the car, it was my turn to be angry. I spotted his mother and father coming out the door.

I looked sternly at Jerry and, through clenched teeth, asked, "Did you plan this?"

"No, I didn't know they'd be here."

"Well, there's nothing like an audience when you just get married," I fussed.

"I didn't know they'd be here. Anyway, I like being with people. I never liked being alone," he said.

I asked myself, What does he think I am, a poodle?

Huge trees shaded the driveway in front of the stately, old farmhouse, and a large porch circled all around it so that, no matter what room you were in, you could always walk outside with little effort. It was absolutely beautiful. I felt like I'd just traveled back in time.

The family came to meet us. Everyone gave me a hug, and Jerry's grandma said, "The day I married Pa-Pa, he brought me to this house, and I've lived every day of my life right here. Some good times. Some hard."

Mrs. Allison overheard the conversation and asked, condescendingly, "Now, Ma-Ma, what bad times have you ever had?"

"Oh, there have been some, Louise. There have been some."

Pa-Pa was a tall man and extremely formal, I thought. Very English. Very cold. Almost stoic.

On the other hand, Ma-Ma was a real character. She had a bubbly, open personality and, like her son, one of the most striking smiles I believed I'd ever seen. She was beautiful. Her silver hair was wrapped in a bun on top of her head, accented by the attractive combs she used to keep it up. She dearly loved to tell jokes, especially when she was sure Pa-Pa wasn't in hearing distance. We sat on the porch swing, and she told us about an incident that happened right after they were married.

"I told him a joke, and he told me never to tell another. He wouldn't have it."

"Did you leave it at that?" I asked, thinking about how many times Jerry had exhibited the same demeanor.

"Only when he walked in the room." Her eyes twinkled.

I laughed. I knew now where Jerry's dad inherited all his wonderful common sense and charm.

It was growing late, and I thought we would be leaving for a motel, but Jerry started getting the luggage out of the car.

"Are we staying here tonight?" I asked.

"Yes, we are."

"It wouldn't be right not to sleep in the wedding bedroom," Ma-Ma said. "It's been a long time since we had a newly married couple in that room. Please stay."

Ma-Ma showed me into the front bedroom. It had a fireplace and hardwood floors that were so shiny, they looked like mirrors. The bed had to be at least a hundred years old, like the other antique furniture in the house. It was covered with the most gorgeous, hand-embroidered sheets and homemade quilts I'd ever seen. It looked just like something out of a history book.

We had dinner and then sat on the porch until bedtime. I was intrigued by everything. I'd never been on a peanut farm before.

"Let's go get a drink of water, Peggy Sue. It's the best water you've ever tasted," Jerry said.

We walked around to the side of the house.

"They have a well? Jerry! You mean to tell me there's no running water," I exclaimed.

"That's right," Jerry informed. "They've always used the well. Pa-Pa says it works good so there's no reason to change it."

"How does she do the dishes?"

"She draws the water out of the well and cooks it."

"I hope he lets her have a gas stove, or is she still using wood?"

Jerry took a deep breath, let it out slowly, and then said, "Cute, Peggy, real cute. Do you want to wash your feet? Ma-Ma won't let us go to bed unless your feet are clean. Those are the house rules. Come wash. Feel how cold the water is."

As I started to put my feet into the bucket, he screamed, "Don't do that, dummy!"

"Do what?"

"Put your feet in the bucket."

"How else do you wash your feet?" I asked.

"You pour the water into the washbowl. They drink from this well and use it for cooking. You have to keep the bucket clean."

By this time, the whole family had gathered to watch the show. I was glad it was dark enough that they couldn't see how embarrassed I was. Nobody had taught me farm etiquette. I was a city girl, and this was like being in another world.

The East Texas night was hot and sticky, and the water did feel good.

As he crawled into bed, Jerry told me it was quite an honor to get to sleep in the wedding room.

"Ma-Ma really likes you. If she didn't, she wouldn't let you sleep in this special room."

"I'm glad someone in your family likes me. I don't seem to be a very big hit with anyone else, mainly you," I said, for once putting a voice to my true feelings.

"That's not true," he said tenderly.

"I have one question. Where's the bathroom?"

Jerry smiled. "Outside in the back."

"Please don't tell me they have an outdoor toilet," I begged.

"That's what I'm going to tell you. Back where the cows are. Pa-Pa thinks it's germy to have a toilet in the house."

"Well, good for Pa-Pa. You're going to get up and go with me, Jerry."

"Oh, no I'm not."

"I'm not going out there alone," I insisted, tugging him out of bed. "Come on. I hate cows. What if they stampede or something?"

Images of cowboy westerns ran through my mind. I envisioned us scurrying under a log for protection as the herd thundered above us.

"They won't hurt you. They're more afraid of you than you are of them."

"I doubt it," I retorted.

As we started out the door, I realized how ridiculous I looked in my long, white-laced nightgown and spiked mules—not quite the proper attire for wearing on a farm, especially for going to an outside john.

We made it back to the bedroom without being attacked by any vicious livestock, and for the first time, we talked. The main thing Jerry wanted out of life was to be Buddy's partner, whether it was playing, touring, writing music, or publishing. He wanted us to have a house in Lubbock that we could call home, but even when he was talking about us, Buddy's and Joe B's names were never far from any sentence, and I knew that if we were going to have a successful marriage, I, too, would have to be committed to their dreams. The magic of the wedding bed seemed to be working. It was the first night everything went right. Maybe marriage wasn't so bad after all.

The next morning, I was awakened by Jerry's mom who was in the bedroom telling him to let me go.

"You're going to hurt her, sleeping that way. You're holding her as if she's trying to run away," she reprimanded.

As Jerry sat up in bed, he scolded, "Mom what are you doing in here?"

"Breakfast is ready," she said teasingly, trying to lessen the tension, but this time, even he was annoyed.

♫

After breakfast, Jerry and I hugged everybody goodbye and hit the road for home. *Home?* It finally dawned on us that we had no home. Jerry's "plan" didn't include our after-marriage living arrangements. I'd assumed we would rent an apartment, but we'd never really discussed where we would live. I realized, for the first time, why parents often give know-it-all teenagers the *What were you thinking?* look.

We drove around Texas for several days, visiting Jerry's classmates and trying to figure out where we could live. We didn't even know what town to pick because that would depend on where The Crickets—actually, where Jerry and Buddy—needed to be to advance their careers. Lubbock, Clovis, and New York were all possibilities, but that was in the future. We needed some place to stay at least until after the double honeymoon with Buddy and Maria. We couldn't stay at my house because Mother still wasn't talking to me, so the only solution was to move in, temporarily, with *his* parents.

Jerry was absolutely thrilled because everybody he loved was now living under one roof. Not surprisingly, my feelings were quite different. Physically and mentally, my life was miserable. Mr. Allison went out of his way to make me comfortable in his home, but Louise treated me like a guest. When I asked if I could help her do anything, she usually answered, "Just go play with Jerry," like we were only six years old. I quit trying to start up conversations, and when I did have to talk to her, I was extremely polite—to the point that it would hurt your ears to listen to me. Louise was always kinder when Jerry was around than when he was away, and Jerry was away most of the time. In fact, married life hadn't stopped him from hanging out with his buddies, sometimes until the wee hours of the morning.

Louise's passion was working with children with birth defects, especially those with cerebral palsy and Down syndrome. She attended classes part-time, while writing her doctoral dissertation. I *loved* the days she went to class. I felt like a bother when she was home because she studied constantly, and my job was to be quiet and stay out of sight. When she did talk, she bombarded me with facts that proved how *extremely brilliant* Jerry was—he'd advanced a whole year in grade school, and he'd always shown a propensity for science and math. Plus, he enjoyed calculus in high school.

Louise was big into IQ testing and wanted to test me. In a pig's eye, I thought. I wasn't about to let that happen.

Living conditions were poor at best. There was only one bathroom. Granted, it was certainly better than having an outdoor toilet like at Ma-Ma's house; still, at times, it could be quite an inconvenience.

Also, I wasn't used to living in a house that was in such disarray. Every room was as cluttered and unkempt as ever, and since I'd moved in, Jerry's room had become even messier. His suitcases and instruments were piled everywhere; and his clothes, some clean, some not-so clean, were heaped on top. Mostly, I lived out of my luggage, which had to be stacked, too, so every time I needed something, I had to unstack my suitcases. I laughed every time I thought about how a baggage cart would create some order in my life. It wasn't long before I embarked on a major, cleaning, picking-up, washing, dusting, and packing-up-things project.

While I was cleaning, Mrs. Allison came to my door and said, "Someone is here to meet you. Oleta Hall lives across the street. She's a close friend of mine, and her son, Ernie, just idolizes Jerry. This is her daughter, Yvonne Hall. I'll leave you two to get acquainted."

Yvonne, a petite, freckle-faced brunette, asked in a schoolgirl voice, "How are you?"

"I'm fine," I said politely, not really knowing what to say to her. I began folding clothes.

"Is Jerry here?" She asked, looking around for him.

"No, he's at the store."

"Did you and Jerry really get married?" She asked skeptically.

"Yes, we did," I said, showing her my ring.

"Well, hum. You deserve each other," she sneered.

"What?" I asked, wondering what she meant.

"You deserve each other because *you* are just as messy as *he* is."

I grinned. "Oh. I haven't had time to clean up yet."

Lifting her eyebrows and slightly tilting her head to the side, she stated brashly, "I'm his girlfriend. Didn't he tell you? Well, I *was* his girlfriend until he met you in California and played a show for you, and the two of you made up." Then, with a self-satisfied jerk of her shoulders, she turned on her heel and left the room.

When Jerry came in, I said, "I met *your* Yvonne Hall. Is she a close friend?"

Jerry rolled his eyes like he usually did when he didn't want to discuss something or was aggravated, and droned out, "I went with her when you and I were *not* together."

"Was she expecting to be Mrs. Jerry I. Allison?" I asked.

"I took her out. That's all," he answered nonchalantly.

"Maybe you need to talk to her; she seems hurt." I was persistent.

"Oh, she'll get over it," he answered, as he vacated the room.

Humph! I had more empathy for her feelings than he did, I thought, and I didn't even know the neighbors. I resumed my housecleaning.

I found a little piece of sanded wood about two inches long and an inch wide. I couldn't figure out what it was, so I threw it away. Well, later that day, Jerry noticed it was missing, and our first real argument ensued. Supposedly, this hand-sanded, well-crafted, little box he'd made in his high-school shop class was his pride and joy. Who would've thought? I hadn't realized it was something fit for the altar. We looked and looked, but we couldn't find it anywhere. Actually, I was amazed that he'd even missed it, considering how much stuff he had strewn around his room. I was sure this would be an important and bitter conversation piece for the rest of our married lives—even more so than our eloping.

Jerry was too busy searching for his "keepsake" to answer the door when Buddy and Joe B dropped by, so I had to let them in.

"How are y'all doing?" Buddy asked, smiling.

"Not well." I answered ill-humoredly.

"Yeah?" His smile faded. "I gotta go now," he said. He backed out of the room as if he was walking on eggshells.

I was *so* looking forward to the trip to Acapulco and *so* ready to leave Jerry's parents' house that every chance I got I told Jerry I didn't want us to continue living with his parents. He always came back with the same story: We had to because we were waiting for Buddy to get married. Lately, Jerry had added, "Well, you're the one who wanted to go to Acapulco, so you'll just have to wait," to his rebuttal.

I could hardly wait to meet Maria. I guess you could say I was very young and impressionable. But I couldn't help it. Jerry had painted a picture of the four of us touring together, with Maria and me working side by side as a part of their ventures. The three of us had always had such fun together, and now I would also have a girlfriend. The double honeymoon to Acapulco would be the first of many exotic adventures we would have together. I truly hoped that Maria would like me, too.

♫

I really missed my family. Every time I tried to talk to my mother, she hung up on me. Finally, a few days before Buddy's wedding, Daddy called.

"What are you doing for dinner tonight?" he asked.

"Oh, the same thing, I suppose," I said drearily.

"We want you and Jerry to come to dinner. Can you make it?"

"Sure," I answered, my spirits soaring higher by the second.

It felt awkward to knock on the door at my parents' house. Our greetings were uncomfortably tense, and dinner conversation was rather cold and formal. Then, Mother dropped the bombshell by asking, "Why weren't we allowed to come to the wedding?"

I was proud of Jerry when he took the responsibility of answering her. He looked her in the eye and replied, "My parents were not supposed to come, Mrs. Gerron. Peggy Sue and I had left in the car alone, and we were getting ready for the wedding when they showed up. I am so sorry, Mrs. Gerron. We had not planned that."

Mother said, "If they'd called and told us they were going, we would've gone with them. Up to that point, your mother acted like she wanted to be friends. I don't see how that can ever happen now."

Jerry nodded his head as if to say, I understand. I completely understood my mother's feelings. I still felt betrayed by both Jerry and Louise, and now that I was living with Jerry's parents, I felt like I had no control over my own life. *They* always made the decisions, not me; and like an unwanted stepchild, I was expected to comply fully. Undoubtedly, my marriage wasn't off to a good start.

♫

CHAPTER FOURTEEN
Mr. and Mrs. Buddy Holly

On Tuesday morning, the phone was ringing off the hook. Jerry kept answering it, so I knew it had to be Buddy or Joe B, or both. He came into the bedroom and said, "Buddy's coming over after he picks Maria up from the airport. He wants you two to get acquainted."

"I can hardly wait to meet her. Now instead of the three of us, it'll be the four of us. That'll be so much fun."

Hurriedly, I put on a pair of Capri pants and a casual shirt, combed my hair (but didn't bother to put on any lipstick), slipped into my shoes, and went into the kitchen to await Maria's arrival.

Buddy's pale-blue Lincoln Continental finally pulled into the driveway. Buddy stepped out of the car and, in a gentlemanly fashion, walked over to the other side to help Maria. As soon as I saw her, I panicked. How could I have been so stupid? Why hadn't I put on a dress, or *at least* some lipstick? "Please, floor, open up and swallow me now," I said under my breath.

In they walked, and there stood Maria right before me. Her appearance screamed *New York career woman*: a fashionable, short hairdo; an immaculately tailored suit; high-heeled shoes with a matching purse to boot; and perfectly applied makeup. She was short, but very beautiful. Standing next to Buddy, I could tell she was older than he was in both age *and* demeanor. I felt a little more at ease when I noticed the gold medal she wore around her neck because I immediately assumed that she was Catholic, too. Maria's appearance reminded me of Buddy's former girlfriend, Echo McGuire. Both Maria and Echo were about the same height; they had similar dark, curly hair; and they flashed identical smiles when they looked at Buddy and Jerry. And...then...Maria began to talk. Her Puerto Rican accent was *so* strong, I could barely understand a word she was saying. I hadn't even considered that she would have an accent. However, the more she talked, the more comfortable I became with it, but I still had to listen *very* carefully to understand everything she said.

We visited for a while, making one another's acquaintance and engaging in small talk. Well...let me clarify. Maria *only* talked to Jerry and Buddy—she didn't acknowledge me at all. Even when I spoke, she made no eye contact with me whatsoever. As far as she was concerned, I was just another piece of dusty furniture in the Allison household. I was very disappointed that our relationship was getting off to this kind of start, but I resolved that maybe Maria was just shy, and maybe, after getting to know me better, she would warm up to me. After all, she didn't even know me, so how could she possibly dislike me already? I was hoping she wouldn't be another mother hen either—I already had one too many of those in my life.

Before they left, Buddy suggested, "How 'bout the four of us going out to dinner tonight? Just some place casual, okay? I'll pick you up at seven."

As we waved goodbye, Jerry asked, "What's the matter?"

"I don't know," I replied. "I guess I just expected someone different. It's like she's from a world I know nothing about."

"Yeah, Buddy's going to have his work cut out for him with her."

"She's so much older than he is." Realizing it was time for me to stop looking like a schoolgirl, I continued, "I need to go shopping for Mexico. I need cocktail dresses. You know, adult clothes. It's time to get rid of the bobby socks."

With a rise in his voice, Jerry asked, "Are you going to buy makeup too?"

"I wouldn't know how to use it if I had it, but I guess I can get some. Do I need to pick anything up for you?"

"No, I have everything I need. Going to Hawaii and Australia fixed my wardrobe right up, Steve," Jerry had begun to call me that every time he was in a really good mood.

Dinner did nothing to make me feel better about Maria. I ate, and Buddy, Maria, and Jerry talked and laughed. When I spoke, I felt invisible to her. Buddy wasn't the only one who had his work cut out for him; I did, too, especially if this *foursome* was going to work.

♪

Early the next morning, Buddy phoned and said, "Hi, Peggy Sue, Jerry said you plan to go shopping today."

"Yeah, I do," I replied.

"Maria needs to pick up some things, too. I thought maybe the two of you could go together. You know more about the Lubbock shops than I do. Would that be okay? That'll give you an opportunity to get to know each other better, too," he said.

"Sure. I'll pick her up a little after lunchtime," I replied.

Mrs. Holley was always the first to answer the door. "Oh, come in, Peggy Sue. Come in. Come in."

"No, thank you. I just came to pick up Maria. We're going shopping," I said, noticing Maria coming toward the door with her purse in hand. Mrs. Holley stepped back, and as Maria walked out the door, I said cheerfully, "Hi, Maria."

"Hello," she said bluntly and unsmiling.

Oh, man, I thought, this excursion is *not* going to be fun. As I backed out of the driveway, I asked, "What kind of store would you like to go to?"

"The best dress shop in Lubbock," she replied.

"What are you looking for? Cocktail dresses? Casual clothes?"

"No, my wedding dress," she replied.

Her answer was one I would've never imagined, even in the deepest recesses of my mind. She'd come across as being so cool and proper that I just couldn't imagine her not already having a wedding dress, especially with the wedding taking place only three days after her arrival.

I stammered, "You didn't buy your dress in New York?"

"No," she replied brusquely.

I took Maria to Margaret's, Lubbock's most elite dress shop, and she became a different person as soon as she stepped through the door. She chattered non-stop, telling the clerks who she was, where she was from, whom she was marrying, and that she had brought nothing with her for the wedding or honeymoon. She needed everything—a wedding dress, hat, panties, a slip, dresses for Acapulco...I was stunned. I guess I just supposed someone close to her would have thrown her a bridal shower of some sort. After all, it wasn't like she was eloping or something. I was eighteen, and Maria was, I guessed, around twenty-five. At least *I* knew to plan and pack what I was going to wear when I got married, and I eloped. I was looking at her like, Why is Buddy buying all this for you? This would not have been something I would've asked Jerry to do for me.

I wondered if her behavior had anything to do with her Latin culture. In some places, I knew the groom was expected to give the bride's family a dowry. Maybe Buddy was supposed to offer her aunt a dowry, but hadn't, and now she was expecting him to pay for everything. I didn't dare ask her, nor did I act like she was doing anything out of the ordinary.

For nearly three hours, Maria remained the center of attention at the store. The clerks set her up in the store's posh, white, bridal dressing room, which had mirrors that circled all around and plush, white carpet on the floor. Because the clerks knew that Buddy Holly had money, they showed Maria the store's very best clothes. It was entertaining to watch them scamper through the store, catering to Maria's every wish and treating her like she was Mrs. Astor.

Meanwhile, she strutted around with her nose in the air as if she was the most important person in the world. She was definitely enjoying the attention. According to Maria, nothing in Margaret's was good enough for her. "Oh no, that won't do. That's not what I'm looking for. Haven't you got something else?"

As I sat outside the dressing room watching all the hoopla, I heard her comment to one of the clerks, "Oh, is this it? Humph!" But, she finally made her selections, and arrangements were made for her alterations to be finished in time for the wedding.

Me? I had bought two dresses and was eagerly waiting to take Maria back to the Holleys. Buddy had wanted us to get to know each other better, but, after this experience, I realized we had absolutely nothing in common, except for Buddy.

When we got into the car, I asked her if she knew how to drive. She replied curtly, "No, I don't drive."

"You don't have a car in New York?" I asked, hardly able to believe it. In Lubbock, children were practically born drooling over the thought of the day they could get behind the wheel for the very first time.

"In New York you don't need a car, so I've never learned to drive."

I helped Maria take her purchases to the door. Mrs. Holley met us and asked, "Won't you come in, Peggy Sue?" Her voice sounded almost as if she were softly pleading rather than merely making a polite gesture. She's going out of her way trying to make Maria comfortable, I thought, but this didn't surprise me. Mrs. Holley was one of the kindest women I'd ever met.

"No, thank you," I said. "Jerry's waiting for me. We need to start packing for the trip."

As I walked back to the car, I noticed that my step was a little lighter, the air was slightly fresher, the sun was a shade brighter, and I could breathe much easier. Whew! This was the first time I was really looking forward to be going back to the Allisons'.

As soon as I walked in, Jerry crushed my spirits by asking, "Well, did Maria help you pick out some clothes?"

"No," I said, feeling betrayed. Had that been the real reason why Jerry and Buddy had sent me shopping with Maria? Did they think I was that uncultured and immature? I continued, "And, thanks a lot. What makes you think I can't pick out my own clothes?"

"Well, she's from New York, and that's where it's all happening. Not Lubbock," he replied.

"Maybe you're right." I smiled mischievously. "But, remember, New York dresses are more expensive. By the way, here's the bill for today."

♫

The next day, I vowed to change my image. I shopped all afternoon, alone, and finally found one suit. Jerry was pacing the floor when I arrived home. I had neglected to tell him I also had a beauty-shop appointment.

I had long hair when I left to go shopping, but when I returned home, I was sporting a pixie hairdo. I wanted a style that would be easy to manage on the trip. When we lived in Fort Worth, I went swimming a lot, and I experienced nothing but trouble with my long, thick hair. I planned to spend a lot of time in the water in Acapulco, and I didn't want any bad-hair days; unfortunately, however, it appeared that bad-hair days were all I was going to have now. My hair looked awful. I looked like the ugliest girl in the world.

Jerry's face paled as soon as he saw me, and he screamed furiously, "You look terrible! What on earth have you done to yourself?"

I tried to explain that the style was much easier to take care of, but he wouldn't listen. He was ranting and raving so much that his mother finally came into the room to calm him down.

"She looks cute. Why are you so mad?" His mother asked, defending *me* for once.

"She looks like hell. Her head looks too small for her body. Why didn't you discuss this with me before you did it?" he screamed at me.

"I didn't know I had to. I thought it was my hair. I didn't realize it belonged to you."

"You are 'Peggy Sue.' You can't run around looking like that."

"I'm sorry. I didn't know my station in life," I shot back at him, realizing that he was referring to me not as a human being and not as his wife, but rather, as a song.

"I don't want to be late. Buddy and Maria will be here in half an hour. Go get ready," he commanded.

"Okay. Okay. I'll get dressed. And, by the way, Jerry, are you *sure* you want to be seen with me?" I asked sarcastically, thinking perhaps he should just take one of his precious "Peggy Sue" records with him instead.

Well, that was the wrong thing to say. He started yelling again, and I headed for the bathtub.

I was just about ready when I heard Buddy and Maria arrive.

"Where's Peggy Sue?" Buddy asked.

"Dressing," Jerry said, still angry. "She was late coming home from shopping."

"I guess she went out and spent all your money considering the mood you're in," Buddy laughed loudly.

"Hell, no! She went and had all her hair cut off, and it looks like hell," Jerry screamed.

Maria and Buddy started to laugh.

"You know, Jerry, it'll grow back," Buddy reminded him.

"Yeah, but I have to look at her until it does."

I walked into the room acting as sophisticated as I could.

"Peggy Sue, I like your hair," Buddy said.

"Thanks Buddy."

Jerry and I got into the back seat, and we left for the restaurant. It was the quietest car ride I'd ever had with Buddy and Jerry; no one said a word. Just before we arrived at the restaurant, Buddy broke the silence and said, "I know what Peggy Sue is going to say next."

"What are you talking about?" Jerry asked.

Buddy's car had a back window that he could roll down. Soon, the wind started blowing in, and I laughed. "Would you roll up the window, please?" I asked. "You're messing up my new hairdo, the one that Jerry likes so much." Buddy laughed hysterically. The ice had been broken.

Our form of a bachelor and bachelorette party, so to speak, was a meal at Lubbock's finest Mexican restaurant, where we also celebrated our upcoming trip. Buddy and Maria were to be married the next day, and we would leave immediately after the ceremony. We discussed their wedding and our trip to Acapulco; Maria, once again, ignored me, and spoke only to Jerry and Buddy.

"You're going to be my best man, aren't you, Jerry?" Buddy asked.

Maria, whose body had remained slightly turned away from me during the whole meal, faced me and, for the first time since she and Buddy picked us up, spoke directly to me and asked if I would stand with her.

"Sure," I said, trying to keep the surprise out of my voice. "It'll be my pleasure."

"You don't have to wear anything special. Just what you are going to travel in will be fine. I have to go to the powder room. Will you excuse me?" Maria asked, as she stood up.

At nice restaurants in Lubbock, ladies didn't go to the powder room by themselves when they were in the company of gentlemen, so I asked, "Me, too?" and followed behind her.

Before leaving the restroom, I commented on the medal she was wearing. "It's beautiful. You're Catholic, aren't you?"

"No, I'm not, and I don't want to talk about it," she snapped.

I was astounded. She had to be Catholic. She was from Puerto Rico, which was a Catholic country, and she *was* wearing the medal. Why would she deny such a thing? Furthermore, what was with that *attitude*?

Not wanting to get off on the wrong foot with Buddy's wife-to-be, I apologized. "I'm sorry. I didn't mean to upset you. I'm Catholic and we're really not all that bad."

Her face softened a little. "That's all right. I'm sorry I snapped at you."

I dropped the subject, but I couldn't keep from analyzing Maria in my mind. I had been taught that respect was not given to you; it had to be earned, and Maria wasn't earning any from me right now. I felt sure she had to have some ties to Catholicism, and being brought up the good Catholic girl I was, I was flabbergasted that anybody would deny their religion. Then, recalling the feud between the Gerrons and Allisons, I thought, perhaps Buddy doesn't want his parents to know. After all, they're Baptist.

Back at the table, Buddy and Jerry were discussing reservations and hotels, and that remained the topic of discussion until we got home. Buddy was very proud of himself for planning this double honeymoon, but his doing so hadn't surprised me. He was always the creative one—the planner, the thinker. Jerry, on the other hand, was more of a manager type. Once a plan was in place, Jerry made sure no detail went unnoticed, but creative leadership had never been his strong suit.

♫

On Friday morning, August 15, 1958, I awoke early and started to pack and dress for the wedding. Around noon, Buddy came over to visit.

"What happened? Did they throw you out of the house so the bride could get ready?" I asked. He seemed depressed and was not his usual happy, perky self.

"No, the house was all in a flutter, so I left. Hey, Jerry, just wear your Levi's."

"No, Buddy. He doesn't have to wear a suit if you don't want him to, but he *does* have to wear a coat and tie."

"Peggy Sue, this is no big thing. He doesn't have to wear a tie."

"Yes, he does, and this *is* a big thing," I said seriously. "Now come on. Go home. Get dressed like you should."

Buddy looked at me and asked hesitantly, "Is my black suit okay?"

"Yes, it's great. We'll see you at the wedding."

He took off on his motorcycle. I couldn't believe his mood. It was as though his mind was elsewhere.

Jerry and I finished dressing, and we left for the wedding.

The Holleys lived in a small, wood-framed house and, in contrast to the Allisons', it was completely spotless. The floors were so clean you could have eaten off of them. We were the first ones to arrive. Mrs. Holley met us at the door, greeting us with her usual, "Come in. Come in."

Joe B arrived right after we did and then came the minister; Buddy's brothers, Larry and Travis; and his sister, Pat. Everyone seemed to be running late. I'd never met Buddy's brothers and sister before, so introductions were made all around. Buddy was smiling from ear to ear and laughing a lot, but his laugh sounded more like a nervous laugh than his usual one. The fact that Mrs. Holley *totally* adored Buddy could be seen in every word she spoke to, and about, him. Buddy's adoration for his parents was also very obvious. Maria was quiet, but she was smiling. I thought she looked a little intimidated and nervous.

The only wedding decoration was a small, spring-cut-flower arrangement that had been placed on the Formica kitchen table. Next to it sat a punch bowl and a small wedding cake. It seemed strange to me that Buddy's wedding ceremony was taking place in his parents' house, considering that Mr. and Mrs. Holley were such devout church people and that Buddy had originally wanted the four of us to have a big church wedding. Why had the ceremony suddenly become, as Buddy said earlier, "no big thing"?

Maria made her entrance wearing a simple, but classy, sheath, which had been altered to fit her perfectly. Her white-lace dress was knee-length and short-sleeved, and it boasted a scooped neckline. It was very tailored and sophisticated. She also donned a fashionable white, beaded-claw hat with a shoulder-length veil, and she was carrying a white-orchid bouquet with streamers.

The ceremony was short. Mr. Weir, Pat's husband, arrived just as it was ending. Jerry put "Now We Are One" on Buddy's record player, and

Maria allowed Joe B—with help from Jerry—to remove her white garter. After pictures had been taken, Buddy and Maria changed their clothes, we all said our goodbyes, and we climbed into the DeSoto dance-band station wagon to drive to El Paso, where we were going to spend the night and catch a plane to Acapulco the next morning.

♫

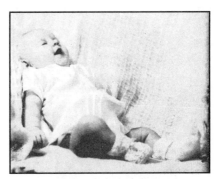

Peggy Sue's baby picture...
Courtesy of Peggy Sue Gerron

Peggy Sue with her baby doll...
Courtesy of Peggy Sue Gerron

Peggy Sue at 5 years...
Courtesy of Peggy Sue Gerron

Peggy Sue on her 9th Birthday with
brother-in-law Von...Courtesy of
Peggy Sue Gerron

Peggy Sue in
Lubbock High School Band...
Courtesy of Peggy Sue Gerron

Peggy Sue 1958 Graduation from
Bishop Armstrong Girls School...
Courtesy of Peggy Sue Gerron

Peggy Sue's Twirling Photo in 1955...
Courtesy of Peggy Sue Gerron

Peggy Sue and Jerry Allison's Wedding Picture...Courtesy of Peggy Sue Gerron July 22, 1958

Jerry, Peggy Sue, Louise & J.D. Allison July 22, 1958, Honey Grove, Texas... Courtesy of Peggy Sue Gerron

Peggy Sue's parents John & Lillie Gerron...Courtesy of Peggy Sue Gerron

Peggy Sue's grandfather Henry Reiger and his date at the Cotton Club...Courtesy of Peggy Sue

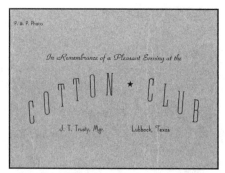

An original Cotton Club photo folder...
Courtesy of Peggy Sue Gerron

Jerry Ivan Allison
"Real Wild Child" Promotional Picture...Courtesy of Peggy Sue Gerron

Jerry and Peggy Sue's
Catholic Wedding in 1964...
Courtesy of Peggy Sue Gerron

Peggy Sue, Uncle Raymond, and Jerry
July 22, 1958, in Honey Grove, TX. ...
Courtesy of Peggy Sue Gerron

*Sister Johneva, Peggy Sue, and
Dick Clark on The Dick Clark Show*

*Dick Clark and Peggy Sue.
Promotional Photo*

*Peggy Sue, Donna Ludwig, and Ger-
aldo Rivera...Backstage Photo*

*Peggy Sue and Oprah...
Courtesy of Peggy Sue Gerron*

Peggy Sue on motorcycle at the Clovis Music Festival...
Courtesy of Peggy Sue Gerron

Ella Holley and Peggy Sue at Carl Perkins Concert...
Courtesy of Peggy Sue

Gary & Ramona Tollett. "That'll Be The Day" backup singers...
Courtesy of The Tolletts

Peggy Sue, Donna Ludwig, and Tommy Allsup at the Surf dressing room in Clear Lake, Iowa .

*Bobby Vee and Peggy Sue.
Surf Ballroom. 2002...
Courtesy Clear Lake Mirror Reporter*

*Peggy Sue. Buddy Holly Center
opening promo*

*Peggy Sue and Maria Elena at the 1996
Buddy Holly Music Festival
in Lubbock, Texas*

*The Foxy Drive In,
Clovis, New Mexico...
Courtesy of Al Omernick*

*Recording Equipment with
photograph of Norman and Vi
Petty...Courtesy of Violet Ann
Petty Estate*

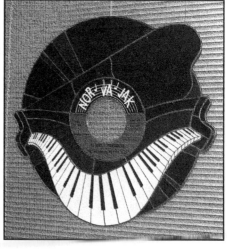

*Studio Front Sign of Nor Va Jak Studios...
Courtesy of Violet Ann Petty Estate*

Jo Harper, Vi Petty, and Georgiana Veit walking up Broadway toward Central Park in New York on June 22, 1958... Courtesy Violet Ann Petty Estate

Picture of the Guitar amp and microphone used by Buddy Holly... Courtesy of Al Omernick

Music truck filling up to go to Oklahoma City...Courtesy Violet Ann Petty Estate

The Original Norman Petty Trio car and music trailer...Courtesy Violet Ann Petty Estate

Alan Freed's Promotional Poster...
Courtesy Violet Ann Petty Estate

Norma Jean Berry at the controls...
Courtesy Violet Ann Petty Estate

Norman und Vi Petty, Jack Vaughn. The
original Norman Petty Trio...
Courtesy Violet Ann Petty Estate

Buddy Knox Promotional Photo

George Atwood on bass...
Courtesy Violet Ann Petty Estate

Eddie Cochran Promotional Photo...
Courtesy of Alan Clark

Paul McCartney and Vi Petty...
Courtesy Violet Ann Petty Estate

Buddy and Ed Sullivan...
Courtesy Michael Ochs

Ritchie Valens Promotional Photo

J.P. Richardson (The Big Bopper)...
Promotional Photo

A young Buddy Holly and his dog
Alonzo...Courtesy Ingrid Kaiter
& Eddie Weir

Buddy and Little Richard...
Courtesy of Violet Ann Petty Estate

Buddy rehearsing for
The Ed Sullivan Show...
Courtesy Michael Ochs

Buddy, Paul Anka, Jerry Lee Lewis, and
Rusty Smith getting on an airplane on the
Australian Tour...Courtesy C.J. Rees.

Alan Freed, Larry Williams, Don Costa, and Buddy...
Courtesy Michael Randolph.
Taken by William Popsie Randolph

Jo Harper, Joe B, Buddy, Vi Petty, Jerry, Georgiana Veit, and Niki in Washington...
Courtesy Georgiana Veit

Jerry, Joe B, Niki, and Buddy...
Courtesy Violet Ann Petty Estate

Joe B, Jerry, Niki, and Buddy...
Courtesy Violet Ann Petty Estate

Buddy Holly's High School Graduation Picture Lubbock High School,
Class of 1955

Niki, Joe B, Buddy and Jerry
in Clovis, NM...Promotional Photo

Lonnie Donegan (English Record Artist) and Buddy In England...Courtesy
Violet Ann Petty Estate.

Buddy on stage at Birmingham Town Hall in
England on March 9th, 1958...
Courtesy Violet Ann Petty Estate

*Buddy signing autographs at South
Hampton, Gaumont on March 3rd,
1958...Courtesy Violet Ann
Petty Estate*

*Joe B, Buddy, and Jerry having Tea in
South Hampton, England...
Courtesy Violet Ann Petty Estate*

*Joe B, Jerry, and Buddy in Australia...
Courtesy Violet Ann Petty Estate*

*Vi Petty, Jerry, Buddy, and Joe B
in England...Courtesy Violet Ann
Petty Estate*

The Crickets.
Courtesy Violet Ann Petty Estate

The Nurse's Memorial Center,
February 5, 1958,
Melbourne Victoria Australia
Photo courtesy of Roddy Jordan

Entrance to the Brevoort Apartments,
New York City. Courtesy Mike Gruber and
Marco Ellman

Glen Campbell and Jerry Naylor, 1969.
Courtesy Jerry Naylor

Robert Linville, David Bigham,
Ray Rush-The Roses

*Jerry and Peggy Sue Allison, Buddy
and Maria Holly at Buddy's wedding in
the Holleys' home, August 15, 1958*

Liberty Records promo shot. Hollywood.
1962. Jerry Naylor, Glen D. Hardin,
Sonny Curtis, JI Allison

*Joe B Mauldin, JI Allison, Jerry Naylor.
1961. Promo copy Liberty Records*

*Buddy Holly in Hawaii on the Australian tour.
1958... Courtesy Violet Ann Petty Estate*

*Photograph of David Box, who recorded "Peggy Sue Got Married"
in Los Angeles after Buddy Holly's death*

George and Barbara Tomsco, 1964... Courtesy of George Tomsco

Carl Bunch was Buddy Holly's replacement drummer for The Crickets Winter Dance Party in 1959... Courtesy of Al Omernick

Beechcraft Airplane that Peggy Sue learned to fly. It is a newer model of the same plane that crashed in 1959 killing Buddy Holly

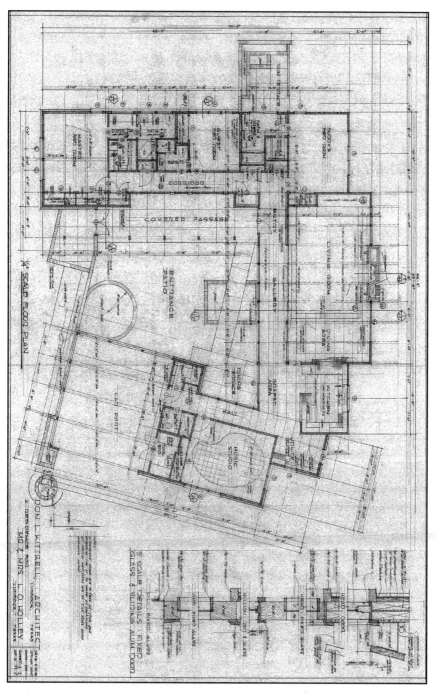

Buddy Holly's proposed Lubbock Studio Plans... Courtesy of Don Kittrell

Buddy Holly's proposed Lubbock Studio Plans... Courtesy of Don Kittrell

CHAPTER FIFTEEN
The Honeymoon

Double Honeymoon in Mexico City with Maria, Buddy, Jerry, and Peggy Sue.

W̃e had barely left Lubbock's city limits when Jerry and Maria fell asleep. As Buddy drove along, he played the radio and sang quietly when he found a song he liked. He changed the stations frequently, trying to find one of his hits, but he never came across a single one. He talked to me about some of the songs we heard. One was Bobby Darin's cover of Buddy's record, "Early in the Morning." We wondered why the DJs were playing Bobby's version instead of Buddy's.

"You know, Peggy Sue, there's no way to tell if what we're doing will last."

"Doesn't it have something to do with destiny, which you're always talking about, Buddy?" I could tell that not finding The Crickets' songs on the radio had made him a little somber. If he didn't have a hit in the top twenty-five, he always seemed worried that no one would buy another record. I continued, "Some of the hits are already standards. They'll never be forgotten."

"That'd be 'Peggy Sue,' right?" Buddy laughed.

"Nobody can sing 'Peggy Sue' the way you do. Rock 'n' roll's just getting started. In ten years, they'll be doing all your music all over again," I said.

"Do you really believe that?" Buddy asked.

"*Our* music will *not* be forgotten," I replied undoubtedly.

He laughed again. "What do you mean *our*?"

"The music belongs to the world. What is it you're always telling me, Buddy? If the music's any good, give it to the people, and they'll tell you. Do you want me to drive so you can get some sleep?" I asked, knowing it was a seven-and-a-half-hour trip to El Paso.

"No, just stay awake and talk with me."

The highway led us straight to downtown El Paso and the hotel Buddy had booked for us. We were almost sitting on top of the border. When we pulled up, I sighed disappointedly. "That's a really old hotel, Buddy."

"I know, but it's the closest one to the airport. We can leave the car here in the garage and take a taxi in the morning. I figured the car would be safer here than in airport parking," he explained.

"Good planning," I said. We both started to laugh.

Just awakening, Jerry and Maria were not in a party mood, so we went straight to our rooms. I knew I was tired, and Jerry was walking around in a complete stupor. He had not awakened completely from his nap. I wondered how he could sleep so much.

I woke up early the next morning to Jerry shouting, "Hurry, or we'll miss the plane. You know how I hate to be late."

"Okay. Okay. Just don't lose your temper. I'm up." I started to dress and pack at the same time. "I'm ready."

The phone rang, and Jerry answered it. "I'll be right down."

"Who was that?" I asked.

"Buddy. He wants me in the lobby, and he wants you to go get Maria. So hurry."

"Yes. Okay." I stacked the suitcases together, grabbed my little square purse, and walked over to Maria's room. I felt funny about knocking on her door, but I did, and then I called out to her, asking if she was ready.

"The guys are about to have an attack in the lobby," I told her when she opened the door.

"We aren't in *that* big of a hurry. Have a cup of coffee while I finish dressing," she said. She'd already ordered room service.

"Thanks, I will. I haven't had anything yet this morning." All of a sudden, she started talking, almost babbling. I was amazed. *This* is the same Maria who wouldn't talk to me in Lubbock?

"We had the most wonderful time last night. Buddy is just wonderful. The most kind and gracious husband in the whole wide world. Being a virgin, I was a little worried how the first night would go." I almost choked on my coffee; I was so embarrassed that I wanted to melt away. "Let me show you something," Maria said as she flipped back the covers on the bed. "See?"

"See what?" I asked.

"The blood on my sheets. Buddy was so pleased that I was a virgin."

I was speechless *and* appalled. What was I supposed to say now? I put down my cup, looked at her, and finally managed to say, "I'm glad you both had such a good time, but I really do think it's time we joined them in the lobby." Meanwhile, I was wondering why she had made such a big deal about this in front of me.

"It's really something to be a virgin, you know," Maria continued as we stepped into the hall.

As I reached for the elevator button, I replied, "The only thing I can say about that is that the first night of marriage can be highly overrated if you're a virgin."

Maria looked at me strangely and then started to laugh, "You really are funny. You have a funny sense of humor."

We met the guys in the lobby and went straight to the airport. In the taxi, I asked, "Jerry, did you buy me some cigarettes?"

"No," he replied.

"Thanks a lot. Can I get some at the airport?"

"Probably not. You can smoke mine or nothing," he said.

"I hate your brand of cigarettes, and you know it."

"*Ladies* aren't supposed to smoke," he snapped.

"Thank you, Father," I said sarcastically, totally annoyed by his attitude.

As soon as we arrived at the airport, I started looking for some cigarettes, and begged, "Jerry, give me some money. Please."

"No," he snarled.

"*Please*. Come on. Don't joke. I don't have that much time before we board," I said.

Jerry said angrily, "I'm not giving you any money."

He had humiliated me once again, in front of Maria and the whole world.

"I'm sorry, Jerry, but I've never had to ask for money before. Between the allowance Daddy gave me and working at the dental office, I had my own spending money, and Daddy bought my cigarettes at the commissary," I explained as I glared at him.

This was my first time flying and my first time outside of the United States. Of course I was thrilled to be going, but I was a little apprehensive, too, which made my desire for a cigarette even stronger.

We boarded the plane, and Jerry and I sat across from Buddy and Maria; I was sitting next to the aisle, and so was Buddy.

"Hey, you excited?" Buddy asked.

"The only thing I am is mad. I don't have any cigarettes."

"You can smoke mine. Don't let this spoil the trip." His brown eyes were smiling as he offered me a cigarette with a filter on it.

"Thanks, Buddy."

As soon as the smoking light went off, we lit our cigarettes, and Buddy asked, "Want some coffee, Peg?"

"Yes. Please."

Jerry had gone to sleep—and so had Maria. Shaking my head, I asked, "Does he sleep every time he starts a trip?"

"Yeah. If he doesn't, he gets airsick," Buddy answered. "We're going to have such a good time. The rooms I got are totally private. We're going to have our own pool and bar, and no people around us. I've been assured complete privacy."

By the time the plane reached Mexico City, Buddy and I were laughing and cutting up—having a great time. He was teaching me all the Spanish he knew, which was basically *cerveza*.

"At least you won't get thirsty," Buddy joked.

"Right, but I don't like beer," I joked back.

We had an hour and a half layover in Mexico City. Jerry was in a good mood when he awoke, and he and Buddy began making up Spanish-sounding words and laughing at their "inventions." Maria, who refused to join the fun, complained, "You act like you're two years old. Stop it. You're calling attention to us." She sounded like a mother correcting her child.

"Who cares what they think," Buddy yelled. "This is my vacation, and I'll do whatever I please."

I thought it was strange that he used the word *vacation* instead of *honeymoon*.

"Okay then," she said, muttered something in Spanish under her breath, and continued angrily, "I will not sit with you, Buddy. I don't want anybody to know that we are married."

I said, "Come on, guys. That's enough. There's no point in making Maria mad. Knock it off."

Just as I said that, I noticed Jerry sitting on the staircase rail acting like a monkey, jumping up and down and making ape-like sounds. I couldn't help it. I started laughing and couldn't stop. Buddy joined the antics; and the two of them began jumping up and down on the seats, scratching under their arms. The only reason they continued their childish antics was to irritate Maria even more. If the world could see Buddy Holly and the Cricket now, I thought. Maria moved to the other side of the room. Boy, was she mad!

"You guys really look like rock idols now," I said laughing. "Mr. Monkey, would you give me some money now so I can buy some cigarettes?"

This changed Jerry's mood. He immediately became angry and said, much too loudly, "No, I'm not going to tell you again," and he went to sit by Maria.

"We'd better get ready to board," Maria suggested. "In a few minutes, we'll be airborne."

We boarded the small Mexican airplane for Acapulco. The land below us looked like a desert. The plane stopped only once in the middle of the vast country to refuel—not at an airport, but at a landing strip with gas tanks. As I watched from the plane window, I wondered how they got the fuel out there; there was nothing else around. We could have been on the moon—it was the same color and that barren.

The flight was very uncomfortable. Everyone on the plane, except the four of us, was Mexican, and the stewards only spoke Spanish. The airplane wasn't even pressurized, and I developed a horrendous earache. Leaning over to me, Buddy reassured, "It'll be okay once we land. Your ears will clear." He laughed. "The plane's old, but the flight was cheap."

It was late when we landed in Acapulco. As soon as we stepped off the plane, the heat and humidity made me think of a tropical jungle. Luckily, the hotel car was waiting for us and took us straight to the Las Brisas. At first glimpse, the hotel looked like a bunch of houses built on tiers, but I really couldn't tell for sure because darkness covered the place like a blanket. At least there were lights around the hotel lobby when we got there, so I could see how really pretty everything was. There were lots of flamingos in the décor, and gold golf carts with pink- and white-striped awnings were parked near the office. We had so much luggage between the four of us that the concierge decided to drive us to our cabana rather than have the bellhops try to carry everything.

"Just think, complete privacy. Isn't this groovy?" Buddy asked, and I agreed. It certainly was groovy.

The swimming pool was right outside our cabana—just two steps and you were in the pool. Buddy ran over to see what his half looked like and then came right back into ours. "Your room is a lot nicer than ours," he noted.

"Do you want this room?" I asked.

"No, no. You keep this one so you can be near the pool."

While I put on my swimsuit, Jerry, Buddy, and Maria went through the bar. It was completely stocked, and there was some food in the refrigerator, too. Jerry mixed me a drink of something, mostly coke, and the party was on; we all sat on the edge of the pool, laughing, talking, and feeling like we were truly in paradise.

"Tomorrow I'm going to have to buy myself a bikini, Jerry. The only thing wrong with this hotel is that there's no air conditioning," I complained.

"Do you wanna leave?" Jerry asked.

I exclaimed, "Oh, no! I've never seen a bathroom like this one before in my life. The shower's an entire room done in marble."

"Don't get too spoiled," Buddy warned. I could tell he was proud that I liked the accommodations.

I laughed. "It's too late for that; I already am."

With that, Buddy and Maria retired to their room.

Buddy laughed. "I think Maria has had a little too much *cerveza*."

"So have I," Jerry confessed.

Jerry was out as soon as his head hit the pillow, but I lay in bed, fully awake, for at least an hour. Hum. Nobody was awake, and I'd have the whole pool to myself. Why not go swimming? I got out of bed, slipped off my gown, and went skinny-dipping. The water felt so good and cool. Whoops! I noticed that the pool light was on. Oh, well, no one was awake anyway. And anyhow, what would it matter? We had complete privacy. I stayed in the water for about an hour, swimming, turning somersaults, and dancing.

The next morning, I awoke to a bellhop beating on Buddy's door, speaking only in Spanish, and I peeked out to see what was going on. Maria came to the door and started talking to him.

He said, "You must leave now."

I could hear Buddy say, "No. We have reservations."

The man persisted, "You must leave now."

"Ask him why," Buddy said, turning to Maria.

Maria said something in Spanish to the bellhop. His answer made her turn white, then red. I saw them all look toward our door, and I jumped away from the window.

In a flash, Buddy and Maria were standing in our room. She gave me a cool stare and then said, "*Someone* went skinny-dipping last night. And now they want us to leave."

Suddenly, all eyes were upon me. Jerry was angry, and I was extremely embarrassed.

Buddy broke the silence with his typical two-toned laugh. "Why didn't you invite me?"

"Hey Man, nobody goes swimming in the nude! Are you crazy?" Jerry yelled.

151

"I thought we had complete privacy. I was hot and sticky and, yes, I went skinny-dipping. It never occurred to me anyone was watching," I replied excitedly.

Jerry's face was red with anger, which seemed to be his natural state these days.

"Still, Peggy, if you had called me I'd have gone with you." Buddy laughed again.

"Wrong thing to say, Buddy. Jerry's not laughing. I'm really sorry I ruined your trip," I said to everybody.

"Now's a nice time for you to think about *us*," Jerry bellowed.

"Look, Jerry. You act like I was having sex out there. All I did was swim. What if it'd been Maria out there?" I countered.

"I don't swim," Maria replied quickly.

I just rolled my eyes and thought, She doesn't drive, she doesn't swim, she doesn't joke, and she doesn't smoke. I wonder, What she does do?

"We'll get a bigger and nicer place to stay, especially one that has an air conditioner. Don't worry, Peggy Sue, you didn't ruin our trip. Don't forget, the next time you go skinny-dipping, invite me, okay?" Buddy said, laughing heartily as he left the room.

Jerry was mad the rest of the day. I started packing my clothes and then decided to take a shower before leaving. You're batting a hundred, Peggy Sue, I thought to myself. As of today, you've received a speeding ticket, you put your feet into the drinking bucket at the well, and now, you've caused the foursome to be thrown out of the hotel for indecent exposure.

As we walked into the Las Brisas lobby together, Maria gave me a smile and said, "Just straighten your back a little, be very indignant, and put your nose in the air like you don't know what they're talking about."

Buddy was kind enough to check us out so we didn't have to stand around with people staring at us. Jerry got the cab, and we were on our way. We drove toward town and found a beautiful American-built hotel called the El Cano, which was delighted to have us as guests. Buddy was checking us in and, as the clerk handed him the keys, he turned to me and said, "Please try to keep your clothes on here." The clerk's eyes opened up wide, and Buddy started laughing hysterically. I could have killed him, and he knew it, too.

Buddy started running for the stores in the lobby, and the rest of us followed right behind him. I found the cutest string bikini ever but, as usual, I had no money of my own to buy it. I grabbed Jerry by the arm and started dragging him over to pay for it, but he pulled away from me and said indifferently, "Just sign it to the room."

After exhausting all the shops, we went to check out our rooms. Jerry's and my room was on the west side, almost at the top of the building. We could see forever. What a beautiful view! Parked out in the harbor was a gigantic white yacht—rumor had it that it belonged to Sammy Davis, Jr. One thing's for certain, whoever owned it was living the good life. I thought to myself, Acapulco must be very near heaven. We'd been in the room only a few minutes when Buddy ran through the door. His and Maria's room was at the opposite end of the same floor.

"I came to see your room," he said. "Yeah, no doubt about it. It's nicer than mine."

"What is it with you and the rooms?" I asked. "Don't you know the grass is always greener on the other side? You can have this room if you want it."

"No, don't be silly," he said, grinning.

"Buddy, can I have another cigarette?" I asked.

As he handed me one, he said, "Let's take a taxi downtown and see what the locals are doing."

We stopped at a little cafe the driver suggested. It didn't look all that inviting from the outside, but, what the hell. We were on an adventure. There were wooden tables and benches, and a jukebox was playing in the corner. Buddy and Maria sat on one side, and we sat on the other. We ordered a planter's punch and began enjoying ourselves. When Jerry got up to go to the jukebox, Maria followed him. At the table, Buddy handed me a cigarette, lit it, and asked, "What are you thinking about?"

"Well, if you must know, I really wanted a cigarette but didn't want to have to ask you for one," I confessed.

Buddy reached across the table and laid his hand on top of mine. "If you belonged to me, I'd give you anything in the entire world, including the world if you wanted it."

Shocked, I jerked my hand back, and just in time. Jerry was standing at the end of the table with Maria.

"Hey, look what I just bought," Jerry said. "Two packs of filter-tip Mexican cigarettes. I decided to help old Buddy's expenses out."

"By buying her two packs, Jerry? That'll last two days. You're the last of the big spenders," Buddy joked.

"Well, you look so nice and suntanned," Jerry said, looking straight at me. "I thought if you're going to smoke, I should start buying them for you."

Now that was a change of attitude. Had he noticed the consideration Buddy had been giving me?

"Thank you from the bottom of my heart. I can't tell you how much I appreciate it," I said Groucho Marx style, wiggling my cigarette as I spoke. We all laughed.

♪

As soon as I pulled the curtains open the next morning and looked out on the beach, I knew it was going to be a great day. This was exactly what I'd requested when Buddy asked me where I wanted to go for our double honeymoon. Jerry and I threw on our bathing suits, grabbed the suntan lotion and beach towels, and headed for a day of fun in the sun and water. Buddy and Maria were already on the beach, and they yelled for us to join them.

As we approached, Maria said, "Look, Jerry, we even have waiters out here on the beach. We don't even have to get up to get our own drinks."

I said, "Terrific. Jerry doesn't have to move to get drunk. He can do it in one spot."

"Now, Peggy, don't sound like a wife," Maria said, as she took another sip of her *cerveza*.

I sat down and started putting on my suntan lotion. We played in the waves, lay in the sun, and talked all day. Most of the time, Jerry and Maria remained under the Palapa drinking their *cervezas* and arguing about politics. Jerry was Republican, and Maria considered herself a liberal Democrat. And me? I was totally bored with the whole conversation after the first twenty minutes. It was obvious that they were never going to find common ground, and that neither would ever concede to an opposing argument. Buddy must have felt the same way because he turned away from their conversation and said, "Peggy Sue, tell me about that Catholic girls school you went to. Jerry told me how nice it was. Did you study religion?"

"Oh, yeah. A lot," I said.

"Did you get to study anything about other religions?" he asked.

"Well, some. I can tell you a little bit about Buddhism. Please, don't take me as an authority because I'm not sure that I understood all of it, but Buddhism is like earth, air, fire. It's belief in the now. It's what's here that we must deal with," I explained.

"What's wrong with that?" Jerry chimed in.

"Well, Christianity is our belief that real life begins after death. Not here on this plane. You know, where God and heaven is. Everything is up. The only thing I know about Zen is how to spell it. Judaism is a very old religion like Catholicism, and we believe in the same fathers in the Bible. You know, like Abraham, but they don't believe that Jesus has come yet." Running out of words of wisdom, I suggested, "Why don't you tell me about the Baptist religion, Buddy. It seems that I have more problems understanding it."

Buddy laughed. "Well, they're not as hard to understand as the Church of Christ," he said, referring to the problems he'd had with Echo McGuire. He continued, "I decided some time ago that I believe what is between me and my God is what counts. Not some man-made rule. I don't understand how any church can believe that music's a sin. Feelings are things that are not of this world. Music's a feeling. How can that not be from God? No one can see how much I love God, but God. There's no man-made measure. As far as the Baptists, they think that Catholics do not have a direct relationship with God. The priest does it for them."

Defensively, I spoke up. "Have they ever asked a Catholic? Because every Catholic I know has a direct relationship with God, not the priest. The priest doesn't talk to God for me. He adds prayer and a state of grace to what I'm doing. But he doesn't forgive me. God has to do that."

"Do you believe in destiny?" Buddy asked.

"Hmmm. Predestination. That's a hard one for me. As Mother Superior would say to me in school, it's about humility. However, I keep thinking that we have some control over our lives," I replied.

155

Buddy laughed. "You have some control; it's just that you don't have control over the big things."

"Wait! Wait! I know what *you're* going to say for a change," I exclaimed.

"What?" Buddy asked.

"Death. We don't have any control over that appointment," I said, proud of myself.

He laughed. "You got it. I'm goin' swimming and cool off."

"Well, I think it's *cerveza* time after that discussion," announced Jerry, looking over at Maria, who agreed and started looking around for the waiter.

I said, "I'm going swimming, too. Come on, Jerry. Let's go in while we have all this great water."

"Okay," he replied, "but just until the beer gets here."

Maria motioned for the waiter, and as Jerry ran out toward Buddy, I asked, "Are you coming, Maria?"

"No, I don't swim," she replied. "I'll stay here."

I saw the waiter coming and hung around like I was looking for seashells or something. As he was leaving our Palapa to get the beers, I asked if he knew whose gorgeous yacht was in the bay, and he replied, "Sí. It has guests on it. So private."

"Do you know who's on the yacht?" Having the curiosity of a cat, I couldn't stand not knowing.

"Sí," he replied. "Mr. Sammy Davis, Jr., and his lady."

"And that would be..."

"Señorita May Britt. They have been in the village to shop."

I rushed into the water where Jerry and Buddy were horsing around. "Guess what I found out. That's Sammy Davis and May Britt on that yacht. That's what the waiter just told me. All the movie magazines are saying that she's about to lose her contract with the studio because of their relationship. You know, because she's a white, blonde, blue-eyed Swede, and she's married, too, I think, and he's black. I think she's very talented," I rattled on. "She sings, dances, and acts. Hollywood sure gave her an easy break..."

Buddy, knowing what went on behind the glamour of performing, broke in, "You mean it *looks* like it was easy."

"Well, at least she already has some money if she gets fired," I said. "That should help the situation a lot."

Jerry noticed the waiter had brought the beer, so we walked back to our Palapa.

♫

A common saying in West Texas was "If you don't like the weather, just stay around a day or two and it'll change." God had truly made Acapulco a beautiful place; the weather was perfect here every day.

Tuesday was another fun day in the sun and water for us, except Jerry and Maria spent even less time in the sun and water and more time under the Palapa drinking their *cervezas*. Toward evening, we went to the hotel bar where we became completely intrigued by a couple dancing. She was a tall blonde; he was a tall Latin, who was extremely graceful and an overall fantastic dancer. We all admired the way he held and turned her. At first, we thought he might be a famous dancer, but then we decided he was probably an actor due to the intense look on his face. We asked the bartender if he knew who the man was.

"Oh, yes. He's a famous matador," he answered proudly.

Now we understood what the dancer was doing. He was maneuvering his partner like he would his cape—bringing her close then, gracefully and artistically, swinging her away. Even the expression on his face, as he flashed his dark-brown eyes, resembled that of a matador engaging in a series of veronicas. After the couple left, Buddy jumped up and started dancing like a matador—solo. Maria laughed. We had a few more drinks and then retired to our rooms.

♫

The next day started out the same—same beach, same waiter, same *cerveza*. Around noon, Maria already had a drink in her hand, and Jerry was on his way to join her. Buddy told me he was bored.

"Me, too," I replied.

"Peggy Sue, what would you like to do today?" Buddy asked.

"I'd like to learn to water ski," I answered matter-of-factly.

Jerry said, "You know I can't go into the water. I'll get an earache."

"Can't you swim, Jerry?" Maria asked, noticing that he hadn't gone very far out into the water during the entire trip.

"Not well, and I don't water ski either," Jerry stated emphatically.

"That's okay. I don't either, but I'm willing to learn," I said.

Buddy said, "I'll get us a boat and a driver." He ran off, calling, "Come on, Jerry, let's go."

Jerry just shrugged his shoulders and yelled back, "Okay, but you're probably going to get us all killed!"

"No, Jerry, I wouldn't do a thing like that. We'll come and get you in the boat, so look for us out there," he said to Maria and me as he motioned toward the bay.

I looked at Maria, lying on the beach under the Palapa, sipping her tall, cool *cerveza*. "Haven't you ever tried to swim, Maria?" I asked.

She snapped, "Very little."

"I can swim well enough to save my life if I don't have to go too far. I'd really like to try to water ski. What the hell. There's nothing else to do." I laughed.

"You *are* crazy," she said, obviously repulsed by the idea of leaving the safety of the Palapa for an excursion in the water.

"Maybe so. There they are. Let's go," I said.

As we waded out to the boat, Maria started yelling at Buddy, "I told you I don't water ski, and I won't! If you try it and get hurt, where will you be then?"

Buddy responded, "Don't be ridiculous. I've been water skiing for years. If you don't want to try it, just get into the boat and enjoy the ride." His voice was lower and more serious than normal. I noticed that he was no longer mincing words with her, or Jerry.

We loaded up and took off. The water was warm, calm, and smooth—perfect for skiing, I thought; but, then, I'd never been skiing. Buddy was the first to go, and he did amazingly well. He and Joe B had been skiing at Lubbock's Buffalo Lake for years. I clapped, Jerry cheered, and Maria just sat there shaking her head in disapproval. Ten minutes later, Buddy dropped his skis, and we circled around and picked him up.

"Okay, Jerry, it's your turn," Buddy said.

"No way, Man! I'll just sit here and watch, and drink my *cerveza*," Jerry replied.

"All right. Who's next?" Buddy asked.

"Me! Me!" I yelled. "Everybody keep in mind I've never done this before."

Motioning to the man sitting beside the driver, Buddy commanded, "Stay with her, Carlos. If she falls off the skis, you fall off too."

"I understand, Sir. Nothing will happen to her," Carlos replied in his beautiful, thick accent.

"Anyone who doesn't want to watch, close your eyes," I yelled, and jumped out of the boat.

Carlos swam over to me and said, "Swim over to the beach, and I will explain how to get up on the skis."

In a few minutes, we were on the warm white sand. Carlos asked, "What is your name?"

"Peggy."

"Is your real name Margaret?" Apparently, he was Catholic because "Margaret" was the saint's name for the nickname "Peggy."

"No, just Peggy. Now what do I do?"

"Just pretend you water ski like you make love," he explained softly.

"I beg your pardon," I said, surprised.

"Well, see, you just relax. Just let it happen," he said.

"Well, let's give this a try, shall we?" I asked.

He lined the ropes out, and we started to move. It took about half a minute for me to realize that I was going to drown if I didn't turn loose of the rope. Did he forget to tell me that? We started over.

"Go up gradually. The skis will float. Let them take you up. You're working too hard," Carlos said.

Buddy drove the boat up beside me. "Have you had enough yet?"

"No. Go away. I'll get it," I said.

The next time I almost got up—I made it to a stooped position before I fell off. When I came up, the boat was next to me.

"Well, Peggy," Jerry said. "You're the first girl to take the longest douche in the Pacific Ocean."

"Thanks a lot. You're so good for my ego. At least *I* tried it which is more than I can say for *you*," I retorted.

We circled around the bay for a while, enjoying the white beaches and green palm trees, the distant mountains, all the fishing boats, and the bluest water I'd ever seen. As the sun went down, casting a photographer's *sweet light* across the picture postcard view, we returned to the beach for a cocktail before dinner.

Not having any cigarettes with me, I asked, "Buddy, may I have a cigarette?"

"Sure, Peggy Sue," he replied.

"Do you always have to call me by both my names?" I inquired.

"Of course. It's the title of my hit record." He began to laugh. "Shall we dress for dinner this evening and dine in the dining room?" he asked in a stilted, formal tone.

"Ah, yes, my good man. We will dine at seven. Meet you there," Jerry replied.

We returned to the hotel rooms and dressed for dinner. Totally out of the blue, Jerry said, "I couldn't stand it if you were married to Buddy. Do you know that?"

"What did you say to me?" I couldn't believe what I had just heard. "What on earth is wrong with you? I'm not married to anyone but *you*."

"I know. But I just had to say that so you'd know how I feel," he replied in a serious tone.

"What did I do to make you even entertain that idea?"

"You didn't do anything. Forget I said it."

I wondered if Jerry's conscience was beginning to bother him.

For once, I beat Jerry dressing. "Now, tell me. How do I look?" I asked as I walked out of the bathroom. "I picked the whole outfit out myself. Did I do well?"

"You look great. Not at all like in high school," he said, smiling.

I had on a strapless, brown taffeta and chiffon dress that fit all the way down and then tapered four inches above the knee. There was a large ruffle that flared as I walked and a black bow just above the ruffle. My shoes matched, of course. I did look all grown up for a change.

Buddy was alone at the table.

"Where's Maria?" I asked.

"She'll be down in a few minutes. She wasn't ready. We don't have to eat right now. We can have a drink and wait for her," Buddy replied, revealing a different mood than he'd been in earlier. He looked annoyed, but managed a slight smile when he said, "You look fantastic. Where did you get that dress?"

"Well, would you believe I bought this little number at Margaret's in Lubbock, Texas? I wish I could say New York, but I'm not that sophisticated yet, damn it," I answered.

Buddy and Jerry laughed. We finished our drinks, and Maria still had not made her entrance. The situation at the table was becoming quite tense.

Buddy said, "I think I'll call the room and see when she'll be down. Excuse me. I'll be right back."

I looked at Jerry and said, "Well, I have one thing to say. I've been waited on here more than any other place I've ever been. Did you know the maids even washed my lingerie while we were out on the beach today?"

"You're kidding," he said.

"No, I'm not. I think I'll stay here forever. What do you think is going on with Buddy and Maria?" I asked.

"Maybe Maria isn't feeling well."

"You mean she's had too much *cerveza*."

"I didn't say that. Be quiet. Here comes Buddy."

Buddy was more than just annoyed now; his anger showed in every step he took.

"What's wrong? Is Maria sick?" I asked politely.

"No, she decided to have dinner alone in her room when she knew we were waiting for her here," Buddy snapped.

"She probably thought we'd already ordered, and she didn't want us to sit and wait for her," I suggested, trying to ease the tension.

"No, that's *not* what she thought," Buddy exclaimed so bluntly that I raised my eyebrows in surprise.

"Well, let's order then and not ruin our dinner," I said. "Come on everybody. Let's get in a good mood."

Buddy flashed me a small smile. "Why do all the waiters run over here to you? Could it be because of your blonde hair?"

"Who cares? Great service—whatever the reason. Let's try everything on the menu, okay?" I suggested impishly.

We ate for two hours and talked non-stop. By the time dinner had ended, Buddy had calmed down and appeared to be in a good mood.

"Let's go downtown and see what kind of night life we can stir up," Buddy suggested.

"You go get Maria," Jerry told Buddy.

"I'll get my purse," I said, "and we'll meet in the lobby."

Jerry followed me to the room, and as soon as we were out of earshot, he said, "I told you the other day that he wasn't happy."

"Don't say that, Jerry. They probably just had their first argument. They'll forget about it in a few hours. Don't say anything to Maria if she goes with us. It'll only make matters worse."

"Okay," he replied, as he batted his eyes. "I'll be good."

"That'll be the day," I joked.

By the time we got to the lobby, Buddy had a taxi waiting, and he waved us on excitedly. "Come on, you guys. What took so long? What were you doing up there?"

Maria's features were tense and her demeanor cold. She was definitely annoyed.

As we climbed into the taxi, Buddy told the driver to take us to a local nightspot.

"Sí, Señor, I know a good place. You will like this one. All American tourists go there." The driver started to laugh and then said, "Tell everyone to hold on. It's a pretty rough ride." Before we could prepare ourselves, we were driving straight up a mountain.

"Is he sure he knows where he's going?" I asked, holding onto the back of the seat in front of me.

"Sí, Señorita. We are almost there," the driver replied.

The taxi started to slow down as we approached a beautiful nightclub that looked like a Spanish mansion with marble and tile steps, columns, and water fountains.

"What is this place?" I asked.

"It's an American-built-and-owned house of prostitution," our taxi driver replied.

Buddy laughed and said, "Stop kidding."

162

"I'm not," the taxi driver said. "This is the place to go. It has a live band and a great bar, and everybody comes here. If you want a little company, it's available here."

"Of course, the Americans own it," I piped in, as Jerry paid the driver and we made our way toward another adventure.

I was awestruck the moment we walked in. This place was beautiful. The girls, all of whom looked Spanish, were sitting together at the bar, sort of in a half circle. They ranged from pretty to—well, I'd have to say, fair. I started to chuckle.

"Why are you laughing?" Jerry asked.

"I'm mentally grading the girls, and I've never even met a prostitute before. I wouldn't know if they're good or not. I mean, I thought they would look different."

"Just shut up," he snarled.

"I'm sorry," I said, realizing I was being rude.

The interior was decorated in jungle decor. Half the building had an indoor look and the other half had that of a veranda. There were hotel-like rooms all around one side on two different floors. The girls' outdated dresses were the only thing I would've changed. Everything else was beautiful.

Buddy ordered drinks, and then he and Maria started dancing. Jerry and I stepped onto the dance floor, too. Suddenly, all the girls came out to the veranda and started watching us and giggling.

"Why are they staring at us, Jerry?" I asked.

"I don't know. Do you want to leave? We can, you know. Buddy and Maria can come when they're ready," he said.

"No, I don't, but I do have to go to the ladies' room."

"No, not here."

"I don't have a choice. I'm sure they have a powder room somewhere," I said as I started across the room, smiling cordially at the girls who were obviously eavesdropping on our conversation.

Maria raced across the room, grabbed me by my arm, and asked curiously, "Where are you going?"

"To the powder room, if I can find one."

Buddy, who had followed right behind her, asked with surprise, "Here?"

"Yes, here," I exclaimed.

As I started toward the bar, one of the girls who'd been watching us intently ever since we'd arrived rushed up to me and asked, "Can I help you?"

"Yes, is there a powder room in the bar?" I asked.

"I would be most honored if you would come to my room and use my bathroom," she said.

"Oh, how nice of you. Are you sure you don't mind? I thought there might be a powder room in the bar," I stated.

"No, not for ladies. Please come this way," she said, as she stretched out her hand.

"Wait a minute," Maria called. "I'm going with you."

We walked into a hallway with wall-to-wall, red carpeting, and the girl opened the door to a large entry hall that was mirrored from ceiling to floor. Then we turned into a bedroom where everything—the bed, drapes, and floor—was made of red velvet. Another room, on the other side of the bathroom, was decorated in gold velvet. Everything looked very clean, but it all felt steamy and sticky from the humidity. I also noticed all the folded towels. Evidently, they had a very busy house. I suppose my fascination was obvious because the girl asked, "Do you want to see the rest of the rooms?"

"No. No, thank you. That's all right," I replied.

"Are you on your honeymoon?" she asked.

"Yes," I nodded.

"You are very beautiful," she said.

"Thank you," I replied. "Your room is very beautiful, also."

"I like...oh...how you say?...Where you from?" she asked.

"Texas."

"Oh, American."

"Yes, I'm American," I said.

"I love your dress," she said, and then started talking in Spanish.

"I'm sorry. I don't speak your language. I don't understand what you're saying."

About that time, Maria came out of the powder room, looking a little annoyed, and explained, "She wants to buy your dress."

The girl nodded her head. "Sí. Sí."

"She will give you a hundred dollars for it," Maria said.

"A hundred dollars for this dress?" I asked in amazement.

"Sí. Sí. I will."

"This dress is not worth a hundred dollars," I told her.

"To me it is. I can't buy one like it here," she stated.

I smiled and said, "I wouldn't have anything to wear back to the hotel, and my husband wouldn't understand if I sold the dress. You see, I've been in enough trouble lately with the whole group. If I walk out in my panties and bra, they'll *all* divorce me."

"I understand," the girl laughed. "I tried, Señorita, I tried."

"Thank you for your compliment. You've been very nice to me," I said.

Maria explained to her what I'd said. The girl laughed and took us back to the dance floor. When we told Buddy and Jerry what had happened, they just shook their heads in disbelief.

"I could have sold my dress to her for a hundred dollars and walked out here nude, but instead, I decided to be a good girl and not embarrass y'all anymore. It was hard for me to turn down the money since I don't have any of my own, even for cigarettes. I could make a fortune over here," I said.

Everybody laughed. Jerry got up and asked Maria to dance, and Buddy extended his hand and said, "Come dance with me, Peggy Sue."

"I'd love to," I answered.

We partied the rest of the night. All evening, every time I looked up, Buddy was staring at me over Maria's shoulder while they were dancing. He looked like he was wondering what I was thinking. I knew we would have to talk again about the comment he had made to me earlier, and I was not looking forward to that. We returned to the hotel about three in the morning. Buddy was wiped out, along with Jerry and Maria. I'd never seen Buddy drink to such a degree before; he was usually the one who remained sober. I managed to get everybody back to the hotel, and I was thankful that we were all staying on the same floor. Even in his condition, Jerry had to help Buddy and Maria to their rooms.

♪

We were extremely kind to each other the next morning. Hell, our hangovers had made us kind to everyone. After breakfast, we felt better and decided to go shopping, although nobody was jumping up and down with enthusiasm. When we returned to the hotel, Jerry and I lay on the beach for about an hour, and then Buddy and Maria joined us.

"Take a nap?" Buddy asked Jerry.

"Yes, and I think I may just live to see another day," he moaned.

"I feel well enough to have another drink. How about you, Jerry?" Maria asked.

"You're on. Let's go get one. A little hair of the dog," Jerry quipped.

"Bring me back a Coke, will you, Jerry?" I asked.

"Sure you don't want your baby bottle?" he snapped.

"At least my head doesn't hurt like yours does today," I sneered.

I was lying with my sunglasses on, facing Buddy. "Boy, are you tan. You really don't need to lie out in the sun," I said.

He laughed. "Did I upset you the other night when I got so personal?"

"No, you were drinking, and you were upset with Maria. I just thought you were feeling a little blue. Should I be mad?" I asked, not expressing my true feelings.

"No, I wasn't drinking then, and I didn't say that because of Maria. I said it because I meant it," Buddy said definitively.

"Jerry is your closest friend."

"I know I should have said something to you a long time ago, but every time I started to, I decided it wasn't fair to Jerry. The only thing I can say is that he doesn't begin to know what he has. He should be married to someone like Maria; and then, maybe, he'd appreciate how damn lucky he is."

His feelings bared, Buddy turned away from me and looked out at the ocean, waiting for me to respond.

Was this for real? Or, I wondered, was he just as disappointed in marriage as I was and wishing he hadn't rushed into it? "I can't talk about this right now," I said, as I stood up and dusted myself off. I continued, "Tell Jerry that I went back to the room to shower and wash off the sand."

166

Buddy started to get up, but I said, "No. Please. Don't get up. Stay put and enjoy the beach."

He pulled his sunglasses off and looked me in the eye. "Peggy Sue, let's have dinner in the dining room tonight."

"No, I don't think so. I think I'll have dinner in my room and go to bed early," I replied, looking around for Jerry and Maria. They hadn't come back from the bar with their beers yet, so I said, "Tell Jerry where I've gone. See you tomorrow."

I turned and headed for the hotel elevator, literally running away from such a tense situation. I couldn't acknowledge what he'd told me. If I did, it would make it real, and it couldn't be real. That would confuse things too much. There were rules we couldn't break no matter what—no matter how unhappy we might be with our lives. I tried to put it out of my mind and pretend Buddy never said a thing.

Jerry and I had dinner alone in our room that evening and later went for a long walk on the beach. The sky sparkled brightly, and looked as if it were patched with large diamonds. This was supposed to be our honeymoon, a time that we would never experience again, and yet, all I could think about was what Buddy had said to me.

"Jerry, are you happy?" I asked.

"Happier than maybe I have the right to be."

"Why's that?"

"Well, all I've ever wanted was to play with Buddy, and then to have you for my own. Now I have both of you. There's nothing else left...except... wanna make love on the beach?"

"Swell. You're the one who got so mad because I went skinny-dipping. And, now, you want me to make love on the beach and get thrown into jail?" I laughed. "I'll race you back to the hotel."

I was running so hard to beat Jerry that I nearly ran into Buddy and Maria on the walkway.

"Where are you going?" Buddy called.

"I'm going to beat Jerry back to our room." And I did.

♪

We spent our last day in Acapulco shopping. After taking a taxi downtown, we walked to each little store in the market. Buddy and Maria argued all day long. Maria felt that everybody in Buddy's family should have a gift from their honeymoon. Buddy said no, only the immediate family—his parents, brothers, and sister would be getting a gift. By the time we got back to the hotel, everybody's patience had been tested. Jerry and I excused ourselves and spent a quiet evening in our room packing.

♫

On Saturday morning, we were all off to another adventure—Mexico City. I hated to leave Acapulco because I knew Mexico City was not going to be as pleasant, as there was no ocean. Besides, it would put us closer to going home and reality—finding another place to live.

We checked into the Hilton Hotel around two o'clock, and Jerry had barely tipped the bellman before Buddy came bouncing in to do his little inspection. He whirled around the room and then said, "Yeah, your room is nicer than ours."

I started to laugh. "You can have this room if you want it, can't he, Jerry?"

Jerry said, "Yes...if he will move all the suitcases."

Buddy laughed and said, as usual, "No thanks. Are ya'll hungry?"

"Not really," Jerry replied.

"Well, then, my man, let's all go for a walk in front of the hotel and see what's out there. We'll meet you in the lobby," Buddy said.

I didn't like Mexico City. There was so much noise. The taxis did nothing but race up and down the narrow streets honking their horns.

"Why do they honk so much? Our taxi drivers never do that. It would be considered rude, and probably illegal," I said.

Another couple, obviously tourists as well, overheard me, and the man laughed and said, "If you notice, just before they get to an intersection, they speed up, too. One of the drivers told us that if there's no light, the first taxi to reach the intersection and honk is the one that gets to go first."

Plus, somebody was always yelling. Merchants were selling their wares on the streets and yelled for shoppers to come over and see what they had. Haggling was going on everywhere. I'd never liked the idea of dealing with car salesmen and this was like the same thing, but here, you even had to bargain over the price of a piece of fruit. Who would want to eat out here? When they weren't haggling, the shopkeepers were shooing flies from their displays.

Maria was in her shopping mood again. I thought she'd already bought enough for every person she'd ever met, but here she was again saying she had to buy, buy, buy. Uncles, aunts, and cousins, you know. It seemed to me that she had an unusual amount of relatives. Finally, Jerry said, "Let's go back to the hotel and see what they suggest for dining tonight."

We went to a very quaint Mexican restaurant not too far from our hotel, and the minute we walked in, my spirits were lifted. The maître d' sat us right in front of a table filled with people who were having a great time. We clearly heard them say, "Oh! Gringos!" and Maria said something back to them in Spanish. All I got out of it was that she was puertoriqueña, not gringa. They all laughed at her because she was so adamant.

Dinner was great. When the strolling mariachis came to our table, Buddy asked the guitar player if he could play "Malagueña." I noticed Buddy intently watching every finger movement, and as soon as the song was over, he threw his head back and said with gusto, "Well, al-l-l-l right."

Back at the hotel, Buddy said, "Don't forget that we're going to the bullfights tomorrow afternoon. We need to get there early so we can get a seat. The show starts around four o'clock. See ya'll tomorrow."

We got up early Sunday morning, went shopping again, ate some lunch, and then attended the bullfights. We were late getting to the arena due to the heavy traffic, and all the preliminary pomp and circumstance had just ended. The stands were very crowded. I was shocked by how steep and erect the rows were because I had expected the arena to resemble the interior of a football stadium. It made me wonder who the crazed architect must have been. I'd never seen a bullfight, so I didn't know what to expect and kept asking question after question.

"I didn't know they rode horses. Look how the horses are padded and blindfolded," I said. "What's the matador doing with those spears?"

Jerry said, "That's the way they kill the bull, I think."

I looked over at Maria, who applauded—along with everyone else— every time the bull was hit. "Olé! Olé!" they screamed. I was aghast! I wished the poor bull would jump the fence and storm into the stands, and then everyone would see how fast *they* could move and how graceful *they* could be.

"This is horrible," I said. "Absolutely the worst thing I've ever seen. How can these people enjoy such cruelty?"

Jerry said, "I think you miss the point. They give this meat to the poor."

"I don't care who they give it to. Can't they find a better way to kill the animal?"

Maria looked at me and said, "You don't understand. The animal died with dignity."

"How do you figure that?" I asked.

"The bull fought till death," she said.

"Yes, but he didn't have a chance. They bled him and weakened him so the big, bad brave matador could get close enough to kill him. I don't call that dignity. Let the bull and matador fight without half killing the bull first, and then we'll see how many matadors show up."

With that, Maria turned up her nose, and we silently left the arena. Man, was I ready to go! The whole place smelled like nothing I'd ever smelled before—a combination of stale tacos, garlic, beer, and bull. By the time we got outside, I was ready to throw up. We went back to the hotel, and called it an evening.

We spent the next two days shopping; I wondered how we were ever going to get all the stuff home. Jerry and I bought Mother and Mrs. Allison a classy set of sterling-silver glass holders. You could slip a glass down into the holder and really dress up a table—great for Thanksgiving and Christmas. I also bought Mother a really pretty china tea and coffee set adorned with red roses. Of course, we couldn't resist buying some big sombreros, and I couldn't pass up the big, straw shopping bags. Maria seemed to buy a massive amount in every store—tablecloths, napkins, purses, jewelry.

During our last night, Buddy made reservations in the hotel's fine-dining area. The hotel photographer came over and asked if he could take a picture of the four of us. I thought, Humph! Even fine dining has its own type of hawker trying to make a buck off the tourists; but Buddy said, "Great. We need this picture," so we gave the photographer a smile as he snapped his camera.

By the time dinner was over, the pictures were ready. The photographer gave one to me and one to Maria. As soon as I saw it, I immediately noticed that the guests at the table next to ours were smiling big, happy smiles, too, and looked like they were actually a part of our party. They'd already left by the time the pictures had arrived, so we couldn't show them the photos and find out who they were.

On Wednesday morning, we left for home. We had to take two taxis because of all our luggage, gifts, and souvenirs. At the airport, Buddy and Jerry didn't repeat their "monkey-business" performance. In fact, we were all quiet; we hardly said a word to one another.

We arrived in El Paso early in the afternoon, picked up our car, and headed back to Lubbock. Buddy drove until we stopped for gas, and then we traded seats. Buddy and Maria fell asleep immediately. We were all tired, but more than that, we were all aware that the honeymoon was over. What did destiny have in store for us now?

♫

CHAPTER SIXTEEN
Jivin' Ivan

*W*e'd been home only one day when Norman called and said, "I've got some good news. I just booked Ivan in Charleston, West Virginia. You'll never guess. 'Real Wild Child' is number ten on the regional charts. Isn't that wonderful?"

After they'd come back to Clovis from Australia, all Jerry and Buddy had talked about was how much they liked Johnny O'Keefe and his hit, "Wild One." They discussed recording it as a novelty song, and finally, Norman suggested, "Let Jerry sing it like he talks." So, Jerry's habit of talking through his teeth was actually what landed him his first position as a vocalist. It was a Crickets' project—with Buddy playing guitar, Joe B playing bass, and The Roses singing backup. But, with Jerry's voice giving The Crickets a new sound, they decided to use his middle name, Ivan, on the label as the artist instead of The Crickets. The record's success spawned quite a bit of speculation in the music world as to who *Ivan* was.

"Yeah, Man. Are Buddy and all of us going to do the show?" Jerry asked.

"No, just you. I think you can play the ukulele and lip sync the record for the fair. You'll only be gone three days. It'll be a nice trip for you and Peggy Sue," Norman said.

Jerry hung up the phone and turned toward his mother and me. With clenched jaws, pursed lips and fury-squinted eyes, he started talking slowly through his teeth, emphasizing each word. "I don't want to do this. I'm not a record act. I play the drums, and Buddy fronts the band.

He knows how. He can sing and play the guitar like a real entertainer. I can't do that. I can't believe how embarrassing this is going to be. Real entertainers don't do things like this."

He was throwing an absolute temper tantrum, and I just looked at him thinking what a spoiled brat he was. Most musicians could only dream of having a hit in the top ten and performing in front of their adoring fans.

Jerry was pacing back and forth in the kitchen.

"This is a fair, Jerry, not the civic auditorium. You only have to do this one song. Why are you so upset? It's great. You should be proud to have another hit record. And, with your voice on it. You made a new sound for The Crickets. How lucky," I said.

"That's not talent. I'm Buddy's drummer. I'm not a singer."

"If you couldn't do this, Norman wouldn't let you. Jerry, if Ivan has a hit, then that makes Buddy Holly and The Crickets that much bigger, and maybe, there'll be even more solo hits from others in the group," I said.

"How would you know anything about this? What you don't understand is that it's embarrassing. If you can't play the guitar when you sing, then the fans think you aren't a real musician. I didn't play the guitar on this number. Buddy Holly did."

"That's just the way you think. It's silly to take along everybody when they only want you to sing the song twice in one day. They probably couldn't afford it. But, you're right. I don't know anything about your business; however, I'm learning quickly. Oh, look. Buddy just drove up. Maybe he knows something."

Buddy bounced into the kitchen, laughing. "Hey Man! Isn't it great, Man! Looks like Ivan has a hit, Man!" He was talking so excitedly that you would have thought he was the one with his first hit.

Jerry was rolling his eyes. "If it's so great, then why don't *you* go do the fair?"

"Hey Man, you can do it, and I can't wait for us to add the act on stage on the road. You might as well make the money, and you don't have to split it with me."

"You can have all of it if you come." Jerry announced.

"Hey Man, you'll be fine; you can do it. Besides, my birthday's coming up, and I need to hang around here. I have a great surprise for my parents. Wait'll you see what I'm drawing up with the architect. Peggy Sue, wait'll you see the recording studio that I'm going to build right here in Lubbock. Hey, I gotta go. I'll talk to you later." Buddy looked at me and laughed. "He'll be all right. He's just in a state of shock." He gave a hearty laugh as he bounced back through the kitchen door and down the drive.

"Jerry, do you know the song?" I asked.

"No," he said very loudly.

"Why don't you practice it and learn the words. There's nothing wrong with the song. Come on. I'll go with you," I said.

I could tell that Jerry would rather go into the backyard and eat worms than to go to Charleston, and especially, with me accompanying him. If he was going to fail, he sure didn't want to do it in front of anyone he knew. Clearly, the thought of my presence there didn't do anything to boost his confidence. At least I was trying to be supportive. He was not even being reasonable.

Well, Norman had already booked it, so a few days later, we found ourselves in a hotel in beautiful West Virginia. Jerry was so insecure about his performance and the audience's acceptance that he wouldn't allow me to go to his first show, so I sat in the hotel, watched TV, and wondered what was happening. Finally, he came through the door saying, "Well, I got through it. It seemed to be all right. You wanna go to the next show?"

"Sure," I said.

I was delighted with *Ivan's* performance on stage. He tried to make people laugh, and they did. He finished to a resounding round of applause from the audience.

"I thought you looked just darling up there," I said.

Jerry laughed. "Did I look like I was singing?"

"Yes, you did."

I knew how hard it had been for him to do the show by himself. I was very proud of my Ivan.

Afterwards, we had a great time strolling through the fair. We threw dimes on dishes until we won a ton of them and then bought a suitcase so we could carry them home to our parents. They were just what any parent would want—a bunch of mismatched dishes that wouldn't match anything in their cabinets.

♫

Buddy was constantly on the move; he was always going somewhere. Because our house was so close to downtown, it was a convenient stop for him when he was out and about. But Maria never came with him.

One day, Buddy dropped by and said, "Hi, Peggy Sue. Hey, did ya hear? Norman's going to help me produce a record for Waylon. My debut as a producer! I'm so excited about it! I think Waylon has lots of talent. He just doesn't know it yet." Buddy chuckled and then announced proudly, "I have King Curtis flying in from New York to play saxophone on the session."

"That's just swell, Buddy," I exclaimed, truly impressed.

King Curtis was *the* sax player of the day. He was originally from Fort Worth, Texas, but now he lived in New York where he was a session musician, playing on numerous artists' albums. Everybody knew how great he was because of the Coasters' 1957 number-one hit "Yakety Yak." I thought the sax had made that song. Secretly, I wondered if there might be a chance I could attend the session and meet King Curtis.

Buddy was serious about becoming a producer. He, Norman Petty, and Ray Rush were setting up a recording label in Clovis called Prism. Buddy was president, Norman was in charge of sales, and Ray handled promotion. Buddy and Ray were equal financial investors, and Norman invested in recording time and equipment. Waylon Jennings was going to be the first artist produced on this new label.

As Jerry—who had been in the bedroom moving suitcases around—came into the kitchen, Buddy continued, "I thought we could get King Curtis to play on our session. We can try to do 'Reminiscing' and 'Come Back Baby' while he's here."

Jerry asked, "What are you going to do for Waylon's backup?"

"I'm going to use studio musicians. We're going to do 'Jole Blon' and 'When Sin Stops.'"

"Did you give the house plans to your parents?" I asked Buddy.

"I sure did. My dad had seen them, but it was a big surprise for Mom. She loved them. I can't say that for anybody else though. I have to run. See y'all later."

Yeah, I thought, I bet Maria was not pleased at all that he wanted to build a studio in Lubbock, Texas.

♪

The next day, Jerry and I drove to Clovis. As usual, we pulled into the driveway at the back of the studio. Jerry went around to the front door, while I entered through the patio where I was thrilled to find Norma Jean sitting in the lounge. Undoubtedly, she was one of my favorite people. Our discussion turned from casual small talk to more personal topics.

"How did you end up working for Norman Petty?"

"Oh, I got to know Norman real well because I was working at the Clovis newspaper. He was in radio and was always at the paper advertising something. One day, I happened to say to him, 'I'm really tired,' and he said, 'What you need is a new job.' I laughed and said, 'What I need is a life.' And, then, he said, 'Come work with me.' And I haven't regretted one minute of it."

It was no secret that, when Norman was away, he knew everything was in great hands with Norma Jean. They trusted each other completely.

She was a fantastic cook, and she loved making pies for the whole group, even if meant for a hundred people. She loved great music and great food, and wanted to be part of the party.

Robert Linville and David Bigham were there to sing backup on Waylon's record. They came into the lounge and said, "Peggy Sue, he's here if you want to meet him."

"King Curtis? I *must* meet him if I can."

We walked through the building to the recording studio. It looked like everyone in Clovis was there. Buddy was talking to Waylon, who was dressed in a white, suit shirt with the sleeves rolled up. I felt sorry for Waylon as soon as I saw him; he looked so scared. I'd never seen his eyes opened that wide—like a deer in the headlights.

As I looked to my left, I saw King Curtis in the control room talking to Jerry and Joe B. George Atwood was there on his bass, and Bo Clark was on the drums. I wondered why Buddy was using session musicians instead of Jerry and Joe B. The studio was so full of people and noise—voices laughing and talking, instruments being tuned, chords being played—that I couldn't move or hear. Slowly, with Robert and David paving the path, we weaved our way to the little reception room up front.

It seemed like there was some concern about the sun going down and Norman not being there yet. Somebody said he was tied up on the phone. I know many people believed that it was normal for musicians to be awake at night and that was why a lot of the recordings were made at the Norman Petty Studio either late in the afternoon or at night. However, in reality, it was better to record at night because there were fewer electrical problems, and less distractions and noise.

Pa, Norman's father, who lived in the downstairs apartment, was a mechanic; and when he was working on a car in the garage or someone brought a huffing, puffing, backfiring vehicle over for him to check out, there would often be power changes and noise that affected the studio. Recording put demands on the little studio's wattage. Even other businesses in the area could affect the amperage, so the best recording time occurred after such businesses had closed for the day. The perfect sound that Norman sought just wasn't possible without consistent electric power.

Also, there was a problematic window in the control room that faced busy 7th Street. Despite the heavy-duty commercial glass that had been installed and thick, sound-absorbing curtains, the noise from the busy street sometimes filtered into the building.

Jerry weaved his way over to me with King Curtis right behind him. My heart pounded with excitement. Jerry was bringing King Curtis to meet *me*. But, then, Jerry opened his mouth and said, "You need to leave. Why don't you go over where Vi is?"

Vi was upstairs in their apartment, across the walkway from the studio—away from where all the excitement was taking place.

"I want to meet Mr. Curtis. Please, Jerry," I begged.

Jerry turned and introduced us.

"Welcome to Clovis," I said, extending my hand.

"Thank you, Ma'am," he said with a hearty handshake and a great big smile.

Jerry looked me sternly in the eye and, without blinking, he said firmly, "You need to leave *now*. We're trying to have a session."

"Why do I have to leave? Why can't I stay for the session?" I asked. It wasn't like I was going to make a scene by stripping off my clothes or yelling obscenities during the recording.

"Everybody's uptight. You have to leave now," Jerry said, clearly peeved.

Robert and David instantly grabbed me, one on each arm. "Come on. Let's go to the Foxy."

The Foxy was *the* place to hang out in Clovis. It was the local drive-in, and it was also on 7th Street, just a few blocks east of the studio.

"Have you guys seen Maria here?" I asked, sipping on my Coke.

"No, I haven't seen her. If she's here, she's staying in one of the motels," Robert said, as he passed out the burgers and fries.

When we got back to the studio, I went into the lounge instead of going to the apartment like Jerry had suggested. Norma Jean was still there, and I asked her if she had seen Maria before the session began.

"No, she stayed in Lubbock with Mr. and Mrs. Holley. Let's walk upstairs and visit with Vi. It looks like this session won't be through any time soon."

Vi greeted me with a large smile and hug, as always, and asked, "Have ya'll decided where you're going to live?"

"No, not yet. There always seems to be one more trip to do."

"Buddy told me that you and Jerry were going to travel with him and Maria in their new car on this next tour," Vi said.

"Oh. Well, no, I'm going to meet Jerry in New York when they're through with the tour. It wouldn't be comfortable traveling that far with all of us in the same car."

"I can certainly understand that," Norma Jean said.

I always thought Norman and Vi's apartment was just the coolest thing. It was so neat and uncluttered—modern almost to the extent of being futuristic. The living room featured a mirrored wall on the south side. There were also bookshelves, a freestanding fireplace, TV, and coffee table, but no chairs. Everyone sat on one of the two daybeds along the north wall or on the floor pillows by the table. The daybeds could be pulled out to make full beds for guests. They were covered with tailor-made, turquoise tweed slipcovers to match the New Mexican turquoise-colored wall behind them. As the night dragged on, I fell asleep on one of the daybeds.

♪

CHAPTER SEVENTEEN
New York! New York!

*L*ike I said, Buddy was *always* on the go. After the session, he and Maria drove to Southern California in the new Cadillac he'd purchased. I knew they were going, but I didn't know why, unless it was to visit Eddie Cochran, since they'd become good friends. Or, maybe Buddy was trying to work something out in his head or "drive off" some anxiety. I knew that he liked to drive around sometimes when he was thinking or upset. Anyway, it was a quick trip. His session had taken place on September 10, and he and Maria had to be back in Lubbock to leave for New York on the 18th.

The Crickets were scheduled to leave New York on October 3, and their tour would last through October 19. Buddy and Phil Everly had set up a recording session with Lou Giordiano at the Beltone Studios in New York for September 30, and that's why Buddy was going early. He and Phil were going to co-produce the session, and Murray Deutch from Southern Publishing was going to be there.

Jerry, Joe B, and Tommy Allsup, who was the leader of the dance band, were going to ride with The Roses to New York. Robert, David, and Ray Rush showed up at the Allisons' house in the DeSoto, pulling a little trailer that Robert's dad, Jim Linville, had made for them. Mr. Linville had painted the trailer white and then had painted a single red rose on it, as well as words, *The Roses, Odessa, TX*. It was way too cool!

As they pulled out of the driveway, I felt really sad. I almost wished I were going with them. But wait a minute. Six guys plus me, instruments, suitcases, 1,811 miles, the whole tour...forget that thought. I was glad I'd be flying to New York to meet them *after* the tour. I sensed that Jerry seemed really happy to be leaving—and to be leaving me in Lubbock with his parents. What was that about? Did he need his mother to report my every movement to him?

The days between the time Jerry left and the time I flew to New York were miserable. With Jerry gone, Mrs. Allison began treating me like a guest again, and I no longer felt as if my parents' home was mine. The highlight of every day was thinking about going to New York. Every movie I'd ever seen glorified it, and I wanted to see the thrill of it for myself. Besides that, I desperately wanted to get out of the house for a while. A married couple living with parents wasn't a very good situation. Maybe that was why Buddy and Maria were leaving early. As sweet as Mr. and Mrs. Holley were, the living conditions were probably uncomfortable there, too, especially for Maria.

Jerry seldom called me, which was quite unlike him. He was probably just very busy, but it did concern me a little. I hoped everything was going okay on the tour.

I had dinner with Mother and Daddy the night before I left. Daddy said, "Don't forget, if you need anything, you call me collect. I'll see that you have it. I couldn't stand to let anything happen to you. Promise me."

"I promise, Daddy. I really don't think you should worry. Jerry's picking me up at the airport, so I won't be alone once I get there."

"Well, things happen, so if he's not there, you call me."

♫

I had packed and unpacked for two weeks, trying to figure out what to take with me. According to Lubbock's news reports, the weather in New York was turning cold; so, I wore an orange wool skirt and sweater, and I carried the Mouton coat that Mother and Daddy had given me for Christmas the year before. I had my makeup bag and purse with me but very little cash and no checks. I guess I should have been scared to death, but I just accepted the fact that Jerry would meet me as planned, and everything would be okay.

Mrs. Allison made my reservations for the trip, and she and Mr. Allison drove me to the airport in Amarillo to catch the flight. The trip was totally silent—nothing but occasional small talk between the three of us.

"Do I have a reservation for coming home?"

"No," Mrs. Allison said, "Jerry'll book it; he has to make one for himself, too—unless the two of you drive back. You can never tell with his schedule."

I noticed that almost everybody at the airport was really dressed up. I felt a little underdressed in my bobby socks and penny loafers, but I thought I looked okay. I thanked Mr. and Mrs. Allison for driving me to Amarillo, checked in, and boarded the plane, hoping I wouldn't get an earache this time.

I was thrilled to find that I'd been assigned a window seat. How lucky! I could see all of New York when we arrived. I was grateful when a lady took the seat beside me because I wanted to be able to talk to someone. About halfway to Chicago, I worked up enough nerve to ask her if she was going to New York.

"Yes, I am," she replied pleasantly.

"Is this your first trip to New York?" I asked.

"Oh, no. I live in New York," she said.

"Super! Is the Statue of Liberty lit up? Will we fly over it when we land?" I asked eagerly.

She smiled. "Is this your first trip to New York?"

"Yes, it is, and I'm so excited about seeing it," I said, bubbling with enthusiasm.

"Do you have someone meeting you when you get off the airplane?" she asked.

"Yes. My husband is there with his business, and he's meeting me," I told her.

"Well, I hope you have a great time while you're there," she said.

"Would you do me a favor? When we start to fly over the statue, would you tell me so I don't miss it?" I asked.

"I would love to," she replied, as she began to thumb through a magazine.

We landed in Chicago to refuel and reload. I was thankful that I didn't have to change planes.

As it turned out, the pilot announced that the Statue of Liberty would be to my right, and sure enough, there she was in all her glory. She was all lit up just like Christmas, and it was only October. The history books hadn't exaggerated; she *was* beautiful. Miss Liberty embodied all that was "America," and I could hardly wait to see her up close. The Statue of Liberty and Carnegie Hall were the two things I wanted to see most. I hoped that someday, Buddy Holly and The Crickets would perform a concert at Carnegie Hall—to prove that rock 'n' roll was here to stay.

I was thrilled to take my first steps on New York ground. As the passengers came down the steps of the airplane, the airline attendants guided us toward a walkway leading into the entrance of the lobby. I hadn't gone very far when I saw David and Robert waving and running toward me on the other side of the divide. It was hard to tell which of us was smiling the most, them or me. I yelled, "Where's Jerry?"

Robert answered, "He's down there where you go through the gate. We just wanted to be the first to say 'Hi' in New York. Guess what? You know that recording contract we got in August? Have you heard? We met with Dot while we were here. 'It Was Almost Paradise' and 'I Kissed an Angel' have been released."

"Cool," I exclaimed.

I said to myself, I love these two guys. No one else would have thought of meeting me and sharing such news but them. They had definitely become my buddies. It was too bad that the other Rose, Ray, wasn't anything like David and Robert. He wasn't very friendly.

As I reached the gate, I noticed Jerry. Barely giving me a hug, Jerry said, "We have to hurry and get your suitcases 'cause Tommy Allsup's circling the airport in the car so we wouldn't have to park."

"Oh," I said.

Robert, David, Jerry, and I made our way to the luggage area and then to the car. I wondered why Jerry sat in the front seat and put me in the back with David and Robert. Wasn't he happy to see me? I thought everyone was a little too quiet as we were driving into New York City, but suddenly, we turned onto the freeway, and I realized why. Everywhere I looked, I saw bumper-to-bumper cars, and I resolved that *maybe* conversation wasn't the best thing at this time. Now I knew why Jerry sat in the front—to help Tommy drive.

"Tommy, how far is it from our hotel to Carnegie Hall?" I asked.

"Not far," he said. "Not far at all. Why?"

"Please drive down the street so I can see it before we go to the hotel."

Jerry turned and rolled his eyes at me. "It's such a hassle to drive here. We can go look at it after we get you to the hotel. We can take a taxi or maybe even walk," he said.

"I wasn't trying to impose," I said.

"It's no trouble, Jerry," Tommy said. "It's on our way to the Edison." David and Robert both agreed.

"Swell," I said. "You're outnumbered."

It wasn't long before we were right beside the concert hall. It looked exactly like I thought it would. The roof extended out all the way down the sidewalk, making it look like a big porch. The only things missing were men dressed in long tails and ladies wearing evening dresses and white gloves.

"Why did you want to see this?" Jerry asked.

"Because someday Buddy Holly and The Crickets will perform a concert here."

Everybody in the car laughed.

"The public barely lets us play now," Jerry said.

"It's for approval. Don't you see that?" I asked.

It didn't take long before Tommy was pulling up in front of the hotel. As we got out my suitcases, I asked David and Robert if I'd see them later.

"No, we're ready to start back to Clovis in the morning," Robert said.

"Where's Ray?"

"Who knows," David exclaimed. "If he isn't here in the morning by noon, we'll leave without him."

"Oh, you wouldn't do that," I said.

Robert replied, "Yes, we would. He's been late during this whole tour, and we've had it."

"Well, I'm glad I got to see both of you. Thanks for meeting me at the airport, and I'll see you in Clovis."

♫

New York was incredibly busy and even more crowded than San Francisco. There were people everywhere, yet no one spoke to one another. It's sure different from Texas where complete strangers speak, nod, or tip hats at one another, I thought.

As we went through the revolving door, Jerry said, "Stay close to me or you'll get lost. Do you need to change? We're going to Buddy's recording session tonight." We rode up in the elevator to the third floor. "This is where our room is."

"Did you get this room for us today?" I asked.

"No, Joe B and I were staying here, and he just moved to another room so you and I could have it."

The room was small and dark, and the carpet, which was a dark-wine color with flowers, looked very old. Maybe that was just its style, but the look of the carpet made me want to make certain I had a pair of shoes handy at all times. The double bed had two nightstands, one on each side of the bed, and a single chair just to the side. On the opposite wall was a dresser with a large mirror on the chest. The bathroom, with white-ceramic tiles covering its floor and wall, was really tiny. Hum, I thought, this huge hotel is in fancy New York City, and its room reminds me of a motel stop on Route 66. I expected the guys to be living a little better than this.

I'd just brushed my hair and was putting on some orange lipstick when Buddy and Joe B came to the room. We all sat down on the bed to visit. Buddy reached into his coat jacket and pulled out a large stack of fifty-dollar bills.

"One for you," he said as he shoved it toward Joe B, "one for Jerry, and one for me." He looked like he was playing Monopoly as he kept dealing the cash. "Okay, guys, you have your part, but, Jerry, I think you should give Peggy Sue that money so she can go shopping." Turning to me, he said, "Maria wants to go with you, so maybe you can get with her tomorrow, and by the way, Jerry, I'm making dinner reservations for you and Peggy Sue to go to Mama Leona's for dinner with me and Maria and Phil Everly and his girlfriend. I'll let you know what night we're going. Don't forget, Peggy Sue, Maria will call you tomorrow to go shopping."

Jerry said, "That'll be great. She needs some new clothes."

Imitating his mannerisms, I rolled my eyes at him.

"Well, I have the session and have to run. All of you will be there, won't you?" Buddy asked.

I spoke up quickly, remembering that I'd been kicked out of Waylon's session. "I'd love to come see it."

As he walked out the door, Buddy smiled and said, "I'm glad you'll be there."

Joe B said, "I'll meet you guys in the lobby."

After Joe B left, I asked, "Jerry, what's wrong? Is there a problem?"

"What kind of problem would I have?" he asked, as he laughed sarcastically.

"I don't know, but you're not your cheery self. Did something go wrong when you were on tour?" I asked.

"Oh, no. Everything was just ducky," Jerry said.

I could tell he was having another crisis that I wasn't in on yet, but quite truthfully, at that moment, I really didn't care. I just wanted to go to the Pythian Temple, wherever that might be, and watch the session.

As we got into the cab, Jerry said, "I'm not on this session."

Joe B replied, "Well, Jerry, I'm not either. I just figured it was because I don't read music."

"Who is on the session?" I asked.

"This is Norman's string session that he just couldn't live without. He's always trying to change Buddy and make him a popular star," Jerry said.

As we stopped in front of a very impressive-looking building, I asked, "Is this where the recording studio's located? It looks like a church or something."

"Yep," Jerry said. "I guess that's why they call it a temple."

We rode up on the elevator to the studio, and as we were stepping out, a girl about my age with windblown, brown hair smiled at Jerry and Joe B, and gave them a casual hug. She had a girlfriend with her.

Jerry said, "I'd like for you to meet Peggy Sue. Peggy Sue, this is the Jo Harper that you have heard us all talk about."

Jo took one look at me in my Mouton coat and exclaimed, "I hope that thing is not alive!"

"Pardon me?" I said. "I don't understand what you're talking about."

"Your coat," she said, throwing her head back and laughing. "Jerry, you have to take this girl shopping. We wear trench coats in New York. You're off the farm now, Honey." Both Jo and her friend laughed. Looking me over from head to toe, she continued, "It's time you got rid of those bobby socks and put some big-girl shoes on, too."

I'm sure that she couldn't see the flames shooting out of my eyes, but they were there. How extremely rude! As calmly as I could, I replied eruditely, "Yes, I hope to go shopping soon." As they walked into the studio, I grabbed Jerry by the arm and slowed his gait. I asked, "What makes her the last word in fashion?"

"Now, Peggy. Don't be that way," he said.

"Well, I don't like your friend, or whatever she is."

"She runs Norman's publishing company here in New York City," Jerry said.

"Then she needs to learn some manners," I exclaimed, and, right then and there, I vowed to ask Norma Jean about this *Jo Harper* the next time I saw her.

As we walked into the room through the thick, school-looking doors, the first thing I noticed was the wooden floor. Oh, this would be fun to dance on, I thought. To my left, a whole string section was set up in concert form. I gasped. Oh, my. This was really impressive. I knew in my heart that these sessions were going to be important to Buddy's career, although I didn't even know what he'd be recording.

The harp was sitting behind the strings. Looking straight ahead, I could also see the engineers' booth, where Dick Jacobs and Norman were fussing with the equipment. Officially, this was Dick Jacobs' session, but Norman was there to help in any way he could. Dick and Norman had become good friends, and they ate lunch together every day when Norman was in New York. There was another young man in the control room who also seemed to be trying to assist—I heard someone say it was Paul Anka. (Be still my heart!) There were some women in the booth, too—one of which was Vi Petty. They motioned us over and seated us in the last row of the string section. Jerry and Joe B were sitting on each side of me. Jerry said, "You have to be totally silent when they're recording, or they'll have to start over, and that will cost more money." And, I thought, it'll get me kicked out. I noticed Jo Harper sitting far behind us, and I wondered if she was still having fun at my expense.

All of a sudden, I saw Buddy walk out of the control room and walk into another room. I thought I wasn't going to be able to see him, but luckily, there was a window, and once the mic was set up, I could see him perfectly. The smell of rosin permeated the air. I looked at the string musicians, and I noticed that they had their noses up in the air and their violins in place, ready to play.

Dick Jacobs counted off "One...Two...Three..." and the music began. I had never heard the song played before, but someone said it was called "Raining in My Heart" and that it had been written by Boudleaux and Felice Bryant—songwriters who were known for writing lyrics for the Everly Brothers.

As the strings were playing, Maria entered the studio. I guess she hadn't seen the studio lights on, indicating that they were in the middle of recording inside. I thought it strange that she wouldn't have noticed, however, since she was in the recording business. The door slammed behind her and echoed throughout the studio. The music slowed spastically to a stop as, without faltering, her high heels clicked sharply all the way to the control room. Once she was seated, everyone took a deep breath and lifted their instruments again. I was so relieved that it hadn't been *me* who'd stopped the session. Jerry would have never ceased telling me how much money I had cost them.

I'd never heard Buddy sound so good. Originally, everyone questioned Norman's decision to mix Buddy's West-Texas drawl and rock 'n' roll mannerisms with strings, but the result was so poetic that I was mesmerized by the sound. It was like a mass of energy had engulfed me, and I could feel the music all the way down to my toes. Buddy's done it again, I thought. Another first. He has integrated strings and rock 'n' roll—a feat no one has ever done before. I was so proud of him. It was the most beautiful song I'd ever heard him sing, and I knew immediately that it was going to be one my favorite songs of all time.

Buddy could not read music, so to have an entire string section there playing while he was learning a new song and arrangement and was recording all at the same time had to be quite a task, even for someone as talented as he was. There were two or three takes, and after each take, they would play most of it back. They would talk a little and play it again. The whole process didn't take long. When it was over, I just wanted to grab him and give him a big kiss. Most of all, I wanted to tell him that rock 'n' roll wasn't going to die. Not now. I wanted to say, "Look what you have done." Of course, I couldn't do any of that, but maybe I would get my chance at least to tell him how I felt at dinner tomorrow.

The next song they started recording was "It Doesn't Matter Any More." I heard someone say, "Paul Anka wrote this song specifically for Buddy's session," and as soon as I heard that, I wondered where he'd gotten the idea for the song. Personally, I knew there was an unhappy Buddy Holly behind all the music and smiles, and since Buddy and Paul had formed an early friendship, I thought maybe Paul knew some of the same things I did.

I knew nothing about "True Love Ways," the next song they were going to record. As they moved the mics, adjusted levels, and tuned violins, Vi told me how the song had come about. She said that back in the spring, Buddy had left the song title, the music, and some lyrics with Norman as he and Mr. and Mrs. Holley passed through Clovis on their way to a family wedding in Portales, New Mexico. He had asked Norman, "Could you finish this by the time I get back here?"

Well, Norman finished it, and Vi wrote the lead sheet. They tape-recorded Vi playing the piano and singing the song so Buddy could listen to the tape when he came back through Clovis on his way home. Buddy absolutely loved the song. He had laughed at Norman and said, "It sounds like you. Vi, you recorded it so well I don't think that I can do it better."

Vi was thrilled that Buddy liked it. She said they had based the tune on one of Buddy's favorite religious songs, "I'll Be Alright" by the Angelic Gospel Singers.

Just as the session for "True Love Ways" was about to begin, Jerry announced, "I'm ready to go. I've stayed as long as I can. I've had enough. I want to leave."

I grabbed my Mouton coat and purse, and glanced over at the recording room window. Buddy was standing there with his earphones on, looking our way. I waved, and he nodded his head and smiled. Joe B followed us out, and we hailed a cab.

Jerry asked, "Are y'all hungry?"

"I am. I've been so excited about being in New York and going to the session that I haven't eaten all day. It's been fun, but now I'm ready to eat."

I could tell that Jerry was not happy. I tried to talk about the session, but only Joe B would join in the conversation. We walked across the street from the Edison Hotel to a delicatessen. Jerry asked, "Have you ever eaten in a restaurant like this?"

I shook my head no.

"Well, I like hot pastrami sandwiches myself," Jerry said.

"That sounds good. I'll try one of those with a Coke, please."

Joe B had the same thing because he knew the rule: Jerry didn't like food orders to be complicated. It took too much time if everybody ordered something different.

After dinner, we went back to our rooms, where I fell in love with the television set. I couldn't believe it. There were channels all the way around the dial. Jerry wasn't interested in conversing, so I eventually fell asleep watching TV.

♫

The next morning around ten o'clock, Maria called to tell me she would be coming to the hotel to pick me up.

"We can have lunch in the coffee shop and then go shopping," she suggested.

"Terrific. I'll meet you in the lobby at noon," I replied.

Immediately, Jerry began talking, and his mood improved the more he spoke. "You need to buy some makeup, high heels, and a really tight skirt. Don't forget, you also need to buy a trench coat for New York."

He gave me most of the cash that Buddy had given him the day before and then left to meet up with the guys. I thought I heard him say they were doing something with American Bandstand as he went out the door.

A little before noon, I left to meet Maria. As I stepped out of the elevator and walked across the lobby, the desk clerk stopped what he was doing and simply stared at me. I felt like saying, "Haven't you ever seen a girl wearing bobby socks and loafers before?"

I noticed Maria walking through the door. "Hi," she said. "Let's go in the coffee shop and have a sandwich and some coffee."

189

I nodded okay. Even though it was busy, as was everyplace in New York, we found a little table and ordered.

"So how are you?" I asked. "We haven't talked in a long time."

"I'm just fine. You and I have a lot to talk about."

"Really? Why don't you start."

Her face turned angry, she pointed her finger at me, and she said, "Well, Peggy Sue, you need to know that Jerry is not paying attention to business. Now, I think he is a really good drummer, but he is just not being professional. He is making Buddy look bad, and The Crickets."

I was completely taken aback. I didn't know what to say, so I just listened to her ramble on about Jerry. I didn't respond except to give her a look like, "What did you say?" She made the same comments over and over, using both hands to accentuate her words.

"You have got to do something about him."

She was telling *me* to get *him* under control? I was his wife—not his boss. Who did she think I was? His mother? And why did she believe it was her business to tell me what I had to do? Surely, she didn't use this controlling attitude of hers with Buddy.

Her tone went through me like cracking a whip—all the nerves down my spine were burning. Finally, I said, "I'm terribly sorry you had to go through that." My apology didn't stop her tirade, so I sat quietly until we finished lunch.

We walked down 47th Street to the area of Madison and 5th Avenue. Maria continued talking the entire time, but due to all the noise of New York's busy streets and Maria's strong Puerto Rican accent, I didn't hear much of what she was saying. However, I could see the look on her face, and it wasn't pleasant. She'd been frowning the whole day.

I bought a skirt, a sweater, and a tan trench coat at Saks. I said, "Now that I have the obligatory trench coat I guess I'm an official New Yorker." My voice lowered, I added, "And off the farm." Maria just looked at me blankly; she didn't have a clue what I was talking about.

"I need some shoes and makeup," I said.

"You can get the makeup here; they can help you," Maria said.

The sales clerk recommended a suitable powder and blush, suggested an appealing shade of lipstick, and then said, "You need some mascara. Your eyelashes are already long. This will make them look thick."

As we left Saks, I said, "Now all I need are shoes and a purse."

Maria said, "It's called a pocketbook in New York."

Well, great, I thought. Am I in a foreign country or what? I don't even seem to know the right words to use.

Maria continued, "There is an exclusive shoe store on Madison Avenue. We'll go there, and then we can go back to my hotel so we can talk."

I purchased some dark-brown, leather high heels and a *pocketbook* to match. It clicked open and shut and had a single strap. The shoes and pocketbook would really complement my brown, pegged-down, oh-so-tight, tight skirt.

Maria said, "We can take a cab to the hotel or walk; it's not that far."

"Let's just walk."

It was a windy, cloudy day, and by the time we arrived, I was freezing cold and totally out of breath. I had on my new trench coat, but my Mouton coat, although unsuitable for New York, would have been warmer.

We took the elevator up to the seventh floor. As soon as Maria opened the door, I thought, Boy, I wish Buddy, not Norman, had made the arrangements for our room. Their room was more of a suite. The off-white walls featured a wine-colored border at the top, the carpet was light gray, and everything looked much newer than in our room. They even had a great view of the city from their windows. Well, Buddy, I thought, on the honeymoon you always said I had the better room. You got it this time.

Maria said, "Put your packages down. I will order us another coffee."

In a few minutes, room service arrived, and Maria signed the bill. Afterwards, she started *her talk*. Her anger made her strong Puerto Rican accent even more difficult to comprehend. Still gesturing with her hands, she said, "I don't think *you* understand how this can affect *your* life, you know. You know, if Jerry Allison thinks he can't be replaced, he should think twice. You need to get a hold of him right now. It is unprofessional to get on stage drunk...or whatever he was doing. You know, Buddy isn't going to let him ruin *his* career. There are a million drummers out there who need a job."

I wanted to scream. How dare she! She'd been talking about this the whole day. If this problem was as serious as she was saying, Buddy and Jerry should work it out—not Maria and me. Dismiss Jerry from the group? This sounded like it had to be Maria's idea. As I recalled, when Niki Sullivan left, everybody was walking on pins and needles because they were afraid of a lawsuit. This was Jerry. He and Buddy were the heart of The Crickets. They always had been. Even if things were as bad as she claimed, it was Buddy's business to take care of them—not Maria's. I had to say something. I couldn't just sit there and let her think that she had the power to talk about dismissing someone from the group. Especially Jerry. But, what could I say?

I just stared at her for a moment and then said, "You know, Maria, Jerry's not an employee. But I think you're right about his conduct. He really needs to clean that up..."

Buddy walked through the door, pulling off his tie. I could tell he was extremely irritated about something. Maria softened her tone immediately and started to smile at him as she asked, "How did it go?"

"I guess fine," he said in a ruffled voice, not even looking at her. He put his briefcase down and started walking toward the closet.

This was my chance. I stood up and began gathering my packages. "I need to go back to the hotel; but thank you, Maria, for taking me shopping today. It was very nice of you. As for what we were talking about, you can rest easy. I will certainly bring it to Jerry's attention," I said brusquely.

Buddy, with a puzzled look on his face, said, "I'm going with Peggy Sue to the lobby and get her a taxi and help her with her packages."

Maria just nodded her head.

I was so angry with Jerry—and Maria—that I couldn't breathe, much less know what to think. This should be the happiest days of their lives. Jerry certainly had everything he had ever dreamed of. Was he going to lose it all now because he was behaving so immaturely?

Buddy and I turned to the left and then made the quick right to the elevator doors.

"This hotel is not as old as the Edison, is it?" I asked coolly.

Buddy said, "I think it's as old; it's just been redone."

The doors opened, and we walked inside. It was just the two of us. The doors shut, and we started our descent.

I said, "Buddy, I'm sorry you had so much trouble with Jerry."

"It doesn't matter now."

192

He reached out and pressed a button. Suddenly, the elevator jerked to a moaning halt between floors. I looked at him, unsure of what was wrong.

"I stopped the elevator," Buddy said, "because I have something I want to say to you."

"Maria told me what a bad tour y'all had."

"That's not what I want to talk about. Listen to me..." He sounded like his song when he said those three words. "I don't have very much time, and I won't get another chance to talk to you alone. I hired two attorneys today—one to get the song credits straightened out so my name is on the song 'Peggy Sue,' which I wrote, and the other to help me get a divorce."

I was so stunned that I gasped.

"I'm not the only one getting a divorce. You need to get a divorce, too. Jerry doesn't love you. He has done nothing but party and get on stage drunk. You need to know...there have been other women, too."

My knees became so weak that I had to lean against the mirrored elevator wall. I was completely stunned that Buddy was confirming everything Maria had said. How could Jerry have done that to me? Words just suddenly began flowing. "I can't get a divorce, Buddy. I don't think you understand. I don't have any money or job. I can't go to my mother and daddy. I can't tell them this marriage hasn't worked and ask them to help me get a divorce. I'd be the first one in my family to get a divorce, and my mother's already told me that it'd better not happen. And, I don't have any money..."

Buddy interrupted. "I will take care of everything. After I get my divorce, I'll help you," he said.

"You're going to help *me*?"

"Yes. I'm going to take care of you." Buddy's eyes were unblinking, and his expression was very sincere. "He's going to ruin your life if you stay with him. I had Norman fly in when we were in Richmond, Virginia. I met with Norman first, and then he met with Jerry and Joe B. He saw firsthand what was going on. He was sitting on the steps of the hotel when they showed up after a night of partying on the tour. Norman knows that Jerry's not doing his best. Peggy Sue, we'll have a publishing company and a record label. Just wait until you see the studio I'm going to build in Lubbock. Just you wait and give me time to get this straightened out. I won't get another chance to talk to you alone for a while, but I will talk to you again later."

The elevator went bing! bing! bing! and we were on our way down to the lobby once again. A million thoughts were racing through my mind, but there wasn't any time to discuss even one of them. Buddy and I always seemed to meet in minutes. Yet, after each of our meetings, I was forced to face decisions that could change my life.

Buddy motioned for the blue-uniformed bellman and told him to get me a taxi to the Edison.

As I climbed into the back seat, I asked Buddy, "Hey, do I tip him?"

"No, I've already done that. Don't say anything to anyone about what I said. I promise I'm going to fix everything."

"I won't," I replied. I was just numb. Every word he had said was permanently embossed on my brain, and I was going to have to consider everything he and Maria had told me that day very carefully.

"Hey, just a minute," I said as the taxi's door started to close. Buddy grabbed the door.

"What?"

"I love the strings you put in rock 'n' roll."

With an enormous smile on his face, he asked me, "You could hear it then?"

"Of course. How could anybody miss it?"

He shut the door and watched me drive off in the taxi.

The dark-skinned driver turned to me and said, "Your young man's intense."

"Oh, yeah, he's intense."

♫

After the short taxi ride to the Edison, I collected my packages and let out a huge sigh of relief when I realized there was a doorman to open the door for me. While waiting for the elevator, two men walked up and stood on each side of me. Once in the elevator, I said, "Third floor, please," and one of them punched the button. I noticed that they were dressed in black suits. I smiled to myself. Of course, why not? This was New York so black suits were probably the norm; in Lubbock, however, men usually

194

only wore black suits to attend such events as a funeral. When the doors opened, I said, "Thank you," and stepped out to walk down the hall to my room. The two gentlemen followed right behind me. I began to get a little nervous as they walked closer and closer.

One of the gentlemen asked, "Oh, Miss. Is this your room? 340?"

I turned to look them in the eye when I talked. I was determined not to let them know they were making me uneasy.

"Yes, Sir, it is. May I ask who you are?"

Both men pulled out their wallets and showed me their impressive NYPD badges.

"What is your name?" the other man asked.

"I'm Peggy Sue Allison. I'm Mrs. Jerry Allison. We're here because my husband is one of The Crickets with Buddy Holly. They were on Bandstand with Mr. Dick Clark today," I said, in an attempt to prove my identity.

"Where are you from?" the first man asked.

"Lubbock, Texas," I replied.

"Can you prove that you're married?" the second man asked.

I flashed my left hand.

"That's a pretty serious wedding ring." Turning to the first man, he continued, "I would say they were married. Aren't you on the register?"

"I don't know anything about that. I don't take care of the traveling arrangements," I answered.

"Okay. Thank you, Mrs. Allison. We'll take it from here," the first man said.

"One question, Officer," I said. "Are you hotel detectives?"

"No, we aren't. We are from the New York Police Department Detective Division," he said.

He gave me a number, but I was so nervous, I immediately forgot it. I could hear a hot bath calling my name. This had been one of the most incredible days of my life.

Jerry was not in the room. Good! This would give me some time to myself to think. Now I knew why he'd been so moody. He didn't want to tell me that Norman had flown in on the last day of the tour for a private meeting with Buddy and him. Not surprisingly, he didn't want to tell me about his one-night stands and nonstop drinking, either. No wonder I hadn't heard from him very often during the tour.

As I stepped out of the bathtub, Jerry came in.

"You'll never guess. I ran into Phil Everly. He may come by our room and visit."

"That would be nice," I said. "I'd love to meet him."

"Well, we're going to dinner tomorrow night, and you'll get to meet him then for sure. How would you like to go see the Empire State Building? Joe B and I thought we would take you to see it."

"I would love to see it," I exclaimed.

Now it was my turn to be quiet. I didn't know what to say to anybody anymore, especially Jerry Ivan. I was deeply hurt that he hadn't even tried to honor his marriage vows. I'd never hated anyone before, but now that I knew Jerry had "other women" and didn't want to be married to me, I hated him for what he'd done. I didn't know how I could even look at him, much less stay married to him. It was completely obvious to me now that the marriage ceremony had been a charade. But this was not the time to bring it up. If I could get Jerry and Joe B to look at apartments with me...and, then, if I could convince Jerry to rent an apartment here in New York...I could solve the problem of living with Jerry's parents. Then, if Buddy opened the publishing company ...maybe I'd get that job. I knew one thing for certain—I did not want to be in Lubbock if Buddy was going to be in New York.

On our way back from the Empire State Building, we drove by the Helen Hayes Theater. Evidently, it was intermission. The theatergoers, decked out in their best evening attire, were milling around outside, sipping glasses of wine and engaging in polite conversation, while pedestrians bustled about, rushing here and there. Couples were talking and smiling. I said to myself, "Humph. I'm glad *somebody* is having fun."

♫

The next night, we went to MaMa Leona's. As Jerry and I walked in, we could see Buddy and Maria sitting at a long, skinny table with two other people. I took one look at *that* face and knew immediately that it was Phil Everly.

Oh, my! He had to be the prettiest young man I'd ever seen! As he stood to greet us, I noticed that his dress pants and jacket were so exquisitely tailored that he looked like he'd just stepped out of a bandbox.

196

He had a very slender build, and when he shook my hand, I noticed that his hands were also long and slender. He had dreamy eyes and long eyelashes, and when he talked, his eyes opened wide as if he were using them to take in everything. He had a million-dollar smile, and his teeth were as white as snow.

I think the thing I loved the most about Phil Everly was his hair. It was dark blonde, windblown in the front, but extremely coiffed. His haircut was so smooth I couldn't see a cut line anywhere on his head. I also noted his abundance of charm, which directly resulted from his Kentucky drawl—he almost sounded like he was singing when he talked. Immediately, I thought of "Bye Bye Love," "Wake Up Little Susie," and "All I Have To Do Is Dream," and I could easily distinguish his voice in the songs. Phil's high voice created the high harmony in the Everly Brothers' music. I thought, if Don Everly's speaking voice sounds the same as his low harmony, I bet even their personal conversations sound musical.

Phil looked and sounded like an extremely classy man. I knew why Buddy liked him—he never acted like a celebrity. He had a wonderful sense of humor, and he made me laugh throughout dinner. I'd really needed an evening like this one.

His date, Jackie, was truly different. She was my first encounter with someone sporting a bohemian look. She had long, brown hair that was parted in the middle. Her facial makeup was a little white and so was her lipstick, but her eye makeup was quite dark. I loved her clothes—they hung loose over her dark stockings and black pumps.

I thought the seating arrangement was a little unusual. Buddy sat at the head of the table with all the boys at his end, and Maria sat at the foot with all the girls. A waiter took our cocktail order, and when he got to me, Buddy ordered my drink.

"She will have a Pink Lady. I hope you don't mind, Peggy Sue. I know you'll like this because I do. It doesn't make my stomach hurt; and if you don't like it, I'll take your drink, too."

My faced flushed. He hadn't ordered for anyone else.

"No, that's fine. I've never tasted one. Thank you," I said, attempting to avoid eye contact with everyone.

When dinner was over, the girls went to the powder room. My heels were so high and my skirt so tight that it was hard for me to walk. Besides,

I wasn't used to walking in high heels. I wondered why New York women considered high heels to be such a great thing.

I put my pocketbook up on the dressing cabinet, and as I turned to the sink to wash my hands, a lady knocked it off onto the floor. Unfortunately, the fall caused the strap to break, so my new purse suddenly became a clutch bag with one long, loose strap. I opened the purse, stuck the strap inside, and forced it shut. Well, now, I thought, if that will just hold for the evening, I have it made. When we returned to the table, I sat down and didn't say a word.

Buddy had tickets for some premiere on Madison Avenue, so we grabbed two taxis and went to the theater. As I stepped out of the taxi and onto the sidewalk, my new, small, high heel became caught in a vent—I guess to the subway. Well, as luck would have it, the heel broke off, and I stumbled and fell forward. As I started to get up, the clasp on my purse popped open, spilling out all the bag's contents and shooting out the broken strap for everyone to see. This was it! I was ready to go back to the hotel. My evening was finished. However, Buddy stated, "No way. I've bought these tickets, and you are going to go in if you have to go barefoot."

I opened the purse, stuck the strap back in, took a deep breath, and walked into the show. I didn't go barefoot, but one shoe had a high heel and the other did not. I just wanted to die.

♫

Buddy called the next day and said they had left their hotel, and were staying at Aunt Provi's apartment at 33 5th Avenue since she was not going to be home. He and Maria wanted us to come by that evening for dinner.

I told Jerry that we should spend some time during the trip looking for an apartment. "After all, Jerry, all everyone's talking about is that Buddy's going to be moving to New York."

So, that afternoon Joe B, Jerry, and I went out to look at, and price, apartments in Greenwich Village, and then later that evening, Jerry and I went over to Aunt Provi's apartment.

She lived upstairs in a fancy, old building. When the elevator opened, and we stepped out, we immediately stopped in our tracks. As we looked down the hall, we saw that every apartment had two doors, side by side.

"What's the second door for, Jerry?" I asked.

"I think it must be the back door. Maybe a kitchen door."

We rang the doorbell, and a smiling Buddy opened the door, saying, "Come on in."

Maria was in the kitchen cooking dinner.

The entry room was big for an older New York apartment—it was a combined living and dining room. From the main room, we turned left and then left again into the kitchen. Sure enough, there was the back door. Outside, it would be right next to the front door. Straight down the hall, I noticed a spacious bedroom and bathroom.

The apartment was carpeted and decorated in good taste. There was a picture of Aunt Provi and Maria together. Compared to Maria's present appearance, I could tell the photo was not current, and that Maria had been a young adult when it was taken. I knew that Maria's aunt had raised her, so I thought it was strange that there were no baby or childhood pictures of Maria anywhere in the apartment.

Buddy asked what we had done that day, and I said, "We looked at apartments."

"Ohhh?" he replied, with a slight glint in his eyes. It seemed as if he suddenly became more lighthearted.

Dinner was strained, to say the least. Maria was unusually quiet. She was probably wondering if I had told Jerry about our conversation, and I was still trying not to make eye contact with Buddy. We left shortly after dinner because the next day, Buddy and Maria would begin driving back to Texas, and we had to be at the airport early. Jerry, Joe B, and I were flying home.

"See you in Lubbock," I said. "Be careful driving."

♫

CHAPTER EIGHTEEN

The Split

*T*he only conversation I had on the flight home was with the stewardess. Jerry slept all the way, and Joe B was his usual, quiet self.

"Would you like something to drink?" she asked.

"Do you have any more of those cigarettes in that cute little package?"

She smiled. "I sure do. I'll get you some."

"And, could I have a Coke?"

"It'll only take a minute," she replied.

When she came back, she handed me five little packages of Viceroy cigarettes. There were only six in a package, but I loved them because they were small enough to fit easily into my pocketbook.

I closed my eyes, but I couldn't sleep for all the images and sounds running through my mind: the Statue of Liberty...Buddy's bombshell speech...the Pythian Temple...Maria's *talk*...Jo Harper...cars...people... Buddy's eyes and face as they appeared in the elevator...Jerry's infidelity... the NYPD detectives...and more.

In just a few days, Buddy and Maria would arrive in Lubbock, and the meetings scheduled with Norman in Clovis, New Mexico, would begin. The future of Buddy Holly and The Crickets was at stake. Buddy's life was music; Jerry's was all about partying. I was certain that Buddy would continue moving forward, but I wasn't certain that Jerry would be moving forward with him.

In the beginning, the four of us were going to work side by side, but I couldn't see that happening now. I didn't like Maria; I didn't trust Jerry; and actually, I was a little angry with Buddy. If he really cared for me as much as he seemed to now, why hadn't he said something *before* I got married? I remembered Buddy's words, "It's destiny, Peggy Sue. It's destiny." Humph. So much for destiny.

♫

Jerry and I spent a couple of days unpacking and doing laundry before we had to pack again and head for Clovis. I asked Jerry if we shouldn't wait for Buddy to go with us, but he said, "No. I want to talk to Norman alone."

Jerry was unaware that I knew anything about what had transpired on the tour. But, considering that Norman had to fly in and mediate the situation because of Jerry's behavior, I believed that Jerry was probably concerned about Norman's feelings toward him and, therefore, wanted to get on his good side.

We stayed in the lounge at the back of the studio, which was actually very comfortable because it included a little kitchen, small dining area, bathroom, and all the amenities of a family room. A sectional sofa curved from the north wall toward the sliding glass doors, and it separated the fireplace and TV area from the two daybeds, which were upholstered with the same turquoise tweed covers as those in Norman and Vi's apartment.

I absolutely loved the studio. Even when no one was recording, a feeling of creative energy permeated the entire building. And the Pettys *always* made me feel welcome at the studio.

Norman and Jerry remained in meetings behind closed doors, and when Jerry was with me, he wouldn't talk any more than he was forced to. He acted extremely upset, and everyone who came into the studio noticed the tension in the air.

As I vowed to myself in New York, I talked to Norma Jean about how rude Jo Harper had been.

"She really didn't like my Mouton coat," I exclaimed.

Norma Jean laughed and explained, "Jo's a spoiled brat. She's the only child of General Harper, who's a close friend of Norman and Vi. The Norman Petty Trio played at officers' clubs for years, and that's where they met the Harpers. And boy, did General Harper love The Norman Petty Trio. He must have been their biggest fan, and I think he would've done anything for them. You know, without General Harper, Norman would've had a tough time buying equipment and starting this studio. The first recorder Norman bought was an Ampex that he purchased from the Air Force when he found out they were upgrading to better sound equipment. Norman and Vi let Jo travel with them when she was little, and they entertained her on summer vacations. She was kinda like the daughter they never had."

"Is General Harper still around?" I asked.

"Oh, yes. He's stationed at Scott Air Force Base," Norma Jean replied.

Jerry walked into the room with his face set, not saying a word. Norma Jean slipped quietly out the sliding doors.

♫

We'd been at the studio for a couple of days when Buddy and Maria drove up in their new taupe Cadillac. Stoically, Maria entered the studio, holding her head high, but with just a hint of a furrowed eyebrow. I was accustomed to her silence because she usually ignored me when we met; however, this time, she wasn't speaking to anyone. I remembered how she used to smile and chatter around the guys, and how she and Jerry had become drinking buddies on the honeymoon. Undoubtedly, things had really changed in the short twelve weeks since Buddy and Maria had married. She didn't even speak to Jerry anymore. He had to notice that she treated him differently, but I didn't expect he would say anything to me about it. He never discussed anything about Maria with anyone. Whenever someone even mentioned Maria, he would simply state, "That's Buddy's wife," and put an end to the conversation. I wondered if Jerry would be as polite if he knew how she was talking about him behind his back.

Buddy followed her in the door, smiling and asking, "Hey, you hungry?"

We ate dinner at a Mexican restaurant, and afterwards, we returned to the studio. Mostly, our conversation comprised polite chitchat. I didn't know if everyone was as uncomfortable as I was, but I did know that the fun, carefree days Buddy, Jerry, and I had shared were a thing of the past.

A car had pulled under the carport, which meant someone was probably recording inside, so we just remained in the car, talking about nothing in particular, until, all of a sudden, Maria said demandingly to Buddy, "You just have to go in there. You have to have a meeting with Norman. You just look him straight in the face, and...you know...you tell him that...you know...you tell him what he needs to be doing because.... Do you want me to have to? Because if you don't do that, Buddy.... I say if you don't do that, Buddy, then I'm going to have to go in and say, 'Norman, I need monies for my panties.' Do you want me to have to ask Norman for money to buy my panties with, Buddy?"

At first, Buddy kind of laughed it off, and Jerry was chuckling, as if what Maria had just said was a joke. However, she began to talk louder, until she was almost shrieking, "You have to do this! You have to do this—this a way!"

She just kept it up until Buddy finally said sternly, "That's enough, Maria Elena! I don't believe you'll have to ask Norman Petty for money for your personal things."

She slowed down a little bit, but she regained her momentum in no time. I was sitting behind her, and Buddy turned and gave me a *Do you understand now why I'm getting a divorce?* look. At this point, I knew exactly what she had been doing to him. It was more than just her drinking. It was *her.* It was her incessant and annoying *Do it my way now or else* haranguing. She had goaded me the same way in New York with her *You had better do something with Jerry, or he's going to get fired* speech.

Maria just wouldn't be quiet. She said, "We're here for the meetings. Now you are just going to have to go in there, Buddy. You just have to go in there." She kept threatening Buddy that she would take charge of the situation if he didn't.

Her ranting became very embarrassing, and finally, Buddy raised his voice again and commanded, "That's enough, Maria Elena! We'll have our meeting tomorrow afternoon as planned. Someone is here now." Jerry and I said our goodbyes and went inside, and Buddy and Maria left to get a hotel room.

The next afternoon, Buddy came back to the studio for his meeting with Norman, and Maria came with him. Shortly after the three of them met, Norman called Jerry in for another meeting. Obviously upset, Norma Jean rushed into the lounge to tell me what Norman had told her.

She said that Maria certainly didn't endear herself to Norman when, rather than sitting in a chair, she plopped herself down on the corner of his desk with an *I'm in charge* attitude and looked straight down her nose at both him and Buddy, who had just sat down.

Gentlemanly, but firmly, Norman had told Maria, "Please get off my desk," which she did.

Buddy told Norman that he felt his experiences in New York had been good for his career, so he was going to move there. He still wanted Norman to help produce his records, but he no longer needed him as a manager.

When Maria piped in with "We don't think you have done enough for Buddy," Norman felt Maria was putting pressure on Buddy to say what he did, so he replied that producing and managing went together. If he didn't do one, he didn't want to do the other.

Norma Jean said that, by the time the meeting had ended, Norman was so upset that he came up to the apartment and told Vi and her what had happened. Buddy was more than just a client to Norman—he was also a fellow artist, a business partner, and a close friend. After all the success they'd shared together, Norman couldn't believe Buddy would just drop him like that. He wanted to talk to Buddy again, without Maria present, so he could figure out what was going on inside Buddy's head. Norma Jean said Norman had waited until he calmed down before he called Jerry in for another meeting.

Then, Norma Jean shared her personal feelings about the situation. She said, "No doubt, Buddy has talent and wants to explore and experiment every musical aspect he can, and he's eager to learn everything he can about the music business, but what he doesn't have is experience. I'm aware that Maria's Aunt Provi is the head of the Latin division of Southern Publishing, but Maria was just the receptionist. Buddy can't do everything a manager does and be the entertainer, too. He needs help. I hope he and Norman can work something out."

"Well," I responded, "Jerry doesn't tell me anything about what goes on during his meetings with Norman. I'm very concerned about the future of The Crickets."

After the meeting, Jerry came into the lounge and said solemnly, "Let's load the car. We're going home."

Norma Jean got off the sofa and, once again, slipped quietly out the sliding doors.

♫

A few days later, Buddy and Jerry set up another meeting with Norman, and this time, Buddy arrived without Maria. While they went into Norman's office, I remained in the lounge and watched TV. They weren't joking around with one another when they came out, as they normally did. Buddy simply said he was hungry, so we went downtown to the Busy Bee Café. The aroma of greasy hamburgers complete with mustard, pickles, and onions hit us as soon as we stepped out of the car. We sat in a booth that had a little jukebox against the wall.

Both Buddy and Jerry were wearing denim jackets with the collars up. They looked so cool! They really looked like musicians. But, they also looked downhearted.

The waitress had just brought our Cokes when Jerry said to Buddy, "I have something to tell you."

"Okay. What?" Buddy asked.

"Man, I just can't go to New York," Jerry said seriously.

Buddy became so quiet and motionless that he didn't even seem to be breathing. I don't know what I looked like, but I know I felt like the breath had just been knocked out of me. Jerry hadn't discussed this with me at all.

Buddy's brown eyes opened wide, and then he said matter-of-factly, "That's where the business is, Jerry."

Jerry rattled, "I just can't go, Buddy. I can't go to New York. I can't live there. I can't have my motorcycle. I couldn't ride it if I took it. I can't move to New York. I don't want to live there."

I stared at Buddy, who was sitting in complete dismay. Well, this was definitely going to complicate our plans. How was everything going to come together now? How would Buddy respond to this bolt from the blue?

After a moment of silence, Buddy said resolutely, "Well, I have to go to New York. That's where the business is. What about Joe B? What are you going to do with Joe B? I'll move him to New York."

"No. I'll take care of Joe B. Joe B will always be a Cricket, and I'll take care of him. We'll be The Crickets, and you go be Buddy Holly," Jerry said boldly.

Buddy was caught completely off guard. When Jerry said he couldn't live in New York, Buddy clearly hadn't imagined that he meant he wanted to break up the group. Buddy's shocked look quickly transformed into a *You mean you don't want me?* expression. His composure melted, and he appeared totally devastated, as if he could cry at any moment.

There would be no attempt to compromise on this day. Buddy was too hurt. Looking straight at Jerry, he said, "All right, Man. If that's what you're going to do. If that's the way you want it."

Buddy Holly got up and, without looking back, walked out of the Busy Bee Café.

♫

I sat there beside Jerry, dumbfounded. I had worried about Maria trying to fire him, and here *he* had fired *Buddy*. If he didn't want to live in New York, that was one thing, but to fire Buddy! I never expected this.

I couldn't understand how Jerry thought he had the right to take over The Crickets' name. The *three* of them were The Crickets, not just Jerry and Joe B. The three of them received equal shares when it came to money earned for personal appearances. Jerry and Joe B each got twenty-five percent of the royalties received for The Crickets' records, and Buddy got fifty. After Niki had left the group, they'd agreed that Buddy should get Niki's part too because of everything he did for the band. To me, that indicated that Jerry and Joe B accepted Buddy Holly as the leader of the band.

I wondered if Maria had anything to do with Jerry's decision not to move to New York. Although he never said anything about her, I was under the impression that he was totally turned off by her domineering nature and uncontrollable ranting. I think he knew that no good would come out of trying to deal with her, and she was certainly having her say in Buddy's business, which was Jerry's business, too. And, because Maria was from New York, Jerry probably thought she had influenced Buddy to move there.

He didn't know Buddy was going to get a divorce and wanted me to get one, too, and I couldn't tell him because Buddy had sworn me to secrecy. I knew I still had Jerry's infidelity to deal with at some point, but I hadn't even addressed that issue with him yet because I was waiting to hear from Buddy again. As soon as I did, I would be ready to unload. In fact, I was ready to unload on him without waiting for Buddy's help.

When Buddy had said he was going to New York for the business, I knew he meant it. In his mind, Maria Elena was no longer a factor. The business was what mattered to Buddy, and if Jerry didn't see it, then he didn't need to go to New York.

Jerry sat in the booth, staring straight ahead, as still and quiet as a church mouse.

"What are we going to do, Jerry?" I asked softly. "If we're not going to New York, what are we going to do?"

There was no discussion. He looked at me and said, "Let's go find an apartment. We're moving to Clovis so I can work with Norman and get The Crickets recorded. You know, The Crickets never made any money until they came to Clovis."

"Oh, I see. And what Crickets would that be?" I asked, unable to keep the irritation out of my voice.

"Earl Sinks, Sonny Curtis, Joe B, and me. Earl can do the vocals, and Sonny can play guitar."

So, on Thursday, November 13, 1958, we moved into Apartment 4 at 2400 North Main Street in Clovis, New Mexico. It was a relatively new two-bedroom and one-bath quadriplex with a kitchen and living room. It was a fairly roomy apartment, or at least it looked spacious since we didn't have much furniture in it. Mrs. Allison had bought us a sofa and bed, and Norman had bought us a housewarming gift—a new washer and dryer. He said we needed some way to keep clean. When I saw it, I hoped he hadn't bought it in vain. I wondered how long we would really live in Clovis, especially since I was contemplating a divorce, and Jerry...well, that was another story. He never seemed to want to be alone with me, and as usual, he spent more time hanging out with his friends and drinking than he did at home. I wondered if the two of us were even compatible enough to live alone together until the divorce.

Well, I didn't have to wonder about that for long. As soon as we moved in, I realized I *still* wouldn't be living alone with Jerry—he asked Joe B to move in with us. I liked Joe B; in fact, he was very pleasant and quiet. But when Jerry had told Buddy that he would take care of him, I never imagined he meant that he would actually take him in like a foster child.

Was Jerry afraid to be alone with me? If he loved me, he'd want just the *two of us* to spend time together, but it never seemed to be part of his plan. I must admit, however, that I was happier living in Clovis than I had been in Lubbock. I kept busy setting up the apartment and finally felt like I belonged somewhere.

Jerry spent most of his time at the studio. He filled in as a session drummer whenever Norman needed him. On November 21, the new Crickets group made their first recording, "Someone Someone." Vi played the piano, and The Roses sang backup.

As I arrived at the studio one day to visit Vi and Norma Jean, Jimmy Self, who was on his way out, asked if I'd seen Buddy and Maria when they dropped by the studio.

"No. I didn't know they'd been here," I said.

Jimmy said, "Buddy asked Norman if he could take the recorder and Fender amplifier to New York, and of course, he told Buddy he could. They came on Sunday, and Norman took everyone to brunch. I was here with Norman when they arrived. When we came through the studio on our way back into the control room—you know that tall speaker in the studio?"

"Yes," I replied.

"Well, Maria sat down on it. Me, Buddy, and Norman were just about halfway to the door where the reception room is, and Maria said, 'Buddy, he looked up my skirt!' We just froze. We absolutely froze. All the blood just drained from Buddy's face, and he kinda turned and looked at her, and she said again, 'Norman. He looked up my skirt, Buddy.' You know how she is. She just keeps going. Buddy looked at her and said, 'That's enough, Maria. Knock it off!' We went on into the office, and got the recorder and talked a bit."

"I guess Buddy and Maria are in New York by now," I said.

"That's what I heard. You know, Norman got some letters from a lawyer in New York. A Harold Orenstein and one of his staff members named George Shiffer. They want Norman to verify the songwriter and artist credits on The Crickets' recordings. Something about making sure the royalties are right. You know, Southern Publishing pays the royalties on their records. Norman doesn't do that. I don't know what Buddy has in mind with that."

My heart leaped all the way into my throat. Everything might still turn out the way Buddy had told me. Knowing him, he'd probably get the business straightened up first and then pursue the divorce. I didn't know anything about filing for divorce, so I'd surely welcome his help. I knew it would be hard for him to contact me without Jerry or Maria finding out, but I hoped I'd hear from him soon.

The only other news I heard about Buddy was secondhand. I heard that he and Norman had absolved Ray Rush's partnership in Prism Records.

Every time Ray's name came up, Robert and David just shook their heads. They had actually left him in New York like they said they would if he didn't show up on time to leave. I just couldn't believe they had left him—they were so nice to everybody. He must have really crossed the line for them to do that.

No one really knew why Ray was no longer going to be a partner in Prism, but there was a lot of speculation going on. Norman paid Ray back his investment of $2,968 from the Prism business account in the Clovis National Bank. At this point, it looked like the company was going to be just Norman and Buddy.

♫

One night, I woke up frantic, covered in cold sweat. I threw off the covers and sat straight up in bed.

Jerry, still half-asleep, raised his head and asked, "What's wrong, Peggy?"

"I had a bad dream," I told him.

"Go back to sleep," he said with a sigh. He fell back on the pillow and was asleep again in no time.

I'd started having lucid dreams when I was seven years old; I was thirteen when I started having prophetic ones.

One time, I dreamed that a friend died in a car accident, and I went to her funeral wearing my new, black summer dress with tiny pink daisies, pink trim, and a pink bow. When I told my mother about the dream, she'd said, "Now, Peggy, it was just a dream."

About a month later, this same friend and her sister were out at Buffalo Springs Lake, which was about ten miles east of town. They caught a ride back to Lubbock with a couple of boys. Somehow, a head-on collision occurred, their car rolled over, and she was killed. Someone said alcohol was a factor in the crash. Sure enough, I attended her funeral wearing that same black dress I had dreamed about. Mother said it was just coincidence.

Closed-casket services were the norm at all the Catholic funerals I had ever attended. However, this being a Protestant funeral, everyone lined up to pass by the casket and view the body. I was feeling a little creepy as I walked up to the casket, but when I looked at my friend, I became completely mortified. She didn't even look like I remembered her, and she was wearing the exact same dress as me. I just stood there in a state of shock until my mother grabbed me and gave me that *Don't you dare say a word* look. Quietly, she said, "I know you're upset. We'll discuss it when we get home."

When we arrived home, I couldn't get out of that dress fast enough. I told Mother that I would never wear it again—I couldn't even bear to look at it.

"Okay, okay," she said. "It'll be all right."

"Why did she look like that?" I began to cry.

"They had to rebuild part of her face because of the accident," Mother replied calmly.

I gasped. "But, Mother, I dreamed this! I told you about it," I exclaimed.

"Yes, I know you did. But we're not going to discuss it. You can discuss it with Daddy. I won't discuss it with you," she said.

Mother took away the dress, and I never saw it again.

When Daddy got home from work, I told him what had happened.

He said, "It's normal, Peggy Sue. People have prophetic dreams all the time. It's just that most people don't even realize that they have

210

them. They don't listen to their dreams. Dreams can be like warnings or messages. You have to realize, Peggy Sue, there's more to life than what you think. You can't just take everything as black and white. You know, just because you can't see something doesn't mean it's not there. It's good to listen to your dreams. Don't be afraid of them. Learn from them."

Tonight's dream was even scarier though. It was the second time I'd had this same dream. Was it prophetic?

It was winter. I could tell by the snow on the ground. I could even see the color of the plane. It was white with a brown stripe down the side, and it had a V tail. I could see Buddy sitting to the right of the pilot, and there were two men in the back seat. I believed it was Jerry and Joe B, but since I couldn't see them, I was just guessing. I could see Buddy standing on the wing to get into the airplane. It took off from the airport, turned left, and started to circle as if it were going to come back to the airport instead of going east like it was supposed to. I saw Buddy turn his face toward the pilot and give him a concerned look. He knew what was happening. Then the plane dove straight down into the snow on the farmland near the airport.

The first time I'd had the dream was in late summer, somewhere around Buddy's birthday. I told him about it one day when he stopped by the house. He just smiled and said, "Don't worry, Peggy Sue. The one thing about a small plane is that you can always land it. You can always glide it in if anything goes wrong. You don't have to worry about the dream."

Now that I'd had the dream again, I *was* worrying about it.

A few weeks later, in December, I dreamed about the crash for the third time. The plane was taking off, turning left, circling the airport, and then it started to turn as if it were coming back to the airport. I saw Buddy turn his head to look out in the direction of the airport and then back toward the pilot. Once again, I could see his concerned expression. The plane was diving into the snow-covered field.

Once again, I woke up in a panic. This time when I told Jerry about it I begged, "Do not rent a small plane. DO NOT fly in a small plane if you are on tour!"

I wished I could warn Buddy once more.

♫

Life had really slowed down for The Crickets. A year ago at this time Buddy and Jerry had been going nonstop from one venue to another. Always another tour, another appearance, another session planned long before the current one ended. They were on top of the world then. Since the end of October, there had been no more appearances for The Crickets. Oh, the new Crickets had gotten together occasionally to work on some songs or to do some writing, and a lot of the time Sonny Curtis was living with us as well as Joe B. However, that was about it for The Crickets.

I kept my ears open for news about Buddy, but heard nothing. He didn't seem to be making any appearances or doing anything that was making the news either. I wondered how his plan was progressing.

♪

My sister, her husband, and their eighteen-month-old little girl drove in from Sacramento for Christmas and stopped by our place on their way to my parents' house. My sister toured the apartment and kindly commented, "Oh, this is cute."

Jerry and I took them to the studio to meet everybody. Von and Norman hit it off right from the beginning—as soon as they discovered they had so much in common. They were nearly the same age, had been in the Air Force during World War II, were musicians, were passionate about big-band music, and their wives had even been born within five days of each other.

Johnnie thought Vi was just precious and, as usual, Vi and Norma Jean were perfect hostesses. We didn't stay long, however, because we could tell that little Kim was making everybody somewhat nervous. The studio was not baby-proofed.

As usual, Christmas was not everything it was typically made out to be. My family thought Jerry and I should spend the holidays with them, and Jerry's parents were upset because they thought we weren't spending enough time at their house. Christmas never seemed to be my mother's favorite time of year anyway, and this year she was in a particularly nasty mood.

"Your sister has driven all the way from California and brought her family," Mother said. "She took care of you when you were in school. You should be with us."

There was no way the Allisons were going to come to the Gerrons' house for Christmas so that everybody could be together—the in-laws just didn't like each other that much. Consequently, we spent Christmas Eve at my parents' house. Jerry played Santa Claus for little Kim Ruth and passed out the presents under the Christmas tree. On Christmas Day, we went to the Allisons'.

After the holidays, I heard from George Atwood, Norman's studio bass player, that Buddy and Maria had visited the Holleys at Christmastime. It hurt my feelings that they hadn't even called us—I guess Buddy was still too upset with Jerry. I wished he had tried to contact me.

Then, George said, "Buddy told me he was going to build a recording studio in Lubbock, and he showed me a sketch of the plans. One of Mr. Holley's friends, Don Kittrell, was the architect who drew them up."

"Yes," I said. "Buddy told me he surprised his mother with the plans on his birthday."

George continued, "The house has over forty-three hundred square feet in it, if you add all the terraces and carport. Buddy said he's going to build it on two lots in the very best part of Lubbock. It's going to cost around two hundred thousand to build, but Decca told Buddy they would pick up the cost for the studio portion."

My heart was beating so fast I could hardly breathe. Buddy was still intending to build his studio in Lubbock.

"That studio's going to be something else," George exclaimed. "Buddy's even put in ponds and gardens with walkways in brick and tile, a private sun terrace just to the east of his rooms, and a swimming pool on the other side. Buddy asked me if I would do public relations for him..."

I couldn't hear anything else he said; I was too absorbed in my own thoughts. Oh, Buddy, you are still moving forward with your plan. I could see that he was building the perfect place in which he could unleash his creativity. He knew exactly where he was going and how to get there.

Later, I became privy to more news about Buddy. I was told that while he was in Lubbock for Christmas, he had told his mother that he was filing for a divorce. Once again, my spirits soared.

I knew that I should tell my parents that I, too, planned to file for a divorce, but telling them wouldn't be so easy. My family was Southern, and in the South, *ladies* don't get divorces. Rather, *they suffa in silence.* But, quite honestly, I'd had enough of silence and enough of Jerry's infidelities.

♪

CHAPTER NINETEEN

January 1959

We rang in 1959 with a real bang at our Clovis apartment—literally. We didn't plan a formal party, but because someone was always dropping by unannounced—to spend the night or, sometimes, to stay for several weeks—we naturally expected guests on New Year's Eve. Jerry bought two bottles of Mumm Cordon Rouge champagne so we could toast to 1959 in style. One thing was certain: We wouldn't be toasting to our marriage. We weren't getting along at all.

"Be sure to put it in the refrigerator so it'll be chilled for tonight," Jerry said.

Well, one thing led to another, and before I knew it, it was later than I realized. Regrettably, I hadn't put the champagne into the refrigerator.

"Hum," I said aloud to myself in a half-questioning tone, "I wonder how long it takes champagne to chill; I better put it in the freezer."

There's a lot to learn when you're only eighteen. For example, if you don't know how long it takes something to freeze, be sure to check on it periodically—or else.

As midnight drew near, I set out our glasses and opened the freezer. The contents had uncorked the bottles with such force that it looked like a bomb had exploded. Champagne coated everything, creating a total mess.

Jerry came into the kitchen as I was wiping off the frozen peas and hamburger meat. His whole body appeared to snap to attention. After he rolled his bulging eyes at me, he sighed deeply; and without a word, he left the room, shaking his head slowly from side to side.

♪

At the onset of 1958, The Crickets had been on top of the world. They were in the midst of TV appearances, and as soon as one tour had ended, another had begun. The future was bright with the promise of more hit records and new admiring fans from countries they'd never even visited. They were living the life that many aspiring musicians could only dream about.

However, by the end of 1958, it all had ended—there was no more Buddy Holly and The Crickets. The Crickets weren't even the same. There'd been no tours of any kind for two months, and as the new year approached, there were no gigs on the horizon for the newly formed Crickets—and no tours spelled disaster for most rock 'n' roll musicians. Musicians depended on loyal, record-buying fans. Furthermore, a musician's life was his music, and he was usually happiest when he was sharing his *creation* with those who appreciated it. If you take this away from him, he quickly becomes miserable.

Jerry's Crickets were writing songs and working on their own music, but the energy that had permeated Buddy Holly and The Crickets was missing. All the sound and feeling were gone. I hated to think it, but I wondered if Jerry was just becoming another one of Norman's session musicians. Jerry was very unhappy, and consequently, he and Norman were always engaged in closed-door meetings.

How had things gotten so out of control? Maybe Norman Petty had been right when he questioned the guys' decisions to get married. The Crickets were never the same after the honeymoon. Had they started to change before then? By late summer, Buddy had pushed forward on his own to produce and record—he'd set up his own label, planned his new Lubbock studio, and made connections in New York. On the other hand, Jerry had continued to party and play the drums. He always said that all he'd ever wanted was to be married to me and to make music with Buddy. Maybe he just couldn't see beyond that, or maybe, he and Buddy just didn't communicate as much now as they did when it was only the two of them.

I say the *two* of them because Joe B was happy just being along for the ride. Heck, he was happy to be anywhere after surviving a near-fatal, motor-scooter crash that occurred when he was thirteen. He and another boy were on their way to a friend's house with some records when they collided with a Ford driven by an unlicensed fourteen-year-old. The car had hit the scooter so hard that the impact had even knocked Joe B's shoes off. He was hospitalized in critical condition with fractures and a head injury, and for a while, we weren't sure if he was going to pull through. Joe B's near-fatal experience was the primary reason why Buddy and Jerry looked after him the way they did.

The apartment continued to keep me busy. We had nonstop company with Sonny Curtis, Joe B, Earl Sinks, and Bo Clark coming in and out at all hours. For a while, David and Robert even lived with us. They had moved to Clovis from Odessa to work as session singers for Norman while he helped them get their own recording contracts as The Roses. David, Robert, and Bo Clark had rented a house together, but it flooded, ruining practically everything they owned, so they lived with us until their landlord said they could move back in. David, Robert, and I became even closer friends during our *laundry time* together. The eight of us created a ton of dirty clothes, so we had to keep the washer and dryer running twenty-four hours a day.

♬

The Norman Petty Trio was scheduled to play a gig at the Officer's Club on Tinker Air Force Base in Oklahoma City. Mike Mitchell, the group's drummer, couldn't go along, so Norman, even though he knew Jerry didn't like organ music, asked if he wouldn't mind playing for just this one job. Reluctantly, he agreed, and then he moped around the house as if he would never be able to play rock 'n' roll again. What a comedown it was for Jerry to be playing bar music.

"You don't understand," he told me. "That's like playing Musak in the elevators. I can't even use my drumsticks. I'll only be able to use brushes. People'll think I'm not a real drummer."

"Jerry, it's only one evening. You'll live through it," I scolded.

The Officer's Club had been mentioned so many times that I was curious to see what it looked like. Often, I'd heard about how The Crickets had recorded there in September 1957. The Norman Petty Trio had been playing a gig at the base, and the guys just happened to be in the area;

so, after Norman's gig, they'd all met at the club to record "Maybe Baby" and three other songs.

Jerry's dreaded day arrived, and it was time for us to leave. I parked in the back driveway and walked around to the front of the studio where Norman and Jerry were loading the big truck with sound equipment and instruments. Jerry was standing next to the electric lift, sporting a pair of heavy-duty cotton gloves.

"What's that big thing in there all covered up, Jerry?" I asked.

"The organ," he said, his voice indicating disbelief that he had just helped load such a thing.

Finally, we were on the road, with Vi and me driving Norman's car behind the truck. Vi was even happier than usual. She loved entertaining, but she *really* loved performing in Oklahoma City because that's where she'd gone to college.

I was extremely impressed with Norman's truck. After Jerry and Norman moved all the gear out, the truck looked just like a mini dressing room or a set on a movie lot. All the amenities Norman and Vi needed were at their fingertips. Vi even had an area with hangers so that all she had to do was hang up her clothes when she left Clovis, and later, when she was ready to dress in her evening gown for a performance, she simply stepped in and zipped up—no wrinkles and no worries. She also had a well-lit table for all her makeup and hair accessories.

"You can never have too much light, Peggy Sue," she said, smiling as she turned on another lamp.

Vi always had trouble styling her hair, so I fixed it for her. I backcombed it, sprayed it, and pulled it up so it would go over her head in a style similar to a ducktail. She called it a drake. She looked positively radiant as she exited the truck to go into the club.

Sometimes her cousin, Georgiana Veit, sang with the group, but on this night, Vi would be doing all the singing. I knew she and Norman were prepared for any audience request when I noticed what they fondly called their *big book* sitting on the piano. It contained all the music they could possibly ever need; it must have been at least five inches thick.

I had a great time watching The Norman Petty Trio perform. Unlike Jerry, I actually loved some of their songs. Plus, they were my friends, and I enjoyed watching them having fun performing.

I'd been seated in a plush leather booth and was told I could order anything I wanted, except, of course, for booze—but alcohol wasn't my thing anyway. I was really quite flattered by all the young officers who came over to meet me and ask me to dance. One by one, I turned them down, saying, "Thank you for asking, but no thank you. You see, my husband is the one playing the drums for you this evening."

"Whoops! You look too young to be married. Thanks anyway," they replied as they backed away.

Sitting there that night, I had an epiphany. I realized how easily I could have said yes to the young officers, but I hadn't. Moreover, it wasn't just because Jerry was there; I was married, and that meant something to me. It meant being loyal to my husband regardless of where he was. Also, I realized just how many women probably had approached Jerry simply because he was a musician. However, if he'd been a loyal husband, he would've turned them down when they asked him to buy them a drink or to dance, but, according to Buddy and Maria, he hadn't. *"You're* the one who's married, not *me."* He seemed to enjoy uttering these disturbing words, and I heard them so clearly in my head on this night that I looked around to ensure that no one was really saying them to me. I could feel our marriage exploding just like the two bottles of champagne on New Year's Eve, and I concluded that it would be just as impossible to put our marriage right again as it would be to try to restore the Mumm Cordon Rouge. At that moment, I decided I could no longer wait for Buddy. I would have to take charge of my life on my own, and I would do it as soon as we returned to Clovis.

The next day, we were all packed and ready to return home when Norman announced that he wanted to stop by a friend's house for a few minutes. Seeing the look on our faces, he laughed. "Don't worry. We won't stay long, and you won't be bored."

It was the most unusual home I'd ever seen—a '50s Frank Lloyd Wright-style house. In the '40s, this famous architect had created houses based on angles, but the new style for the '50s was circles. This house looked like a wall from the outside, but on the inside, it contained a park, complete with grass and vegetation going up the side of a mountain. Furthermore, there was a pond on the bottom floor. The floor itself was made of something that looked like quarry tile in a garden. Instead of vacuuming, the home's occupants could just hose off the floor.

We ascended a spiral staircase to look at the living room and bedrooms that were on a column standing in the middle of the house. From the outside, these rooms looked just like mixing bowls; on the inside, they had the atmosphere of a cave. The living room sported a very futuristic sofa built all the way around the edge of the bowl, and the bedrooms contained mattresses built into the carpeted floors. There were no ceilings in any of the rooms.

I'd always believed that Norman and Vi's decorating sense was very cutting-edge, but this house was unlike anything I'd ever seen—or imagined.

When we arrived in Amarillo, Norman pulled off the road, and he and Jerry walked back to our car with Cheshire-cat smiles on their faces.

"It's only fair that we take turns driving the truck on this trip," Norman said.

"Oh, Norman," Vi said, as we gathered our purses and headed for the truck. I must say, the rest of the trip was an absolute blast. We laughed all the way to Clovis as we bumped along in the truck and screamed "What did you say?" every time we tried to carry on a conversation over the roar of the road and the truck's engine. I hated to see the Clovis City Limits sign. I hadn't had this much fun in a long time.

♬

"Jerry, I want to know what happened on that last tour. Why are you acting differently?" I asked, with my hands on my hips.

"What? Buddy hasn't called me, has he?" Jerry asked. I guess he thought Buddy had called and told me about all his escapades during that last tour.

"No, no one's called you. Don't change the subject. Was there another girl on the tour that you were interested in?"

"I don't know what you're talking about," he said, obviously annoyed.

"Yes, you do. Did you tell her you were married?"

"What? You're crazy. Where are you getting this idea?"

For hours, I pursued the conversation, while he tried to dodge it. I wanted him to admit what he had done so I wouldn't have to divulge how

I'd found out about it. I didn't seem to be getting anywhere with my line of arguing, but I was relentless because I didn't have any other plan.

At last, he said, "Okay, there was a woman on the road. And, yes, we partied together, but that's all."

"I'm glad you finally admitted it, and just so you know, I'm filing for a divorce. I know your mother holds all your money for you, and she'll be afraid of any settlement, but she won't have to worry about that since we haven't been married very long." I turned toward the phone. "I have to tell my parents that I'm coming home."

Jerry said, "I won't let you do that."

"You won't let me do what?"

"Tell your folks."

"This doesn't have anything to do with you. This is my life. This may come as a big shock to you, Jerry, but I don't intend to waste my life in this marriage. Maybe I can still go to school, which is what my father wanted me to do..." Why did I say that? I don't even want to go to nursing school. Peggy Sue, be careful what you say. You don't want to get yourself out of one problem just to go into another. With that, I headed off to bed, yelling back at him, "And this conversation is not over! We *will* talk about this again tomorrow!"

I got up early the next morning and straightened up the apartment. When Jerry came into the kitchen, I asked, "Have you heard from Buddy at all. Has he called you?"

"No, he hasn't."

"I know that you and Norman have been having closed-door conversations. I thought that maybe you'd heard from him. I know you keep asking if Buddy has called you, but don't you think that maybe you should call him?"

"Yes, if I don't hear from him soon, I'll try to reach him. By the way, Mom and Dad are coming over to spend the weekend with us. They can sleep on the daybed Norman bought us. We'll go out to dinner this evening so you don't have to cook. I know cooking is such a task for you."

"Thanks for your vote of confidence. Why are they coming? Did you call them and invite them to come?" I asked.

"Yes, I called them. They think we should have a family meeting about your wanting a divorce."

"That's just great, Jerry. Don't you think maybe you should have talked to me before you brought them into it?"

He raised his voice and said, "Well, I did mention it to you. I'm telling you now."

"Excuse me. And since we're having a family meeting, don't you think that my mother and father should also be here?"

"They're not invited," Jerry snapped.

In other words, he was going to spring some secret plan on me once his parents got here. I stormed out of the room.

Mr. and Mrs. Allison arrived not too long after our discussion, and as always when they came to see us, they were pleasant. We went out to dinner, then came back to the apartment, and sat down in the living room so that we could all make eye contact. I was still silent, just as I had been all evening, while Jerry and his parents engaged in small talk. Finally, Mrs. Allison said, "We know that the two of you are having problems. Jerry tells us that you want a divorce, Peggy Sue. Is that right?"

"Yes, that's right," I replied, staring at her.

"I see," said Mrs. Allison. "Don't you think that's a bit premature on your part?"

"What do you mean 'premature,' Mrs. Allison?" I asked calmly. I'd been preparing myself for this conversation.

"Well, don't you think that you owe the marriage some time to see if you can save it? You've only been married six months, and Jerry was touring during one of those months. I realize how hurt you are right now because Jerry's had an affair, but..."

Jerry interrupted her, speaking much too fast. "I told her that I didn't love her. That I only loved one woman, and it was you."

My eyes narrowed, the muscles in my face tightened, and I snapped, "So you didn't *just* party with her? You broke your wedding vows?"

He looked down at the floor like he'd just been slapped in the face.

Something inside me had wanted to believe that Jerry hadn't really gone *that* far with his infidelity. However, the blatant truth was that he hadn't been honest with me from the very beginning. I'd just been deceiving myself when I gave him the benefit of the doubt every time I questioned his motives.

221

I threw his words back into his face. "What about how much we have in common and our families having so much in common that we must've been a match made in heaven?"

Mrs. Allison interrupted. "You can't get a divorce now. You need to give this some time. I know if your mother were here, she would tell you the same thing. I know that it'll be hard, but you must learn to forgive, and then you'll forget."

"*You* know what my mother would say? I don't see her standing here. But, of course, *you* never invite her when there's a family event, do you? And what do you know about forgiving and forgetting? Has *your* husband ever broken *your* wedding vows?"

"Well, of course not," she responded, taken aback by my outburst.

"So *I'm* the one who's supposed to be mature and turn the other cheek," I said.

By that time, Jerry had broken into the conversation again. "You have such middle-class morals," he snarled, with his nose turned up in the air.

"What's that supposed to mean?" I snapped.

At this point, Mr. Allison interrupted the conversation. "Louise, the kids need to work this out by themselves. *You* can't fix this for Jerry." He turned to look at Jerry. "If you really want this marriage to work, then you'll do whatever it takes to save it since it's *you* who broke it. I think it's time we went home and let them take care of their problems, Louise." Then Mr. Allison looked at me and said, "I love you, and I'm so glad you're my daughter-in-law. I hope that you decide you can stay with us."

Jerry walked his parents to their car; I remained inside—silent and hurting. Daddy's words, "You make your bed hard, you'll have to sleep in it," raced through my mind. I was appalled at what Jerry had done, but somehow, I still felt like it was partially my fault. After all, I'd disappointed my parents, I'd married Jerry even though I knew in my heart it was wrong, and I'd continued to fall for his line every time he'd given me one of his spiels. Obviously, I still didn't understand what love was, but at least I'd honored my marriage vows. Meanwhile, Jerry had made a mockery of his vows and our marriage—a marriage made in hell. Oops! There go my middle-class morals again.

♪

CHAPTER TWENTY
The Crash

*J*erry and I traveled to Lubbock so often that our car practically cruised down US 84 on its own. Besides our parents living there, that's where we did most of our shopping, and that's where Jerry's money resided; his mother had continued being his accountant after we'd married. Sometimes, Norman even wrote Jerry's checks out in Mrs. Allison's name with a notation that it was money for Jerry's account. I was never privy to how much money he was or was not making; I was not a part of the financial equation in our marriage. The only cash I ever had was what Jerry gave me to spend. I thanked my lucky stars for checkbooks.

On February 2, Jerry, Sonny, and I packed some clothes, piled into the car, and once again, made our way to Lubbock. Jerry and I frequently visited the Allisons, sometimes spending several days with them, and since Sonny was staying at our house at the time, Jerry invited him along so they could continue their talk—they were trying to determine the next step toward getting The Crickets back into action. Joe B had already left for Lubbock the day before.

For the entire ninety-mile trip, Jerry and Sonny talked nonstop about Norman. Poor Norman. These days, he just couldn't do anything to please Jerry—nothing was happening fast enough. Jerry was upset that Norman hadn't booked The Crickets anywhere, especially since we'd heard through the grapevine that Buddy was already working or was about to start. The rumor that Buddy had hired Waylon Jennings made its way to Clovis pretty fast, especially since Waylon lived in Littlefield, Texas, a small community about halfway between Lubbock and Clovis.

The next morning, February 3, Sonny woke us up saying emphatically, "Jerry! Get up! There seems to be some kind of rumor going around that Buddy Holly and The Crickets have been killed in a small plane crash in Clear Lake, Iowa. Man, you need to find out what happened!"

Jerry leaped out of bed and started dressing. I jumped up, put on my robe, and went into the kitchen. Jerry turned on the radio, and then he grabbed the phone and phone book. I sat down at the kitchen table with a cup of coffee. My heart was pounding a thousand beats a minute, even though such news had to be just that—a rumor. Jerry and Joe B were right here in Lubbock, not in Iowa; and since The Crickets weren't in a plane crash, Buddy Holly couldn't have been either.

All we heard on the radio was a short blurb saying a small plane carrying three rock 'n' roll stars had gone down in Iowa. Jerry called several radio stations and everyone else he could think of but didn't learn any further information than what had come over the teletype. As a result, he decided to call the Holleys. We all listened intently as Buddy's mother answered the phone. I could hear her voice coming faintly through the receiver.

"Yes, Jerry. It's true. Buddy and Ritchie Valens and another young man by the name of Big Bopper—you know, Jerry, that 'Chantilly Lace' song. The Crickets were not on the plane with Buddy...by The Crickets, I don't mean you and Joe B. I mean his new group of The Crickets—Waylon, Tommy, and the young drummer, Carl Bunch. Do you know him?"

Jerry's eyes opened wide in surprise. Besides learning of Buddy's death, he'd also discovered Buddy had put together a new group and was calling *them* The Crickets, too.

He managed to choke out, "Yes, I think I do." By this time, his face had lost all its color. "So...Buddy Holly *and The Crickets* were booked on this tour? Is that right, Mrs. Holley?"

"Yes, Jerry, that's right."

Jerry paused a moment and then asked, "I have Sonny Curtis here. Is it all right if we come by?"

"Yes, come by any time, and, Jerry, I'd like for you, Joe B, and Sonny to be pallbearers. Please consider it."

"Yes, of course I will, and I'm sure that's fine with Joe B. I'll let you go, and we'll be over later today." Jerry paused again, and then he took a deep breath and said, "When will the service be, Mrs. Holley?"

"Right now, we're not sure. The authorities won't let us bring Buddy home until there's positive identification by a family member. As soon as we work that out, we'll know when the funeral will be."

"Okay, we'll see you this afternoon," Jerry said.

The phone started to ring just as Jerry placed the receiver back on the hook.

I melted into my own nightmare. I could see a girl—was it me?— wearing a new black summer dress with tiny pink daisies, pink trim, and a pink bow. As she turned to look at me, part of her monochrome face began to transform. I closed my eyes and shook my head as if I were warding off flies. I opened them quickly though because I heard my father's voice saying, "Yes, dreams can be like warnings or messages. You have to realize, Peggy Sue, there's more to life than what you think. You can't just take everything as black and white. You know, just because you can't see something doesn't mean it's not there. It's good to listen to your dreams."

His voice gave me comfort. I wanted to say, "Oh, Daddy. I'm so glad you're here," but I couldn't because he was nowhere in sight.

Instead, I saw a white V-tail plane with a brown stripe down the side, Buddy sitting next to the pilot, and two faceless men in the back. Buddy turned his face toward the pilot, giving him a concerned look, and then the plane swooped straight down into the snow...again...and again. I heard Buddy's voice say, "Don't worry, Peggy Sue. The one thing about a small plane is that you can always land it. You can always glide it in if anything goes wrong. You don't have to worry about the dream." But the plane still went down...again...and again.

I could hear my voice saying, "Daddy, what do you mean by 'Don't be afraid of your dreams; learn from them'? Daddy? Daddy? Buddy's dead? He can't be. Make it go away. Daddy?"

When the phone rang again, I was jolted back into reality, astonished that I was still sitting at the Allisons' kitchen table with my hands wrapped around my coffee cup.

225

"Hello. What did you say, Norman?" Jerry asked. "Okay. I just got off the phone with Mrs. Holley, and they won't know when the funeral's going to be for another day or two. Yes, I'll let you know when I hear."

Jerry's face was white when he hung up the phone, which started to ring again. I heard him say, "Yes, Operator. This is Jerry Allison. Oh, great. You're coming to the funeral? Great. What time will you be in? Okay, call me when you check into the hotel. Give me a number, and I'll call you as soon as we know when the service will be."

"Who was that, Jerry?" I asked.

"Phil Everly."

Before he could say anything else, the phone rang again. After answering several back-to-back calls, Jerry turned his still-pale face toward Sonny and said in a low, hesitant voice, "Would you answer the phone for awhile? You can tell them that I'm not dead."

I sat frozen at the table, staring off into space, still bombarded by flashes of dreams about a plane crash and fragments of conversations. Only periodically did the shrill ring of the telephone, or the inflection of a spoken word, draw my mind back into consciousness. I couldn't believe this was happening. It all seemed as surreal to me as a Dali painting. I couldn't move away from the phone. Something inside me kept expecting the next caller to say that someone had located Buddy and that this had been an awful case of mistaken identity.

I watched the clock tick away the minutes; yet, somehow, time seemed out of sequence. It was as though I was watching a 78 spin round and round on my Pilot, with its perpetual *shh shh* sound keeping beats to the seconds ticking off the clock. But, the record player was broken. Its music echoed in my ears, dragging with the speed of a 33. How many times we'd laughed at the funny sound a song made when it was played too fast or too slow. Today, however, there was no laughter about this sound pulsating in my head or this nightmare draining my very soul.

Buddy Holly had spun to the top. He had lived fast—always pushing his music forward as if he somehow knew that he had to get as much accomplished as he could, as fast as he could. I remembered our drive to El Paso and his concern that *the music* would be forgotten some day. I remembered asking him, "Doesn't it have something to do with destiny, which you are always talking about, Buddy?" Destiny. Was this his fate? To be snatched away before he and The Crickets could reconcile? To never be able to completely fulfill his dreams? To be taken from his family and friends at such a young age? I knew Buddy believed in God and that God had a plan for his people on earth. At this point though, I just didn't understand, I couldn't understand, how this could be Buddy's destiny.

Finally, I accepted the fact that the call I'd been hoping for wasn't coming, and I went into the bedroom where Jerry's mother was. Shortly afterwards, Jerry came in bellowing, "You know what Norman said to me when I was on the phone with him? The first thing out of his mouth was, 'God has strange ways of solving problems.'"

The way Jerry was talking, it sounded like he believed Norman was saying that God had caused the airplane crash.

"No, Jerry. That's not what Norman meant." I started to explain that I understood what Norman was trying to say, but Jerry just went off on a tangent; so, I left him alone with his mother and went into our room to get dressed.

It was obvious to me that Norman was thinking the same way I was. It seemed natural that he and Buddy would have discussed religious matters, too, since Norman was a very devout man. Jerry always took everything literally. While I was away at school, I'd learned that God didn't think the same way humans did. It had something to do with His ways not being like our ways, and His thoughts not being like our thoughts because He thought on a higher plane. Only He knew the whole plan, and we just had to pick up and go on with life based on what we knew. *God's plan. Destiny.* I wasn't even sure I liked that word any more. The crash hadn't just been Buddy's destiny. In one swift moment, all the lives touched by Buddy's life, had been changed, too. That's what Norman was trying to say.

The days I spent waiting for Buddy's funeral passed by me like a blur. The reality of what was happening continued to mix with nightmares and reflections from the past. I coped by inking everything I could out of my mind. I remember Jerry telling me that Buddy's brother, Larry, and his brother-in-law, J. E. (John Edward) Weir, had flown to Mason City to identify Buddy's body so they could make arrangements to bring him home. I had met J. E. at Buddy and Maria's wedding. At the mortuary, Larry was warned that the identification would be emotionally difficult, so he asked J. E. to identify the body for him. When J. E. came out of the room, he'd said, "Be glad you didn't do it, Larry." The Holleys said J. E. and Larry had planned to bring Buddy back immediately, but due to inclement weather, the plane carrying Buddy had been grounded in Des Moines. We were still waiting for the exact time of the funeral.

TV stations, radio DJs, and newspapers all over the country provided updates on the crash, as well as biographies of the victims. It was as if music lovers everywhere *needed* to understand why these four lives had been snuffed out in their prime.

I read a short article about Ritchie Valens in one of our papers which stated that he'd written his hit song, "Donna," about his girlfriend, Donna Ludwig. A small picture of her appeared beside the article. I had assumed the song was written about someone in particular because, after all, "Peggy Sue" had been; but I hadn't really thought about the person behind the song. I stared at her picture for a long time, transfixed that her name, like mine, was the title of a hit record. I was quite aware of my own pain, but I could only surmise what she was going through.

The first news article we read stated the plane had burned, but that account proved untrue once we saw pictures of the crash scene. Speculation about what had caused the crash seemed to change with every news edition. According to one report, it had been snowing heavily when the plane took off; another report, however, indicated it was only spitting a few light flakes, if any at all. Moreover, one article stated that the pilot, Roger Peterson, wasn't sufficiently trained to fly in such bad conditions or capable of flying by instruments. According to another report, Roger Peterson had initially failed his instrument-rating test but had passed it during his second attempt. We also heard that he was skilled enough to fly by instruments, and that he'd trained other pilots. Furthermore, some reports indicated that the plane wasn't even in the air long enough to run into bad weather and warrant flying by instruments. According to Jerry Dwyer, the plane's owner, the night had been clear enough to allow him to watch the plane take off and watch the taillights descend in the distance. Reporters stated that, apparently, the engine was running okay because farmers living in the houses below the flight path had said they clearly heard the engine before the crash.

One story blamed the gyroscope, which was not American-made, and therefore, opposite from what American pilots used; in other words, up could look like down. However, another story rebutted this idea, stating that the fatal flight was not the first time Roger Peterson had flown this plane; the Beechcraft Bonanza had been in service for months, so he would have known how to read its gyroscope.

Finally, every source seemed to arrive at the same catchall conclusion— pilot error. Pilot error? I wondered what that meant. Jerry Dwyer did not believe that the crash had been a result of pilot error. According to him, Roger Peterson had been incapacitated in some way or he would have been able to land the airplane. In my opinion, it seemed too easy to only blame the pilot. All this was enough to make my head spin, but there was no need to try to analyze the crash at this time. Surely, I thought, we'll eventually know the real reasons behind this tragedy.

Learning about the details of the crash was a nightmare for me because of its many similarities to my three dreams. Seeing images of the crushed plane in the snow-covered Iowa field jolted me to my very core. I had difficulty breathing when I heard that, according to eyewitnesses, the plane had taken off, turned left, circled once around the airport, and then crashed about five miles from the Mason City Municipal Airport. The plane also had a V tail, but instead of a brown stripe, like in my dream, it had a red one. I'd never seen Ritchie Valens or The Big Bopper before, and I wondered if maybe that was why, in my dreams, the faces of the young men in the back seats had been indistinguishable.

I went to my church, lit a candle, and prayed.

When I got back to the house, Jerry was there. With all the commotion caused by the numerous phone calls, and people coming and going, we'd hardly even acknowledged one another. Once again, he was in a hurry.

"Phil Everly's coming to the funeral. He's going to be a pallbearer," Jerry said.

"It's really nice of him to come. I know Buddy's smiling. He liked him," I said as my mind flashed to a happier time at Mama Leona's in New York—when we were *all* alive.

Jerry interrupted my thoughts. "Maria came in yesterday. One of her aunts is with her."

"Have you seen her?"

"Yes."

"And how is she doing?"

"She looked great...as she always does," he said.

"That's good. She has a lot to go through now." I wondered if Buddy had ever told her he wanted a divorce.

By February 6, Buddy's body was finally back in Lubbock and had been taken to Sanders Funeral Home.

In the *Lubbock Avalanche Journal*, I read that The Big Bopper's funeral was scheduled for two o'clock because his teenaged fans would be in school at that time and, therefore, unable to attend. The reason for this was to avoid student demonstrations during the funeral. What a putdown, I thought. The only reason they're doing this is because he was a rock 'n' roll musician.

♫

I woke up...and I was still Peggy Sue...and it was the worst day of my life. It was February 7, the day I had to watch them put Buddy into the ground and cover the casket.

Mrs. Holley had made sure all the arrangements were in order. She had seen to it that Mr. Holley had gotten her baby home, and she'd taken care of planning all the formalities of the services and picking the location where Buddy would be laid to rest.

Norman, Vi, Robert Linville, and David Bigham arrived at the Allisons' around 12:30. We all hugged each other, and I was glad because I really needed some hugs from friends. We milled around making small talk in quiet voices and low tones for about an hour.

"Where's the church?" Norman asked me.

"Just go south down College Avenue until you reach 34th Street. Turn left. Go about a mile. It'll be on your right. There's a sign like a small billboard that says Tabernacle Baptist Church," I told him.

Everybody left at the same time. Jerry rode with some of the other pallbearers, and I drove our car by myself. I can't explain why, but instead of going directly to the church, I felt as though I just had to stop by the Holleys' to see if there was anything I could do for Maria. Their house was on 39th Street—not far from the church.

The Holleys' car was gone, but I decided to go to the door anyway to see if someone might still be home. Sure enough, the door was unlocked.

I knocked on the screen door and called, "Hello?" as I stepped into the kitchen. Immediately, Maria's aunt came to meet me.

"Can I help you?" she asked.

"I'm Peggy Sue Allison, and I just stopped by to check on Maria."

"I'm Iris Rodriquez," Maria's aunt replied.

About that time, I noticed Maria coming out of the bedroom and walking down the hall. She was wearing a tight, straight black wool skirt, a matching sweater, black hose, and black pumps. She always had good fashion sense, and she always looked like *money*. I couldn't help wondering, though, if she'd brought her outfit with her from New York or if she had bought it since she'd been in Lubbock.

"Do you need a ride to the church or someone to drive for you?" I asked.

"No," she replied in that snippy tone I'd grown accustomed to. When Maria spoke, it always sounded as if anger were seething right below the surface, like lava, ready to erupt at any moment. I guess I just hadn't expected it *today*. Feeling the need to portray herself as a woman in control, she continued, "I am just fine. I don't need anything."

"Well, I must leave, or I'll be late. It was nice meeting you, Mrs. Rodriguez," I said as I walked to the back door.

My brow wrinkled and my lips pursed as I marched to the car. How could she be so obnoxious and so ugly? We should've been able to come together, especially in this time of sorrow. I'd taken the time to check on her, and she couldn't even be polite. She's certainly not a Texan, I thought, and she acts like everything and everyone from New York are so much better. Has she never heard of *friendly* before? The first time I'd met Maria, she acted like she was mad, but at that point, who could've even had the opportunity to have upset her? It was as if someone had forced her to come to Lubbock the first time, and I believed she felt the same way now. Humph!

It took longer to find a parking place once I arrived at the church than it did to drive there. Cars were parked everywhere. Walking toward the church, I noticed the sign—Tabernacle Baptist Church, Independent and Fundamental. I wondered, Independent of what? And what does *Fundamental* mean? I wasn't familiar with Protestant churches, and I sure didn't understand what that sign meant...then, I realized I was trying to think of anything rather than the fact that I was attending Buddy's funeral.

I walked up the steps and opened the big glass door. Walking to the left side, I went down the aisle until I found a row where I could fit. I spotted Norman, Vi, David, and Robert sitting close to the section reserved for the family, almost in the middle of the church. They were all looking straight ahead, staring into space. I looked for the pallbearers, but I couldn't see them because they were also sitting on the left side of the church. I closed my eyes for a moment hoping I was dreaming, but when I reopened them, the casket and flowers were still there, and so was the picture of Buddy, which rested atop the casket near the pulpit.

Betty Lou Drury was playing the organ, and Carolyn Cosby was sitting at the piano. They were the regular accompanists at Tabernacle Baptist Church. When Mrs. Holley had asked Betty Lou to play at Buddy's funeral, Betty Lou told me she became nervous and replied, "There are going to be so many professional performers in the church, don't you think you should ask one of them?"

Mrs. Holley said, "No, I don't. We've brought Buddy home now. I think it should be the way it normally is when Buddy and the family come to church."

In a few minutes, the minister walked to the pulpit, and at about the same time, the Holley family appeared in the doorway on the right side of the church. The music continued to play as they began to wend their way to the front rows to be seated. I saw Mr. and Mrs. Holley, Larry and his wife, Travis, a little of the back of Patricia's head, and then some more family members. But there was no Maria. NO MARIA!

I heard the minister say that Charles Hardin Holley was survived by his parents, two brothers, and a sister. Why didn't he say by his wife, Maria Elena Holly, too? I never heard him say it.

I'm sure those seated around me wondered what I was doing when I rose to my feet and stared at the front row where *she* should have been seated. As quietly as possible, I left the church and drove back to the Holleys' house. I was almost out of the car before it came to a complete stop. I ran to the kitchen door, and there was Maria's aunt, just standing there, as Maria placed her suitcases into a pile so they could easily be picked up.

"Maria! What are you doing here? I came to see about you again. You obviously are not at the church," I exclaimed anxiously.

I looked at her in disbelief. Only thirty minutes earlier, she'd been wearing black, like a mourning widow, but here she was now wearing a white angora sweater; a straight, tight-fitting, white wool skirt, white pearl earrings (I couldn't help noticing how nice they looked with her dark hair), and of course, the pocketbook that matched her black-suede, high-heel pumps—and the funeral wasn't even over.

"What are you doing, Maria?" I asked demandingly.

She started her little singsong. "I am going back to New York. I am going to get the man who killed Buddy." She said it over...and over. "I will show him he can't push me around. He isn't getting by with killing Buddy."

"Who," I yelled irritably, "are you talking about?"

"You know," she said as she waved that stupid finger at me. "You know. Norman Petty. I will get him. I will have him audited until he can't stand it any longer. I will never let him get away with this."

I shook my head in disbelief. "Maria, Norman Petty did *not* kill Buddy. What are you thinking?"

"Buddy had to go on the tour to make money because Norman had it all and would not give it to Buddy," she said.

I scolded, "And you can't wait? You don't have time to attend the funeral? What about Buddy? Are you going to the cemetery?"

"No," she stormed at me. "Buddy is dead! There is nothing I can do for him now! I'm leaving today for New York with my aunt."

In total disgust and feeling no respect for the widowed bride, I glared at her, turned my back, and started walking toward the door. I didn't want to talk to her any more. She was a done deal as far as I was concerned. She obviously didn't care for anybody but herself—certainly not for the family that had just lost a loved one. I wondered why she even bothered to come to Lubbock.

"Where are you going?" she barked at me. She wasn't through with her tirade, and here I was walking away from her.

Killed Buddy? No one had killed Buddy. I turned toward her and said distinctly and firmly through clenched teeth, "I am going to bury Buddy and try to give my support to his mother." Then, in the same tone of

233

voice I'd heard Buddy use, I added, "Maria Elena!" I turned my back to her again and left, hoping it would be a very long time before I'd have to talk to her again—if ever.

I returned to the church in a very bad mood. While listening to the black gospel song, "I'll Be All Right," being played on a record player, I found my way back to my abandoned seat and sat down as quietly as possible, trying not to make eye contact with anyone. How stupid, I thought. All these musicians here, and they're using a record player. Surely, Norman would've played the organ if he'd been asked, but I'm sure no one asked him, especially since Maria had started her hate campaign against him. I heard somebody say that the gospel song being played was Buddy's favorite. I'd never heard him talk about that particular song, but Buddy seemed to love all music.

As soon as the services ended, I went to my car and turned on the motor. I was so cold that I was shaking and having a hard time taking a deep breath. I'd heard someone at the house say it was 58 degrees, but I think my emotions played as much a part (maybe even more) in my physical discomfort as did the weather. I just couldn't seem to warm up. My body and all my senses were numb, well, except for one—my anger toward Maria.

It looked like everybody who had attended the funeral was going to the cemetery. I watched the cars jockey for positions in the procession. My car was blocked from getting in line because of where I'd parked, so I pretty much brought up the rear in the long line of cars, on a lonesome drive, to the City of Lubbock Cemetery. By the time I arrived, I couldn't even get close to the cemetery gates because of all the cars and people. There was no way I could be near the burial plot where I'd wanted to be. I'd have to watch from a distance and wouldn't be able to hear or see what was going on. But I didn't want to do that, so I went back to my car and drove to St. Elizabeth's, where I went in, lit another candle, and prayed, thanking God for letting me be a part of Buddy's short life.

When I returned to the Allisons', I was alone with my thoughts—no one else had arrived yet. I tried to make some kind of sense out of everything, but I just couldn't. It was as if Buddy wasn't really dead. I had the feeling he was still with me, and if I went to the phone, I could find him through information. I couldn't sense that he'd gone beyond. But what I really couldn't understand was why Maria Elena hadn't attended her own husband's funeral.

The house started to fill with people, and after a while, Jerry asked, "Wanna go over to Phil's hotel room with me and Joe B?"

"Sure," I said.

As we sat solemnly in the hotel room, Jerry, Joe B, and Phil talked about the plane crash, Buddy being only twenty-two years old, and what *going beyond* might be like. They tried to answer the unanswerable question: "What do you think was going though Buddy's mind when the plane crashed?" No one really acknowledged me during the conversation, but that was okay with me. I was in my own world. After all, what was there to say?

♫

Sometimes, Sundays can be abnormally long and quiet. The day after Buddy's funeral was one of those days. I didn't know where Jerry had gone, but actually, I wasn't in the mood to be around anybody anyway. That afternoon, I decided to drive to Buddy's grave.

The old City of Lubbock Cemetery on the east side of town had always been an eerie place to me. A weathered aboveground vault located in the center of the cemetery was a favorite haunt for thrill-seeking, female band students. Supposedly, the vault was inhabited by ghosts. We'd drive to the cemetery just after dusk, park directly in front of the vault, turn off our car lights, wait a short while, and then flash them back on twice. Shortly afterwards, two flashes of blue light would appear from the iron-gated door. Remembering how it gave us goose bumps and how we would shriek and peel out of there like Satan himself was chasing us, seemed rather juvenile to me now. But, hey, there wasn't a whole lot for girls to do for fun in Lubbock, Texas.

Because of all the flowers that had been left, it wasn't difficult to spot Buddy's grave. It was located at the very front of the cemetery, right beside the road. Ella Holley, in all her wisdom, had picked a site where his friends and fans could easily find him.

There were no mourners around, just maintenance men working across the way, picking up debris and shoveling fresh dirt onto sunken graves. I parked and watched the men for a while. I noticed that, actually, for such harsh conditions as those created by the relentless West Texas winds, the cemetery grounds were pretty well-maintained. The perimeter was landscaped with cedars to help protect it from the elements outside, and inside, the shrubs and lawn were perfectly manicured. Buddy was buried in the new part where the headstones were flat to make mowing easier. Big elms lined the lanes that wound through the graves. The cemetery was one of the few places in Lubbock where there were trees.

Finally, I decided to get out of the car. The weather had not been cold on this February evening, but the temperature was beginning to drop as the sun lowered in the horizon. As I stepped out of the car, a slight chilling breeze cut across the cemetery, so I reached back in for my jacket.

I was just amazed by the huge mound of flowers. I spent quite a while reading the cards still attached to some of the arrangements and staring to the south at the tall grain elevators that kept watch over the cemetery.

Indeed, I was saddened by my grandfather's death, but Buddy's death had left me feeling like I was waking up from an anesthesia-induced sleep—it all seemed so unreal.

I wondered how Maria could just walk away from the responsibility of the funeral and all the people who had come to show their respect, and I wondered just how much support she'd given to Mrs. Holley, who'd just lost her baby boy.

I also wondered what it was like to be put six feet into the ground. Buddy was so young. It was all so final. Nothing good could ever happen again. The show was over, completed, finished. Buddy was gone, and I was devastated.

♫

Jerry didn't seem anxious to go back home to Clovis, so we stayed with the Allisons for a few days following Buddy's funeral. Often, when Mr. and Mrs. Allison were home, we'd all sit around the kitchen table so we could *visit* with one another. However, we usually just played cards or dominos so we could focus on the game rather than have to talk to each other. On this particular evening, we were playing 42.

Without saying a word, Jerry got up and left the room. He was only gone a few minutes before he returned revealing his familiar set jaw and squinty-eyed look, which warned everyone that he was about to say something significant. Unfalteringly, he announced, "I don't want anybody to call me Jerry again. From now on, my name is JI."

We all looked at each other, and I rolled my eyes at him. I thought to myself, it's going to take more than a name change to help the way you're feeling.

♫

CHAPTER TWENTY-ONE
New York Settlements

*T*erry was livid when he heard that Buddy's new Crickets had played the show scheduled in Moorhead, Minnesota, on the very day Buddy died. We read in the paper that, at first, the bookers had said they were going to cancel the show because they were short three performers and were concerned that The Crickets wouldn't perform without Buddy. But, when Waylon and Tommy said they'd stay, the promoters decided to turn the show into a tribute program and held an impromptu audition for talent to fill in for the missing artists. Newspaper articles said the night's performance was very emotional for both the performers and the two-thousand audience members, especially when The Crickets went on stage.

A group of teenagers from Central High School in Fargo, North Dakota, just across the river from Moorhead, had been selected as the fill-in band. They called themselves The Shadows, and their lead singer was a fifteen-year-old named Bobby Velline. As soon as they'd been chosen, they ran out to purchase sweaters like Buddy had worn for his promotion photos. Several reviews complimented the performance of the young Velline and his Shadows.

Waylon, Tommy, and Carl, who had been in the hospital with frostbitten feet at the time of the crash, completed the contract for The Winter Dance Party Tour as The Crickets at the request of the General Artists Corporation (GAC) bookers who had set up the tour. Waylon tried to step into the group's vocal position, but someone, probably Tommy Allsup, sent for Ronnie Smith of the Poor Boys to fly in from Odessa and fill Buddy's

238

spot. Even with such new talent, the group members continued to sing original Crickets songs, as that was what the audiences wanted to hear. Hum, I thought, first there were four Crickets...and then three...and then two. And, now, it seemed there was a whole plague of them.

Norman and Jerry were adamant that Jerry and Joe B were the only ones who deserved to be recognized as The Crickets, and since the new group might continue to perform indefinitely as if they were, immediate action had to be taken to get exclusive control of the name. Also, The Crickets were under contract to produce another album for Decca, and if they didn't complete the contract on time, they wouldn't be in good standing with the record label, which would surely affect the possibility of ever getting another contract with Decca or any other label. Jerry and Norman were engaged in frequent phone conferences regarding this issue; finally, Norman told Jerry, "Get prepared to go to New York."

When Jerry had told Buddy to go on to New York and be Buddy Holly, and that he would stay in Texas and be The Crickets, he never dreamed Buddy would hire anyone else and call them The Crickets, too. As time passed, we learned more about how this new group had been formed.

Buddy had hired his new band while he was in Lubbock at Christmastime. He'd hired Waylon first, and on the day before he flew back to New York, he left Maria in Lubbock and drove with Ray Rush to Odessa so he could ask Tommy Allsup, who was playing at the Silver Saddle Club, to join the group. In fact, while at the Silver Saddle, Buddy had taken off his glasses so no one would recognize him and had filled in when Tommy's drummer didn't show up on time.

That night, Tommy suggested that Buddy hire Carl Bunch as the drummer for the tour. Buddy had heard Carl play with Ronnie Smith and the Poor Boys once at Norman Petty's studio, and he had been quite impressed. Only seventeen and still in high school, Carl immediately dropped out of school for what he considered a once-in-a-lifetime opportunity.

Several times a day Jerry would complain about the new Crickets. One day when he was groaning, "How can they call themselves Buddy's Crickets? They didn't even come to his funeral," I said, "Jerry..."

He glared at me and stated venomously, "I said don't ever call me that again!"

"Okay," I replied, returning his look.

"And another thing, Peggy Sue," he declared, "we're moving back to Lubbock."

"Oh, really? And where in Lubbock would that be? With your mother and father?" I asked sarcastically.

"I've talked to my parents, and they want to buy the house next door to them. We can rent it then. I have five-thousand dollars I can loan to my parents, which they'll pay back. We can pay them rent, and everything will be just swell."

"So, you're loaning them money to buy the house, and then you're going to pay them rent for living in the house so that you can be paid back. Is that right?" I asked, mystified by his logic.

"Yep. I think you've got it," he said with a self-satisfied smile.

I closed my eyes tightly, took a deep breath, and let it out slowly as my head bowed to my chest. If only *you had it*, JI, I thought, shaking my head in disbelief. I knew there was no way he'd let me explain the fallacy of what made perfect sense to him. I'd have to try another way to discourage him from this fiasco, so I said, "I really hate to tell you this, but I don't want to live in that old house."

"Mother said you can paint it and fix it up any way you want," he said, as if that would solve everything.

I lashed out, "I don't want to live next door to your parents. In fact, I don't want to live with you!"

"Now, Peggy, you're not trying to get along," he said condescendingly.

Once again, Jerry—correction, JI—would get his own way. There was never any discussion—it was always his way or my fault.

I didn't want to leave Clovis and what few friends I'd made. Undoubtedly, I would miss Vi and her silly little dog that thought he was guarding her, Norma Jean, Robert, and David. Robert and David wouldn't be around as much though because, now that they had a record contract, they'd be busy in the studio and touring. Maybe they'd rise to the top, too, just like Buddy had.

In Lubbock, I wouldn't have any friends. Everything would be focused around JI's parents and JI's needs. Also, I could forget about having any thoughts of my own because I'd never be permitted to express them. My role was strictly that of the dutiful wife. For me, living so close to JI's parents would be like living under lock and key, while the Allisons could continue to live however they pleased.

♫

Norman set up a meeting at the GAC office in New York with Irving Feld, Decca, Maria Elena, and the new Crickets. Since Sonny Curtis and Earl Sinks were part of JI's Crickets, they, along with Joe B, were going to go with us. While we were waiting for Sonny to drive in from Meadow, Texas, JI and I went to say goodbye to Mr. and Mrs. Holley and tell them that we were on our way to New York.

Mrs. Holley put her arms around me and spoke quietly into my ear, "We need to talk more when you have some time to spend with me."

"I know we do, and I'll make the time," I whispered back. "We'll be back in Lubbock soon."

We waved goodbye and drove back to the Allisons'.

♫

The drive from Lubbock to New York was very long, and the comfort level had almost reached unbearable by the time we neared New York State. I was sitting, smushed and bored, in the middle of the back seat. All the guys talked about was Cricket business, and since it seemed that neither my opinion nor I really mattered, I'd spent the entire trip sitting quietly, lost in my own thoughts. I'd never driven through this part of the United States before, and I really was enjoying the scenery.

Looking out the windshield, I transfigured the hood ornament into a replica of myself. Here I was away from the others, leaning forward in eager anticipation of what was ahead, the wind blowing through my hair, and nothing around me but the terrific view—What? I sat up straight, my eyes wide open. We'd arrived at the Lincoln tunnel.

Suddenly, I wanted to become the most miniscule object in the world, hidden in the back somewhere, far away from all those cars darting in and out. I really thought that we could all die in such traffic. Thank goodness that Joe B was driving because he was probably the best driver in the group.

Joe B asked calmly, "Where are we staying?"

"Go to the Forrest Hotel. We need to save all the money we can," JI said.

"That's right off Tin Pan Alley, isn't it?" Joe B asked.

"Yeah," JI replied, without taking his eyes off the highway as we dodged the traffic.

When we arrived at the Forrest, Joe B let us out at the entrance, and JI checked us in as Sonny and the bellman handled the luggage.

"I'll go find a parking place for the station wagon and then meet up with you later," Joe B said.

We took the elevator up to about the third floor and found our rooms. The hotel was really old and in desperate need of new paint and carpet. JI had rented a suite with one bedroom and another large room with a daybed, chair, and TV. It was a perfect setup for business meetings. That room attached, via a locked entrance, to another bedroom where Earl and Joe B would be staying. Sonny's room was somewhere down the hall.

The next day, JI and Joe B planned to meet with Maria and Norman at her attorney's office. Sonny and Earl decided to get a feel for the situation before making an appearance.

As we were unpacking our suitcases, I turned to JI and said, "Let me go to this meeting with you."

Out of his mouth came the most obnoxious "No!" I'd ever heard.

"Please, JI, let me go."

"This is a very important meeting, and the only people who can be there are those involved in the business," he said.

"What do you think I am?"

"I make the decisions in this family, and you'll abide by them. If it's the wrong decision, then I have no one but myself to blame," he said.

"I hope you remember later that you, and you alone, are to blame," I said. "The only thing wrong with you making all the decisions is Joe B and I will have to live with them, too. Could you give me some money so I have some in my pocket to at least buy a Coke?"

"They don't have room service here. You have to go out to eat," he said.

"Well, I'll still need some money," I reminded him.

"Okay. Okay. I'll try to get you some when I go to the meeting," he grumbled.

The next morning, JI and Joe B left to meet with Norman and face Maria and her attorneys. By cocktail time, I still hadn't heard from anyone. I had no money and I wasn't about to go out on the streets of New York alone when I didn't even know where I was.

I heard a knock at my door and called, "Who is it?"

"It's Sonny. Would you mind if I come in?"

"Just a minute. Let me unlock the door. I'd forgotten about you not going to the meeting. I'm glad you came. Where's Earl?" I asked.

"I think he said something about a movie," Sonny said.

As usual, he had his guitar with him; he took it everywhere he went. He was always writing a song.

Sonny asked, "Have you heard anything from JI?"

"Nope. I haven't."

"Well, that surely has been a long meeting, hasn't it?"

"Seems to me like it has been. Would you like to change the TV station? That's all there is to do. I just love all the different stations you can get here. I'll watch anything you want to watch," I said.

It was dark now, and I'd gone all day without eating. The more I thought about not having any money to buy a Coke, the more I wanted one. I wondered why the meeting was lasting so long and was really getting anxious to hear from JI. I could tell that Sonny was on pins and needles, too. Finally, the phone rang.

"Hi. I just wanted you to know that Joe B, Maria and I are going out to dinner," JI said cheerfully.

"Do you want me to meet you?" I asked.

"Oh, no. It's a business dinner," he quickly added.

"I see. How long do you think your meeting will last?"

"Wow...I just couldn't say. I'll get back to the hotel as soon as I can, but it probably won't be early," he hedged.

"I haven't had anything to eat all day, JI."

"Well, this is important, Peggy Sue. I'll be in later," he said insolently.

"I guess I'll talk to you later then," I said, banging the receiver down onto the hook.

Almost sheepishly, Sonny asked, "Did JI say what happened?"

"No," I said despondently.

243

"Hey. How would you like to go get something to eat?" he asked, with a smile.

"Thanks, Sonny, but I have no money on me."

"You know what? I have enough to buy us a sandwich and probably a Coke. Do you like hot pastrami sandwiches?"

"I love them."

In only a few minutes, Sonny returned to the room and said, "I got us two Cokes, but I only had enough money for one sandwich. Wanna share?"

I could have kissed the man. From that moment on, Sonny Curtis was *my* friend.

After our *picnic* in the Forrest Hotel, Sonny picked up his guitar and asked, "Have you heard this song, Peggy Sue?"

He strummed his fingers up and down the fretboard, tuned the guitar, and then started singing "If you want to get in trouble, I can tell you how to do it. Just buy you a guitar and then you're in to it."

I started to laugh, and suddenly, I remembered that I hadn't laughed in what seemed like a lifetime.

Around ten o'clock, Sonny said, "I think I'll go back to my room, but if JI comes in, have him give me a ring."

"I sure will, and thanks for sharing your hot pastrami with me."

I watched TV until midnight but still no JI. Finally, I went to bed. Somewhere between two and three o'clock, JI came back to the hotel.

"That was really some business dinner all of you had," I scoffed.

"Yes, but *I* own The Crickets," Jerry said proudly.

"What do you mean?"

"I gave the Holley Estate forty percent of my royalties on 'Peggy Sue.' They'll take my name off of the song and put Buddy's on it, since he wrote it. I didn't."

"So you paid for the The Crickets name by giving up your ownership of the song?"

"Yes, I did."

"Don't you think that was a lot of money to pay? After all, the royalties will keep coming in."

He rolled his eyes at me as if I were completely incapable of understanding anything in the business world and said, "It's The Crickets name that's the moneymaker, Peggy Sue. We've had more hits under that name than Buddy Holly has. Buddy's only had two records with just his name on it. There still seems to be some confusion over who The Crickets really are. Everybody knows it's me, Joe B and Buddy Holly, not the guys who were on the road with Buddy. We'll have another meeting to see what to do about them."

I wondered how JI thought that he and Joe B, a drummer and a bass player, could be The Crickets by themselves. They didn't even sing backup. In my opinion, without Buddy Holly, The Crickets couldn't exist.

"Oh. You should know that Maria wants you to spend the night with her. I told her that would be fine. That you could do that."

"Does it ever occur to you to let me answer for myself?" I asked. Spend the night with her? Even *seeing* Maria was just about the last thing I wanted to do in New York City.

"No, I guess it doesn't," he smarted.

"Did you bring me any money?"

"I'll get some tomorrow."

♫

A little after noon, JI, Sonny, and Joe B left for meetings at GAC with Norman, Decca, and Buddy's Crickets. Regrettably, I was on my way to meet Maria. For the life of me, I had no idea why she would want me to spend the night with her after the way she had acted the day of Buddy's funeral.

Just as we stepped out of the hotel elevator, my thoughts were interrupted by a loud voice booming, "Joe B, my man!" I immediately recognized the smiling, wide-eyed source of the jovial greeting as Little Richard. I couldn't help but smile. He looked so cute with that platinum curl pinned right in front on his forehead and the way his whole body moved like he was ready to dance. After a few minutes of friendly chatter, he and his band picked up their luggage and left the Forrest. JI put me into a taxi, and I was off to Maria's apartment.

I dreaded every minute the taxi's wheels brought me closer to Maria. I'd never wanted to talk to her again, but here I was, doing what I was told to do, going over to Maria's to spend the afternoon and night with her. I wasn't sure how I would react if she started one of her outbursts again. Before I was ready, the taxi pulled up at her apartment, not too far from the Village.

She was very hospitable. Soon after I got my things settled, she said, "I'm trying to sublet the apartment where Buddy and I lived at 11 5th Avenue. I need to go over there and pick up something. Would you mind?"

"No, certainly not," I said.

We entered the Brevoort Apartments complex through the garage and went into the building from the back. As we walked down the dark hall, I noticed the laundry room and thought what a dreary place to have to do your laundry. We got into the elevator and went to the fourth floor.

"Here we are," said Maria. "Our apartment is right on the end. We even had a balcony off the bedroom. It was such a nice apartment, and I special ordered wonderful furniture for it."

"Oh," I said. "Where's the furniture?"

"I sent it back because I could not keep this apartment after Buddy died, and the furniture would not fit in my smaller apartment. You know I have a job, don't you?"

"No, I didn't. Where are you working?"

"I have a job at the Puerto Rican Embassy."

"That should be nice for you, Maria."

"Oh, it is. I have met someone I like already. He is with the Embassy."

I couldn't say a word, but my heart was silently shouting, "Yeah, she really misses Buddy a lot, doesn't she? A proper time of mourning hasn't even passed yet. She didn't even see him put into the grave, and here she is interested in someone else already."

Maria opened the door to the empty apartment. There was a small tiled entryway and then the rest of the apartment was carpeted except for the kitchen. The dining area and kitchen ran together. Between the kitchen and living room was a half wall so you could cook and talk to your guests simultaneously. Buddy's reel-to-reel recorder, his guitar with the red flowers on it, and the amplifier that he'd brought from Clovis were sitting in the empty dining room.

Maria said, "Listen to these songs that Buddy wrote," as she turned on the recorder.

I sat down on the carpet so I could listen. First, Buddy and Maria were talking and giggling on the tape, saying something like..."Jack...Jack Neghren...the one I told you...he's an old man...fifty something..." Maria said.

"You can talk in a normal voice," I heard Buddy say.

The chopped-up conversation continued. "...I axe you...I axe you, are you going to play this when Tina comes back?...Are you playing this when Tina comes back?...It's terrible...and Anna...hello...hello...uno, dos, tres, cuatro, cinco, seis, siete, ocho, nueve, diez." Then Buddy started to sing "That's What They Say." Next came "What To Do."

When the third song began, I absolutely thought I would die. It was as if my body had forgotten how to breathe when I heard the words, "Peggy Sue got married not long ago." Tears came to my eyes, and I noticed Maria watching me as she walked in and out of the room, going into the bedroom and checking the mail. I didn't want to reveal my emotions in front of her, so I forced back my tears and swallowed my cries. I was so stunned. Why hadn't he told me? A couple of tears trickled unbidden down my cheek, and my head started booming.

The next song was "That Makes It Tough," and then there was a blues song called "Crying, Waiting, Hoping." The last song on the reel was "Learning the Game."

Maria reached down and turned the recorder off. She made no comment at all except to say simply, "I thought you'd like to hear them." Then, very coldly, she said, "Let's go find something to eat and get out of here."

"Yes, of course, let's," I replied quickly.

I didn't discuss the music with Maria. After we left the apartment, she seemed oblivious to it. She was all atwitter over her new apartment and her new life. But I couldn't forget what I'd heard. In my heart, I believed that Buddy had left the music on purpose so there'd be no forgetting...ever.

Maria and I shopped the rest of the day. I bought a great new dress and a leather Village handmade *pocketbook*. JI had finally given me some money before we'd left the Forrest. I kept thinking, though, that he'd probably never give me any more after this shopping spree.

Maria still was in the habit of trying to talk as we walked, which meant that between her strong accent and the street noise, I had trouble following her conversation. It seemed she was trying to confide in me, but I didn't understand why she'd picked me to be the one to listen to her or what she thought she would gain by talking to me. By the time I left the next morning, there was one thing I was absolutely sure about. Maria had made it quite clear that she would never have tied Buddy down with what she referred to as *a snotty-nosed kid* because his career was the most important thing. And, had he lived, Maria would have made sure that when Buddy walked down the street, everybody would have known who he was. *She* would've made him a star. *She* would've done all this. *She*...I looked her straight in the eyes and said, "Buddy Holly was already a star, Maria Elena, and he will always be one." I couldn't wait until I could say goodbye, and just maybe, if I were lucky, I'd never have to be around her again.

As soon as I met back up with JI, I told him about the wonderful songs that Buddy had written, that one of them was "Peggy Sue Got Married," and that they'd been recorded on the Ampex. "They're just great, JI," I bubbled.

"Don't go making anything out of that song. It's only a follow-up to his hit 'Peggy Sue.'"

How could he be so cold? He hadn't even heard any of the songs yet.

"Why can't you take those songs in and record with them? They could be Buddy Holly and The Crickets, couldn't they? Then they would be out and..."

"They're none of my business," he snapped. Then he continued, "We're leaving in the morning. We got The Crickets name settled. Me and Joe B told them that Buddy had given us the name, and Norman said he was ready to sue anybody else that tried to call themselves The Crickets. I think Sonny was pretty upset because GAC said they would recognize us and Waylon, but not him. The other guys made it real clear that they still wanted to be The Crickets and thought they had a right to be because Buddy had hired them for that tour. Tommy said Buddy had talked to him about all the problems he was having with everybody, and that he'd gone on three tours with Buddy, so he felt that he was a Cricket. But, they all backed down when talk about a lawsuit came up.

"We kinda made a deal with them. They can do some recording in Coral under another name if they don't go to court with us. I think they realized they were beat. They took the deal. They knew Maria was backing us. They were pretty upset though. Waylon just seemed to want to go his own way now, but Tommy, he's anxious to keep going. He's going to use the name The Jitters instead of The Crickets from now on.

"I don't know. It sounds like they really had some problems on the road. They haven't gotten paid yet. GAC told them they'd get Buddy's share of the money if they continued the tour and that they'd fly them to Buddy's funeral, but neither one happened. They have really been having problems collecting their money. GAC told them that they gave the money to Maria Elena and that the band was supposed to collect it from her. Of course, she told 'em that she hadn't gotten it. They're broke. The drummer, Carl Bunch, had to go into the hospital for frostbite because their bus kept breaking down, and Tommy paid all the money for the hospital and Carl's airfare to rejoin them when he got out. They can't afford to fight a lawsuit. They have no money for a lawyer. But, we're cool. I'm gonna let them drive back with us and use our Diner's card to get them home."

So, the next morning, JI, Joe B, Earl, Tommy, and I piled into one car, while Waylon, Sonny, Carl Bunch, and Ronnie Smith got into another. In no time, we were all on our way back to Lubbock, Texas, and I could hardly wait to get there...even if I had to live next door to JI's parents...paying rent for a rent house we had purchased.

The trip back turned out to be anything but a smooth ride. JI had no money on him. He'd gotten one of the new Diner's Club credit cards and planned to use it, so he didn't bring any cash with him for the return trip. Oh, we could use the card all right, but not all restaurants took the Diner's card. In fact, not all states honored it. So, throughout the entire trip, we remained on the lookout for states and restaurants that would honor the card—without it, the nine of us couldn't eat. I honestly believed we might starve to death before we made it to Lubbock, but we didn't.

♪

In New York, Maria didn't say anything to me about Norman or what she was going to do to him because he had *killed Buddy*, but she did keep her promise to have him audited until he couldn't stand it any longer. Soon after we returned to Lubbock, the auditors arrived, and apparently, they were following her wishes to the letter. They came in pairs—in black suits. After about a week, one pair would leave, and a new pair would arrive. No one at the studio was smiling, and no one was talking.

JI should've just kept the apartment in Clovis. Since the studio was still where most of the musicians in the area gathered, we were always there, too. Of course, I was eager to go every chance I got so I could visit with my dear friends. When the auditors were around, I simply went to the back of the studio so I wouldn't disturb anyone, but Norma Jean would always raise her finger to her lips anyway as if to warn me not to even *think* about speaking.

Although JI really wasn't at odds with Norman, he wasn't very happy with him either. He was upset because he wasn't working, and he was still holding a grudge over what he perceived to be Norman's callous attitude toward Buddy's death. However, Norman didn't have time to deal with JI's wants or his attitude. The auditors were keeping him so busy that he didn't have time to record or schedule gigs for The Crickets or anybody else for that matter.

Finally, after what seemed like an eternity, Norman announced that the black suits had completed their audit—unless Maria decided to send some more; but, for now, these auditors were satisfied, and there'd be no more auditing. I wasn't surprised that they hadn't found anything illegal or improper with Norman Petty's accounting. Norman always conducted his business in a professional manner, and Norma Jean pretty much served as his right hand.

Maria continued to claim that Buddy would never have gone on that fatal tour except that *Norman* was keeping his record royalties from him, and *they* had needed money. I wondered if Maria had needed more panties. Also, if she'd known they were so broke, why had she ordered all that new furniture for the apartment?

I understood enough about what had happened with the royalties to know that Norman hadn't withheld anything just to be mean to Buddy or to teach him a lesson. JI wasn't given his share either. True, the royalties went through Norman, but he couldn't pay out what he hadn't yet received.

In New York, Buddy had made a West Texas good ol' boy handshake deal with a promoter named Manny Greenfield. According to the agreement, Manny would receive a small percentage of any bookings he'd make for the band. When the time came to pay up, Manny said the deal was for a lot more money than Buddy offered to pay him because he was acting as Buddy's manager at the time. Buddy said that hadn't been the deal and that Manny had never been his manager. He refused to pay Manny for what Manny claimed he deserved and Manny, in turn, sued Buddy for the money. Unfortunately, the Texans weren't familiar with New York law. When a lawsuit originated in New York, any money owed to the writer or artist *in New York* could be legally attached until the dispute was settled. As a result, Manny had all the royalty revenues coming out of New York frozen until his claim could be settled.

Another problem arose when Buddy filed to get the song credits straightened out and his name on "Peggy Sue." Buddy's New York entertainment lawyer, Harold Orenstein, told Norman that The Crickets' assets had to be frozen until all the song credits and royalty percentages were settled—they had to know who would receive what before any more money could be paid. Consequently, the lawyers had tied Norman's hands. Norman said he'd tried to explain to Buddy that there was going to be a delay in receiving funds, but either Buddy didn't listen to what he was trying to tell him or just didn't think it was important at the time. Buddy was an artist and he was young, and because he was an artist and not a businessman, he didn't understand the detailed intricacies of the deals he was making. On the other hand, New Yorkers were accustomed to dealing in such business matters and went by the book instead of the handshake. It hadn't even occurred to Buddy to worry about whether the money was coming in. As usual, he was operating on automatic, always assuming that the money would be there because it always had been before. However, when it wasn't, Norman suffered the blame. After all, Norman was the one who had always given Buddy his money in the past. Considering the way Maria had reacted in the car, in Norman's office, and on the day of Buddy's funeral, I couldn't help but feel that she hadn't helped the situation at all. She claimed that she was knowledgeable and was going to make Buddy a star. But, what knowledge did she have to make that happen? She'd only worked at Southern Music a short while...and that was filling in as a receptionist when someone else had quit.

Once the auditing was finished and the lawsuits settled, the royalties, JI's included, started flowing in again.

♫

Question: If you pack four guys and one girl into a car, and then add all their luggage plus the instruments musicians just can't be without, what do you have? Answer: Four Crickets and one Peggy Sue on their way to New York City—again.

This time around, JI put us up at the Edison Hotel, where we'd stayed on my very first trip to New York. I was thrilled. I had room service, so I didn't have to worry about JI not giving me any money for food, plus I had a TV with a huge selection of nonstop movie channels. In Lubbock, we still only had three channels, and they were all local and network. I was in TV heaven.

JI let me accompany them to their first recording session on May 18. I wasn't impressed with the studio; it was a dark, ugly, dirty little thing called Bell Sound on West 54th Street. After that first day, I decided I'd rather stay in my comfy hotel room.

About the best thing that came out of the sessions was a song Sonny wrote called "I Fought the Law."

"I've really been working, and this is all I've come up with," Sonny said apologetically.

JI looked at the song and exclaimed, "Man, that's a great song!"

I loved it, too.

♫

It wasn't a great time for the West Texas Crickets. Tommy Allsup's The Jitters hadn't gone anywhere with their music, so they'd already broken up. Tommy was out playing gigs wherever he could, Carl Bunch and Ronnie Smith were working together, and Waylon Jennings had become so disheartened with the whole thing that he'd begun working as a DJ in Lubbock, just doing a little music on the side.

JI had come home from New York terribly depressed. It had been well over six months since the break with Buddy, and his Crickets hadn't even been on one tour. Disappointed in Norman's leadership, JI decided to sever The Crickets' management contract with him and take care of business himself.

Oh, JI, I thought. You've never been a leader. Is your mother still going to be your financial advisor? You haven't even learned to take care of your own finances; how are you going to take care of an entire group's? I hoped things wouldn't become too much worse than they already were.

Even though we lived next door to JI's parents, he might as well have moved in with them. As I'd expected he'd do when we moved back to Lubbock, he stayed at their house almost all the time...that is, when he wasn't out with the guys...or maybe someone else I didn't know about. When he was home, he usually moped around with a forlorn look and complained about everything under the sun.

I'll always be grateful to Phil and Don Everly for the day they called and asked him to come to Nashville for one of their sessions. They had two great songs called "Till I Kissed You" and "Cathy's Clown" that they wanted to record, but they wanted something different on the drums this time, something like Buddy always had. With JI gone, I'd finally have the freedom to go a few places I wanted to go.

I went out to the cemetery to see the simple, flat marker Mrs. Holley had picked for Buddy's grave. At first glance, I thought it was made of cement, but as I looked closer, I noticed it was gray marble. When she'd been asked about picking out the resting plot for Buddy, she'd replied, "What's important is going to heaven, not the grave," and I thought this marker perfectly reflected her words.

Next, I went to visit Mrs. Holley. Until now, I hadn't had the opportunity to visit her alone so we could have our heart-to-heart talk. She was happy to see me and, as always, had a smile on her face. Also, she was happy to hear that JI was in Nashville recording with Phil and Don.

"That's good for him," she said, nodding her head approvingly.

"We saw Maria when we were in New York. Did she tell you?" I asked.

"Oh, yes. She told me," Mrs. Holley said. "How did she look?"

"Great, as always, and she has a job at the Puerto Rican Embassy."

"Oh, I didn't know that," she said.

"Mrs. Holley, did you know that I came over the day of Buddy's funeral to see if Maria needed anything?" I asked.

"No. She didn't tell me."

"When I realized she wasn't at the church with the rest of the family, I left and went back to your house. Maria was dressed in white and packing to go to the airport."

"I know, my dear. I can't explain her behavior, but I have something I want to tell you. Buddy wrote a song called 'Peggy Sue Got Married.' It was supposed to be a surprise for you when he came home for Christmas, but then everything got so confusing. He took me for a ride, just the two of us, so we could talk. Buddy was getting a divorce, Peggy Sue."

I let out a huge sigh of relief, and said, "I know, Mrs. Holley. He told me that he had hired two attorneys. One for the divorce and one to straighten out his song credits."

"I'm so glad he told you, my dear," Mrs. Holley said. "Buddy thought you were so special. I'm just so glad he told you."

"Oh, Mrs. Holley, I'm so glad he told you, too. I was afraid that I might be the only one who knew," I exclaimed.

"While he was here, he talked about the studio he planned to build in Lubbock, too. Remember? He surprised me with those plans on his birthday. Decca had told him they would help finance it. He planned to live in New York for two years and learn everything he could about the music business, and then he would be ready to open his own recording studio," Mrs. Holley informed me.

"I knew about the studio, but I didn't know when he planned to have it open. I'd better go, Mrs. Holley. I'll try to come back when we can visit longer," I said.

"You tell Jerry to come by so we can talk. Buddy was so hurt by the breakup, and I know Jerry was, too. But, any time he feels like it, he's welcome."

As I drove away, I thought, how great to be that kind of mother. Mrs. Holley was so supportive of her children and had such a loving nature.

When JI returned home, his spirits seemed a little better.

"How was it playing with Phil and Don?" I asked.

"Just swell, Peggy Suuuu," he joked.

"Was it anything like playing with Buddy?" I inquired.

JI's voice lowered, and he said, "No, and it never will be. There's no feeling that can ever come close to playing with Bud."

Sadness overwhelmed him. He cleared his throat as he hung on the refrigerator door.

♫

Chapter Twenty-two
California Calling

*N*ow that JI had accepted full responsibility for making The Crickets a success, he had some important decisions to make, the biggest being where he would record. He didn't feel comfortable going back to the Norman Petty Studio after just severing management with Norman, so that left him with two options: New York and Los Angeles. JI heard Hollywood calling his name louder and louder each day.

The label was in New York, but JI hated that city with a passion. Besides, everybody in the recording business in New York knew Buddy Holly, which meant establishing The Crickets' identity as a group detached from Buddy would be more difficult than in Los Angeles, where neither Buddy nor The Crickets had previously recorded. Also in the plus column for California, the Everly Brothers had received a new record contract for a million dollars. Artists, hoping success would breed success, always wanted to be where the stars were. That's why so many musicians had flocked to the Norman Petty Studio and to New York. At this time in music production, it looked like California was *the* place to be. Ultimately, though, the most influential factor in JI's decision to go to Hollywood was Liberty Records' ambitious A&R (Artist & Repertoire) man, Snuff Garrett.

Snuffy started out in radio in Wichita Falls, Texas, but he decided he wanted to produce records, so he went to California, got a job with Liberty, and began working with some of the leading artists of the day—including Gene McDaniels, Eddie Cochran, and the young Bobby Vee. Bobby was the Bobby Velline who had burst into fame in Moorhead, Wisconsin, and played with his group, The Shadows, the night Buddy, Ritchie, and the Big Bopper died. Snuffy, a big follower and friend of Buddy Holly and The Crickets, was anxious to sign The Crickets with Liberty, as he believed it would boost his own career.

JI, Sonny, and Joe B went to Los Angeles to talk to Snuffy and to "get a feel for the place," as they were constantly saying. In the end, they signed with Snuff, rented a house in the Hollywood Hills, and began looking for a lead singer. Several months later, JI came back to Lubbock to get me. He rented an apartment on Larrabee Street between west Hollywood and Sunset Strip, and we began decorating—ultramodern, Hollywood style in blacks and whites. I could hardly believe it. We were actually enjoying each other's company as we decorated together. Maybe the move to California was just what our marriage had needed.

♪

I adored LA. The weather was always beautiful and everything was so clean—and there was no West Texas sand to deal with. About three blocks south of our apartment was restaurant row on North La Cienega Blvd. My most favorite restaurant, however, was a place called Hamburger Hamlet on Sunset. I loved sitting on their veranda as I ate lobster bisque (Oh, it was to die for!) and seeing Susanne Pleshette and Troy Donohue or some other famous person walk in for lunch. It was easy to get caught up in Hollywood's magical feeling.

Everybody was an actor, photographer, model, dancer, or screenwriter—even though they'd made no movies yet. JI, being a professional musician, fit right in with that crowd as they were constantly looking for connections. From the waitress to the paperboy, they were always *camera ready*—just in case they met the right person. Female realtors wore their hair backcombed four inches atop their head, and guys would walk down the street carrying reflectors just to get that all-perfect tan on their faces.

Most of the men in the music business, including The Crickets, kept their hair coiffured at Sebring's. The really cool ones made an appointment with Jay Sebring himself, who, I might add, did have the best haircut in town.

There was also the real side to La-La-Land, where nothing was real. One night we'd be invited to a record executive's home, where his wife played the role of hostess, and we'd play charades with three other couples—everything appeared normal. However, the next night, we would run into the same man with his *girlfriend,* and then the following night, we would run into the girlfriend and discover that she was married to a record-label owner or a publisher.

Next, there was the side of Hollywood that was not pretty at all, or fun—rather, it was dirty and sleazy. Walking down the street, we would see the actress who had not made the limelight, had run out of money, and had turned to whatever was available to her to make a living. Or, we'd encounter the old actor, dressed in a frayed, dirty costume from bygone days, stumbling down the sidewalk into an alley to spend the night. I also discovered that the later it became in Hollywood, Beverly Hills, and Studio City, the weirder it became. The streets would fill with characters right out of a pretend, circus world.

I learned another hard lesson about Hollywood, too. I thought of myself as just an ordinary girl from Lubbock, Texas, and I always believed if I was nice to people, they'd be nice to me in return. Not true. Coming to Hollywood with a title like "Peggy Sue" made me a trophy, and almost everybody around me wanted something. Most saw me as their next step to a recording contract—by getting close to me, they could get close to JI, who just might get them close to somebody who would make them a hit. But, the worst part was being made to feel that I was in competition with every one of these young starlets, or was that just plain bad manners on my husband's part?

JI criticized my hair for not ever being the right style or length, my clothes for not fitting tight enough, me for not wearing makeup or not applying it properly, and, worst of all, my speech. He corrected almost every word I said, saying that I didn't know how to enunciate my words. I thought, Oh, now this really makes me want to carry on a conversation with you, JI. I'd give him the silent treatment, and then, he'd come back with, "Why are you so bashful? Are you just ignorant?"

I wondered what else he expected from a *middle-class* wife.

♫

JI was received extremely well as a session player due to his love for playing games and his connections with Snuff Garrett. He was a hit at all the Hollywood gin parties—a real people person. However, his being a session player didn't get The Crickets before an audience, and he was constantly complaining about not being a real musician anymore. As far as I could see, there was nothing wrong with being just a session player. That's what Glen Campbell was, and it looked to me like he and his wife had a great lifestyle. Besides, in my opinion, playing that many sessions honed a musician's talent and his ability to create music. But, of course, JI didn't agree with me.

I was shocked when he hired Danny Whitman from Dallas, Texas, as The Crickets' new personal manager. The way he'd complained about managers before he broke things off with Norman Petty made me think he'd never use another one. I guess he saw things differently now that he'd made himself responsible for the success of The Crickets, who still didn't have a lead singer, and who still weren't touring.

JI decided to bring David Box from Lubbock to Hollywood to do a session with The Crickets. David played with a high-school group called The Ravens, organized by Ernie Hall, who lived across the street from the Allisons and had grown up watching JI perform. Because Ernie and David were only teenagers, Mr. and Mrs. Allison drove them to Hollywood. They were just three years younger than I was, but they made me feel much older because they always said "Yes, ma'am" and "No, ma'am" to me. David looked like the perfect Hollywood actor. All he needed was a tan to go with that natural wisp of blonde hair hanging on his forehead, his big eyes, and the long eyelashes that accentuated his personality.

On August 11, 1960, David had a seventeenth birthday he'd never forget. He and The Crickets recorded "Peggy Sue Got Married" and "Don't Cha Know," and then they all came back to the apartment for a birthday swim party, complete with a birthday cake. His parents and little sister, Rita, were there. They had come to drive the boys home.

I was elated that JI had chosen to record "Peggy Sue Got Married," and when I heard the demo for the first time, I almost got chills. I couldn't believe how much David sounded like Buddy. JI wanted to sign David on as the permanent singer for The Crickets, but there was one little hitch—his parents wanted him to return to Lubbock to finish high school. So, the search resumed.

Gil Turner's Liquor Store and Deli wasn't far from our apartment on Larrabee. It was the only deli around where the proprietor would allow his customers to run a tab for lunch everyday. This made it a fabulous hangout for musicians. Danny Whitman, JI's new manager, met a young songwriter named Jerry Naylor there. Jerry was writing for American Music Publishing Company, recording for Skyla Records, and working for KRLA radio. American Music Publishing's offices were right across the street from Whitman's office on Sunset. Mr. Whitman thought Jerry had the look of an entertainer, and after learning about his experience in radio and performing at live shows, he encouraged him to talk to JI about being the singer and front man for The Crickets.

Talk about synchronicity. Jerry Naylor was from San Angelo, Texas. Before his mother died from cancer in 1955, she made arrangements with Joe and Tille Treadway to give her sixteen-year-old son a home. Joe Treadway co-owned San Angelo radio station KPEP, the sister station to KDAV in Lubbock where Buddy Holly and Bob Montgomery did their "Sunday Party" radio program. Joe took Jerry under his wing and taught him all about the radio business. Besides letting him DJ, Joe took Jerry on his business trips to Lubbock, too, and there, Jerry became acquainted with Buddy Holly. Now, in 1960, Jerry Naylor was the front man for The Crickets.

There's a difference between putting on a *real* rock 'n' roll show and just being a rock 'n' roll band. A real rock 'n' roll show makes audience members want to move, to get out of their seats, to dance in the aisles, to share in the music. A good front man creates that atmosphere for a band to follow. Jerry Naylor was such an entertainer. He never stood still when he was on stage, and he captivated his audience as he danced around and sang. He truly had *the look* of an entertainer, too. He was cute, well coiffed, impeccably dressed, and had a great smile and tremendous personality. He never had a problem finding something to say. I was sure his radio experience had given him the gift of the silver tongue.

Mr. Cricket, JI, never seemed to like Jerry Naylor though because all he did was yell at him and berate him every chance he got. From firsthand experience, I knew how hard such verbal abuse was to take and wondered just how long it would be before Jerry Naylor would quit the band. We seemed to be the only two on the receiving end of JI's madness, and that started a friendship between us that I was sure would last the rest of my life.

♫

Not long after the session with David Box, JI brought a guest from Liberty Records home. He was dressed in jeans and boots and, naturally, was carrying a guitar. He sported an enormous amount of curly hair hanging down on his forehead. As he came through the doorway, he gave a huge smile and said, "So you're Peggy Sue? I'm Buddy Knox. I'm from Canyon, or Happy, Texas."

I started to laugh. He looked as if he should come from a place called Happy. He was a total doll.

His cheerful voice continued to make me smile all through dinner. He said he, Donnie Lanier, and Jimmy Bowen had met in college and put their group together, and since they had bought orchid stage shirts, they called themselves the Rhythm Orchids. They had spent three days recording in Clovis with Norman Petty. One of the songs they recorded was "Party Doll," which he had written. After a few records were pressed, they managed to get the attention of Morris Levy in New York, thanks to Tuddy, Donnie's cousin who was a shoe model and a personal friend of Morris Levy.

As he continued to talk, I thought, here we are in Hollywood, California, and almost everybody we're associated with has come from Texas. I was astounded by all the connections. Donnie Lanier was related to June Clark, who was supposed to have sung backup on "That'll Be The Day," however, she became ill and called her cousin Gary Tollett and his wife Ramona to fill in for her. The song they did turned out to be the one that launched The Crickets. And, then, there was Snuff Garrett, Jerry Naylor, and Danny Whitman. I wondered who'd be next to show up from Texas.

Buddy Knox, with his twinkling Santa Claus eyes, had not stopped a beat in telling his story. He said he'd just gotten out of the Army and that he and Elvis Presley had been together at Fort Hood. Anyway, he was out of the Army now, was a newlywed, and was trying to get himself organized to produce a new album and get back on the road.

JI told him about all the trouble he'd had getting The Crickets back on tour, and Buddy said he'd be glad to show him how to do it. JI could go with him on his next tour so he'd make connections and see firsthand how easy it was.

"Once you meet all these guys, you'll have no trouble booking dances," Buddy said.

JI asked, "How do you get paid when you're booking like that?"

Buddy said, "I put my wife, Glenda, at the door with a counter. The owner knows what we're doing. That way, there's no argument about what my share is. I get paid on the amount of people who attend. If it turns out to be slow, then I always make sure that my ballroom owner gets a little something. It'll be a big advantage for you to have Peggy Sue there. The people are going to love her. They are really nice to Glenda, but you have the real 'Peggy Sue.'"

JI just sort of laughed at that.

The thought flashed through my mind that this would be the first time JI had ever needed me to help him. I was very grateful to Buddy for taking the time to show him how to set up a tour. One would have thought the new manager would have already done this, or set the tours up for The Crickets himself, but I guess this wasn't his forte.

When JI got back from Buddy Knox's tour, he was not too excited about going out and doing one-night stands. He was moody and seldom home. Buddy Knox went to Macon, Georgia, to bring his wife back to Hollywood, and when he returned, I could see why he called her a Georgia peach. She was the perfect match for the man from Happy, Texas. If I had to pick a marriage that was going to last for all eternity, I would've picked theirs.

Glenda stood about 5'2." She had just the cutest little figure, and she dressed like a doll. When she talked to Buddy, her brown eyes sparkled, just like his, and she would refer to him as *Bubby*. Her thick southern drawl was absolutely charming. Indeed, she was truly a Southern belle.

Buddy and Glenda rented an apartment upstairs, and for the first time, I finally had a friend in LA. We shopped for her apartment and talked until we couldn't talk anymore. One day when we pulled into the garage after one of our shopping sprees, I hit the support column in the middle of the garage and scraped some of the chrome off JI's new Cadillac—which I frequently did. When I told Glenda that I would have to order some more new strips to replace the damaged ones before he noticed what I had done to *his* new car, she said, "Don't buy new parts. Let's go to the used-parts place and buy them. They're cheaper that way. I know from experience." She was right; they were a lot cheaper.

Before long, she and Buddy left for another tour, and I really missed her.

♪

JI was always moody, and when he was awake, he was either on the phone or getting ready to leave to go somewhere. He wasn't home much because he was really busy playing sessions—and that was a good thing. I was so bored, though, that I couldn't stand myself. I felt like I had a leash around my neck and could no longer breathe.

When we did have some time together, the silence was either deafening or JI would continually talk about himself, saying only if he *coulda, woulda*, or that he *shoulda* done such and such, then....Finally he'd look at me and say, "I'm tired of talking about me and what the real me wants. You talk, and tell me what you think about the real me."

I'd just roll my eyes, and the argument would really get heated. If I ever said anything about wanting to get a job or going back to school, he would just get livid, and rant and rave, saying, "You're 'Peggy Sue.' How would that look? Besides, when we go on one-night stands, you have to go with me."

After years of talking about divorce, in the spring of 1962 I finally got the courage to leave JI and went back to Texas. I managed to get a job at a dental office in Lubbock and planned to save up enough money to file for divorce. JI called every night, saying, "You need to think about this, Steve. You know you will come back."

Well, about a week after I began working, JI came to Lubbock, unannounced, and showed up at my job. I say unannounced, but I was the only one who didn't know he was coming. He had concocted another one of his plans. In front of all my co-workers, he asked, "Would you do me the honor of marrying me in the Catholic Church?"

Back when we'd married in Honey Grove, Texas, he'd promised to give me a Catholic marriage one day—well, here it was. *Everybody* thought this would give the marriage a new start, except for me. I felt trapped again since everyone was siding with JI and saying how hard he was trying to make our marriage work, so on April 4, 1962, Jerry Ivan Allison and Peggy

Sue Gerron, according to the right of the Roman Catholic Church and in conformity with the laws of the State of Texas, were married again.

♪

Click. Click. Another promotional picture of the new Crickets.

It took a while, but the fourth Cricket was finally added. And he was from—where else? Lubbock, Texas, of course. He was a young family man, named Glen D. Hardin, who could play the ivory off the piano keys. His wife had religious issues about being married to a musician and his playing in nightclubs, but, at JI's request, they moved to Hollywood, and Glen D. got a job playing at the Palomino Club as part of the house band. His new job built his confidence and sharpened his talent like a needle.

Click. Click. The photos of The Crickets changed depending on which young man was doing military duty at the time. Sonny and Joe B spent two years in the Army, and JI was in the Air Force Reserve. JI's periodic military obligations kept us driving in and out of Riverside, California, where he was stationed.

Although The Crickets had a hard time getting on the charts in the U. S. in the post-Holly days, the story was different in England. There, "Bobby Vee Meets The Crickets" became a number one album and "Please Don't Ever Change" became their first top-charted hit. JI was absolutely devastated when The Crickets got booked with Bobby Vee in England, Sweden, and Holland, and he couldn't go because of Uncle Sam. On that 1962 tour, The Crickets comprised Sonny Curtis, Jerry Naylor, and Glen D. Hardin; to replace JI, the bookers hired a man named Don Groom to play the drums. Bobby and The Crickets had a great tour and were received really well. While in London, they made an appearance in the movie, *Just for Fun.* I wasn't sure JI would live through not being in that movie.

Once his stint with Uncle Sam had ended, JI began setting up The Crickets for tours in the Midwest. This time, the group comprised Sonny Curtis, Jerry Naylor, Glen D. Hardin, JI, and Steve—me. I was thrilled to be a part of the group.

I was going to miss Joe B though. Things just hadn't been going well for him. He bought a nightclub, which he named after his sister LaRue, but it went broke; he lost custody of his baby girl when his first marriage ended in divorce; and he got stationed in Germany for his military service. For now, Glen D. was playing bass on a keyboard.

I loved the Midwest. I thought it was so romantic—probably because I'd always associated it with all the big bands that had played their ballrooms. I thought, *This* is where a musician learns to be an entertainer. But things didn't turn out as expected. The bookers seemed to intentionally book the towns at least three hundred miles apart. We'd drive all day, set up, play a four-hour dance, tear down, double-check the list so we wouldn't leave any equipment behind, settle up with the ballroom operator, get into the car, and drive another three hundred miles. Only if we were lucky, did we get to sleep in something that wasn't moving. And, when it's winter in the Midwest—oh, my! Is it ever cold!

On our way back to Los Angeles one time, we stopped somewhere in Utah for breakfast. We walked in—four guys and one girl, donning our black trench coats and large black sunglasses—sat down together in a large booth, and ordered breakfast. When the waitress came with the check, JI got up, put his briefcase full of money on the seat, opened it, and gave her enough money to cover the check plus a nice tip.

Just as we pulled back onto the highway, a local policeman turned on a siren and pulled us over. One cop walked up to the back of our car, while the other walked over to Glen D.'s door. Glen D. asked, "What did I do, Sir?"

The officer said, "You didn't do anything, but, to tell you the truth, the owner of the little restaurant said you had a suitcase full of money. I'd like to see your driver's license, young lady, since you're the only girl traveling with this group."

JI said, "That's my wife, Sir," with a tone of preponderance. "Our name is The Crickets, and I'm the owner of the group. We just finished a tour through the Midwest and are on our way back to Los Angeles."

As soon as I saw the officer look down at the ground and then back at us, I knew what he wanted, so, with a smile, I asked, "Would you like to see the case of money?"

His face lit up. "I've never seen a briefcase full of money before. Yes, I'd like to see it." JI hopped out of the car and opened the case. "I'll be doggone. It *is* full of money," the officer said. He laughed and then said, "Now you be careful driving, young man."

We laughed for the longest time after that.

♫

In 1963, we were living in a new, small duplex, which hung off the mountain in the Hollywood Hills. The whole back of the apartment was glass and the view was more entertaining than anything on TV. President Kennedy was frequently a guest of Peter Lawford, his brother-in-law, and Bobby Kennedy. I would hang off the large balcony and watch the President's motorcade pull into Paramount to pick up a guest, and then later, it would boggle my mind to read in our newspaper that JFK had come to LA to party and that he even tried LSD. The whole world was becoming submerged in the drug culture. To myself, I asked the newspaper reporters, Can you spell amphetamines and count all the different personalities one person can have from these drugs? I most certainly could. When it came to the drug culture, musicians were way ahead of everyone else.

Bored to death with my mundane life at the duplex, I kept hounding JI to help me learn to do something musical—play a guitar, sing—anything. Finally, one day, he said, "If you can give me a song title worth writing about, I'll show you how to write a song."

Well, I thought, I've heard it's good to write about something you know. Hum. Here I am in LA with no friends, no family, no job, and JI's mad at me most of the time. I feel so lost and alone...lost and alone. That's it! That's my song title. I even formed a little bit of the song's melody in my head.

When I told JI, he said, "Okay. Now, let's write the lyrics."

He helped me write the lyrics, and then we wrote the music for it. I was so proud of my song, but the first chance JI had to mention it, he obnoxiously announced in front of everyone, "If I had to write songs with Peggy Sue, we'd starve to death waiting for them—she's so slow," and everyone had laughed.

It made me proud as a peacock when Snuff Garrett put *my song* on an album. He'd been looking through The Crickets' music to find something to record for their upcoming session when he ran across "Lost and Alone," and as they say, the rest is history—Peggy Sue Allison became a published songwriter—well—co-writer.

♫

By the end of 1963, we were moving again, and the house we chose this time turned out to be haunted. I swear. There were cold spots that would come and go all over the house for absolutely no reason, and it wasn't uncommon for me to get a person-to-person call from London asking specifically for Peggy Sue. When I asked, "Who's calling?" the young man would reply, "Buddy Holly." The calls never came when JI was home, and, of course, I never accepted one, but I always wondered how London could know JI wasn't there every time the call came in.

JI was still touring and, at the same time, trying to get into TV or the movies, like everybody else in Hollywood. In the spring of 1964, we were on the road doing one-night stands in the Midwest again. The snow started to fall during our last engagement, and since we had only a few days to make it back to Hollywood because The Crickets were scheduled to be in a movie called *The Girls on the Beach*, JI decided he would charter an airplane for the flight home. I looked at him and said, "I'm not flying in a little plane in the snow. I'm not the one in the movie, so feel free to go. I'll come back later."

He changed his mind and made travel arrangements for us to take a train to Minneapolis and, then, catch a commercial plane to Los Angeles. When we got on the train and settled in, we couldn't find Sonny. After an extensive hunt, Jerry Naylor and Glen D. found him locked in the baggage car, freezing. I thought it was pretty funny, and we all laughed—even Sonny—after he quit shivering enough to laugh. It was a good thing he was such a good sport.

We barely got home in time for JI to change clothes and go to the movie set where the Beach Boys and Leslie Gore were waiting for The Crickets.

♫

JI was no longer even close to being the young man I'd married. He was either depressed or angry, and there was no getting along with him. Most of the time, I didn't feel as if I even knew who he was anymore.

One evening when he came home, I was cooking some double-baked potatoes with shrimp in them. He asked what I was doing and I replied, "I'm cooking dinner. We have company coming."

"Who?" he asked.

"Don Everly and his new wife. They'll be here around seven."

As I was putting the shrimp into a bowl to rinse them, I heard a *ping, ping* noise and saw all my cookbooks dancing across the cabinet, only inches from me. I whirled around and saw JI holding a gun.

"What are you doing?" I screamed. "Do you feel better now that you've murdered my cookbooks?"

I ran past him, avoiding eye contact, thinking I might be his next target.

"I'm sorry," he yelled. "I'll never do it again. I promise. Hey, by the way, Jerry Naylor had a heart attack today."

"Is he going to be okay?"

"Who knows? He's at St. John's Hospital in Santa Monica," he answered almost pleasantly. In a flash, his mood had changed.

The next day, I went to visit Naylor. We'd started calling him that because, even though JI didn't want to be called Jerry anymore, whenever he heard that name, he would usually look up or answer, and then he'd be irritated for a while.

Naylor looked like he only weighed a hundred pounds at the most. I knew as soon as I saw him that the tour and awful, rushed trip home to do the movie had been too much. The biggest problem with musicians like him was their use of uppers to stay awake during their drive to the next gig. Unfortunately, in Naylor's case, the amphetamines had caused possible, permanent heart damage.

There were two young ladies in the room, so I gave him a kiss, told him to call me if I could do anything, and I left. I knew it would be a long time before Jerry Naylor would be able to work again, and going on the road would not *even* be an option.

♫

By the fall of 1964, I'd pretty much had all this so-called *church* marriage that I could tolerate. Instead of bringing us closer together, it had made another wedge between us because JI used it to continually remind me of my religious responsibilities to the marriage. My brother-in-law was retiring after thirty years in the Air Force, and when my sister called to ask if I could help them move back to Lubbock, I jumped at the chance.

I could ride to Lubbock with them and file for a divorce once I got there. Little did I know what JI had in store for me once I got to Lubbock.

When we went into the house, JI was sitting on the sofa next to my Mother.

Mother said, "Sit down. I have something very important to tell you." We all sat down without saying a word, and then she announced, "JI wants to be baptized in the Catholic Church, and, Johnnie, I want you and Von to be his godparents. We have an appointment with the priest tomorrow so he can get baptized."

You could have knocked me over with a feather. "Did JI tell you, Mother, that I was coming home to file for a divorce?" I asked.

"Now in all fairness to JI, he told me everything he did, and he is so sorry. He's gone to confession and has been forgiven by God. You have to forgive JI, and then forget what he has done to you. Do you think you can do that?" she asked.

My dad had always been the one to make decisions and say, "Now, Lillie," if he thought she was wrong, but he had died from a heart attack the year before, and I had no one to argue my case. I looked at JI, sitting on the sofa next to my mother, impeccably dressed and sporting that Cheshire-cat smile of his. Instantly, I knew that, once again, he had won.

"What about your parents?" I asked. "Don't even try to tell me that they approve."

"They think we've been married long enough that I should know what I want," JI said.

Mother said, "Now, Peggy, all that's in the past. JI is going to buy you a home right here in Lubbock so you don't have to live in California. You can just visit when you go."

As JI got up to leave, he smiled at me and said, feigning politeness, "I'll pick you up tomorrow. Our appointment is at two o'clock. The priest wants to talk to you."

The next day, the priest said, "JI has told me all the problems that the two of you have had. I truly feel that JI becoming Catholic will be the saving grace between the two of you. You can't be serious about a divorce since I'm about to baptize him. That would ruin his religion forever. I don't think you can do anything except try this arrangement for both your sakes."

What could I say? On September 3, 1964, Jerry Ivan Allison was baptized into the Catholic Church and my sister and brother-in-law became his godparents. Once again, JI had saved the marriage, and things would continue to be his way.

♫

"Listen, we can start over now that I'm Catholic. Your mother gave me your dad's part of the estate, your five thousand dollars, and now, I have enough cash to make a down payment on that house I showed you," JI said.

"You mean that if we bought that house, you'd have room for a recording studio," I said.

He laughed. "I'm not an engineer. I need to go back over to Clovis and try to record in Norman's studio."

A few days later, we found ourselves on the road to Clovis once again. As soon as I walked into the lounge, I got that same warm, comfortable feeling I used to get whenever I was at the Norman Petty Studio—the feeling that reassured me that everything was right with the world. For the first time in a long time, I felt at peace.

Norman, Vi, and Norma Jean seemed to be as thrilled to see us as I was to see them. As always, an aspiring musician was with them. Norman introduced us to George and Barbara Tomsco, explaining that George was one of the Fireballs; he and Barbara wrote songs together. I thought it was really neat how Norman Petty had continued to record young groups and create hits.

Norman and Vi were making plans to go to New York with George and Barbara, and I think JI was as excited as I was when they invited us to go along and stay in their new apartment. So, a few days later, we made another trip to New York—this time in the car with Norman, Vi, and Speedy. George and Barbara would be traveling via airplane.

We only spent a few days at the Pettys' apartment, but we were busy the whole time; we even went to the *Johnny Carson Show* and *West Side Story*. Chita Rivera was appearing in *West Side Story*, and she and Jo Harper actually came by the apartment to give us tickets. I couldn't get over how giddy Norman was when the two of them dropped by. I'd never seen him quite so sociable before. Norman was going to produce an album with Chita; I wondered how he was *ever* going to get through it.

Carolyn Hester, one of the artists Norman had produced in Clovis and in New York, was performing at Carnegie Hall. The whole show comprised folk artists, and I loved every moment of it. I was very impressed with Carolyn. She was totally unpretentious and full of fun. She only stood about 5'3," which made her guitar look bigger than she was.

She and Buddy Holly had been friends; in fact, she was the last close friend he had lunch with before he went on the final tour. Carolyn commented that Buddy had the Ampex recorder, on which he had recorded the apartment tapes, with him that day. I wondered why he'd been carrying that heavy recorder around with him.

I loved Carolyn's apartment in Greenwich Village—it was exactly like I imagined it would be. The whole building looked like it was haunted. We entered through a dark front door and got on this really old elevator that creaked as it went up. In addition to a kitchen, a small bed and a few chairs, Carolyn's one-room apartment featured a light bulb that hung straight down with no shade on it. The apartment had a comfortable feeling to it, in contrast to the eeriness outside.

As we walked back to the Pettys' apartment on our last night in New York, a buggy with a young couple inside passed us. Oh, how I would have loved a buggy ride through Central Park with someone special. I shrugged my shoulders and continued to walk behind JI.

♪

CHAPTER TWENTY-THREE
Goodbye, Crickets! Goodbye, JI!

*I*n September 1965, with The Crickets disbanded, JI got a contract with Jerry Naylor's friend, Roger Miller, as his personal drummer. Roger's "King of the Road" career was so hot that I was surprised he didn't melt when he walked. We rented a house out in the valley in an average neighborhood, and amazingly, the person-to-person calls from Buddy Holly stopped.

I absolutely fell in love with the Millers. Roger was always very nice to me, and when we were on the road, he would make sure that JI and I traveled in the same comfort as he and his wife, Leah, did, whether that meant a Learjet or posh hotel suite. Now that JI was on call as a drummer for Roger twenty-four/seven, he'd developed so many personalities that I felt I didn't know him at all. Whenever I was around him, I had to walk on eggshells, so to speak, for fear that it wouldn't take much provocation on my part for me to be the next one in the hospital. Finally, I left JI again and went to stay with my sister who had returned to Sacramento to live.

Shortly thereafter, JI called to say that he'd be playing a dinner show with Roger at the Fairmont Hotel, which was close by, and he wanted me to come so we could spend some time together and maybe settle our differences. Feeling I had imposed on my sister and brother-in-law enough, I agreed.

The Fairmont Hotel was as old as San Francisco's first earthquake and fire, and not only was it still standing, but it had also been renovated through the years. At its grand opening, the hotel had served six-hundred pounds of turtle, thirteen thousand oysters, and five-thousand dollars worth of California and French wines. Now that's what I called a party. Even I felt like royalty walking into the lobby. JI took my arm and led me to the old part of the hotel. Our suite, which was on the same floor as the dinner shows, contained a side room that was filled with instruments.

JI said, "This was the band room. I made the other guys move to another room so I could have this one. I can get to the stage faster, and besides, I can take the back elevator straight to Roger's room if he needs anything."

"Is Leah here?" I asked.

"No, she didn't come."

We kept the conversation light and went to the bar for a cocktail. I thought JI seemed a little nervous but, maybe, it was just my imagination. When we returned to the room, he picked up his jacket off the bed and said, "I'll get back as soon as I can after the show."

"What? I don't get to go see the show?" I asked.

"No. I'd have to clear that with Roger, and I didn't have time today. He's been busy."

"Oh," I said, shocked. Roger had never had a problem with me attending shows before. It seemed strange that now JI had to consult him before I could go.

I watched TV to kill some time, and then around 8:30, figuring the show was almost over, I opened the drapes to look out. I saw a young woman walk toward the swinging doors across the way. Just about the time she reached them, they flew open, and JI walked out with his jacket on his shoulder. He put his arm around her, they kissed, and then they walked to the elevator and disappeared. Shortly afterward, the phone rang. JI said, "Hey, I'm going to be a little late."

"Oh? How come?" I asked calmly.

"Roger wants to have a meeting. I'll be back as soon as the meeting's over."

"Would you tell him I said hello and ask if I can catch the show tomorrow since it's the last one?"

"Sure, Peggeee Suee. I'll do that," he said in a happy, southern, sing-songy drawl.

I ordered a sandwich and some of the Fairmont's famous cookies, and then, I turned on the TV again. You have really changed, Peggy Sue,

I thought to myself. This time, there were no tears, no *how could you do that to me?* pain, and no shock over his disrespect for the marriage. It was around three o'clock when JI returned to the room and went to bed. I pretended to be asleep.

The next day, I asked if I was going to get to see the show, and JI replied, "Roger had rather that you didn't. There's no way he can get us a table."

I knew it was a lie; JI had probably not even been in a meeting with Roger because, if he had, Roger would've insisted on a table and thought nothing about it. JI was probably having a private party with his young woman. I held my tongue, realizing that what he did or didn't do really didn't matter any more. This marriage *would* be coming to an end—but I didn't realize how soon.

♪

We'd barely walked into the house when the phone started ringing. Buddy Knox and Glenda were about to go on tour again and wanted instructions on how to get to our house so they could visit before they left. By nighttime, the house was full of people. *Bubby* and Glenda left somewhere around midnight, and I went to bed around one. When I woke up the next morning, the house was much too hot. I heard JI talking to someone and wondered why he hadn't turned down the thermostat. I walked down the hall to do it myself and was about three steps away from the kitchen when I saw he had a woman pushed up against the refrigerator—obviously, they where having a very private moment. For a few seconds, I listened to their conversation, and then, as hard as I could, I hit the wall with my hand to unstick the thermostat. Naturally, there was a quick response. JI stepped into the hallway with a scared look on his face and asked, "What is it? What's going on, Steve?"

"Nothing's going on with me, but what do you think is your problem?"

Our *housequest* decided it was time for her to leave—in a hurry.

JI bringing his fun and games into our home had been the last straw for me. I just could *not* get my emotions under control. I was angry, and I felt it in every inch of my body. I knew that I had to be free—that I'd rather be dead than to be married to this man any longer. In life, there are moments when a person can see things crystal-clear, and for me, this was one of them. Suddenly, I understood JI. Having a wife was not on his list of personal achievements—it never had been. JI loved games, and I was the pawn that he had to win in his own game. The only problem: No one knew the rules, except him.

That night we went out to dinner, and when we came home, I went to bed early. I don't know what time JI came to bed, or if he even did. All I knew was that the game would end tomorrow. No more *charades*.

♫

I awoke around noon, and put on a cute, green dress. I was more than just nervous because I realized I didn't know how to leave. I had no car, no money, no credit cards, and no place to go. My family lived too far way, and I was too embarrassed to call them again and tell them I was leaving JI. I had done that so many times and then gone back to him that they wouldn't believe I was serious about it this time. The only way I knew to make it really happen was to announce to Jerry what my plan was. I hoped to civilly inform him that I was definitely leaving this time and civilly insist that he get me to my family. After all, he had promised my dad that if things didn't work out, he would see that I got home. JI had been somewhere with Roger Miller, and when he walked through the front door, I said, "I want to talk. I have something to say to you."

"Well, I don't have time. Can it wait?"

"No."

"Why are you wearing that dress?" he asked.

"I like this dress. What's wrong with it?" I asked calmly.

"You know that I don't like you in that color. You do that intentionally to upset me."

Oh, JI, I thought. This is part of your game, changing the subject so I won't talk about what I really want to. Well, it's not going to work this time. "This will only take a minute of your time, JI. I'm going back to Sacramento. I'll have an attorney get in touch with you. I don't want your publishing company or anything else—just my freedom."

"Why do you want a divorce?" JI asked, as if he were completely shocked.

"I'm not in love with you, and I don't want this marriage now or ever."

"Is there someone else?"

Of course, I thought. JI couldn't possibly think I wanted a divorce from him unless there was someone else. I could have said a million other things than what I did, but in my stress and desire to end this conversation, I answered in the terms I thought he'd understand. "Yes, I am. I'm in love with someone else."

Completely outraged, he rose from his chair, grabbed me, and began hitting me in the middle of my forehead with the diamond ring on his fist, over and over, until I no longer sensed pain—my whole body just felt numb. Then, he turned and jabbed his fist against the wall so hard that he broke his hand. He insisted that I take him to the emergency room, and fearful for my life, I did as he said. The doctor set his cast and gave him some more pills to add to his collection. No one said anything about *my* injuries.

From that point on, I became a prisoner in my own house. I was forbidden to answer the phone or call my sister. I fought to stay awake because I was sure he was going to kill me at any moment. I had to find a way to escape.

JI took out some of his *special weed*, as he called it, and demanded I try it. When I resisted, he said, "You and I are going to have *something* in common from here on out. And, when you learn to smoke this, we'll enjoy *something* together."

All I could think about was running as fast as I could, but my head was hurting all the time now. I'd never smoked weed before, but I knew I wouldn't be able to fight back if he attacked me again, so I put it to my lips and acted like I was trying to smoke it. Then I looked at him and asked, "How do you do that thing where you hold your breath?" and handed it back to him.

"Here." He grabbed the joint and, demonstrating, took a long, deep puff. "Just inhale and hold your breath."

I hoped that he'd eventually fall asleep from the weed and painkillers and I would be able to escape. Finally, he did.

I turned in the bed to see if he would wake up. There was no movement on his side, but I had to be cautious because I knew that if he caught me leaving this time, he *would* kill me. Quietly, I sat up on the edge of the bed, and then, I *bounced* the bed with both hands. He still didn't wake up. I reached inside my closet, pulled out a pair of pants and a shirt, and slowly and quietly, I dressed. I couldn't find my shoes, so I had to wear my fuzzy bed slippers instead. I gathered up my purse, the keys to the car, and my toy poodle Whiskey. Then I went to the garage. I put Whiskey and my purse on the car seat, locked the doors, started the car, and hit the automatic door opener. Even if he came for me now, I could still escape. I headed for the only friend I had, Leah Miller—she'd listen to me; she'd believe me.

In LA, everything is timed in minutes, not miles. Leah and Roger lived in Woodland Hills, which was only about fifteen minutes away. Her driveway curved straight up a hill and had an iron fence and gate at the top. I wondered how I was going to get in. It was three in the morning, and since Leah had a new baby, Roger Dean, to care for, I knew she'd be sleeping. I drove to the speaker, but no one answered my ring; so, I put on the emergency brake, got out of the car, climbed the six-foot fence, walked to the front door, and rang the doorbell.

Leah answered the door laughing. "What on earth are you doing? Well, so much for security. How did you get on this side of the gate?"

"I'm so sorry. I climbed your gate. I need help, and there's no one else I can ask. I hope you aren't upset with me. My dog is in your driveway, and I'd like to drive the car inside."

"Of course, you can." Leah hit the buttons and the gate opened. I ran out and drove the car in.

"Leah, I need to borrow some money. I have to get to the airport and go to Sacramento. You can tell by the way I look that this is an emergency."

"Yes, Sweetheart, I think I certainly can validate that," Leah said, smiling that beautiful smile of hers. "Don't you think you should tell me what's going on?"

"JI and I got into a disagreement...and...Oh! My God! JI has broken his hand *and* my head. Please, Leah! Just help me get home to my sister. She's moved back to Sacramento. My mother is there, too."

"You lie down right here and listen to me make the arrangements," Leah said.

"I can't leave Whiskey with JI," I said, rising up.

"Okay. Okay. Don't you worry." Then, speaking on the phone, she said, "I need one ticket to Sacramento for a young lady and another ticket for her poodle. Can you take care of this for us? Let me give you my credit card...Yes...and leaves at eleven o'clock this morning...Right. We'll be there." Then, handing the phone to me, she said, "Now give me your sister's phone number so I can call her and tell her when to meet the plane."

277

I dialed the phone and handed it back to her. "I'm Leah Miller, Peggy and JI's friend. Well, I'm a better friend to Peggy Sue. Listen, there's been a little problem here, and I'm putting Peggy on a plane. It leaves at eleven and will be in Sacramento by noon. Could you have someone meet her? She probably needs to see a doctor. Well...well...I'll let her tell you about it when you pick her up. I am sorry that I had to meet you this way. I'll call JI and get him to send her some clothes. What does she have on?" Leah smiled. "It's not quite how Peggy dresses; she's wearing her bed slippers. Whiskey is coming with her. Would you give me a call when you have her home safe and sound?"

God took care of me that night. He gave me a friend who would make all the necessary arrangements and help remove me from an unbearable situation. I knew I'd always feel indebted to Leah and Roger Miller.

By the time I arrived at my sister's house, I had a constant headache and could not bend over without losing my balance, so she took me to see my doctor, Dr. Raulf Hanson, in Carmichael. I had a concussion, broken tailbone, and bruised ribs.

Dr. Hanson said, "You'll be fine in about a month. Let me see you again in a week. If you can't quit sleeping or if any blood appears, call me at once. I'm afraid there's nothing I can do about the mark on your forehead."

"That's okay," I said. "I'll just have to watch where I'm walking next time."

♫

I was sleeping soundly when I felt someone touched my shoulder. Thinking it was my sister or mother, I stretched, slowly opened my eyes, and—JI! I bolted upright, my head throbbing from my sudden movement, and leaned against the headboard. "What are you doing here?" I asked, frightened.

Mother, standing in the doorway behind JI, said, "I let him in. He said he just wanted to look at you and see if you were really here. He promised that there would be no violence."

"Not with my hand in a cast, Mrs. Gerron," he said sweetly. "There'll be no violence." Mother left the room, and JI continued, "I had a dream that I put your body in the pool."

"Why didn't you just look in the pool? Wouldn't that have been easier than coming all this way?" I asked.

"I couldn't bear to look," he said and began to sob.

"Please don't do that. I'm here and, no thanks to you, in one piece. How did you know I was here?" I asked.

"Leah Miller called and told me."

"Oh. You can leave now," I said.

"Now, Steve, let me just talk to you for a while."

I now realized that he wasn't calling me *Steve* just as his term of endearment, or just when he was in a good mood, but he used it every time he was being manipulative, too. I said, "No, JI. No more games. I want you to leave this house now. If you want to talk to me, try the phone."

"Okay." He was no longer teary; his face had immediately changed into that hard, set look I'd come to know only too well. "I'll leave for now, but you *will* come back, and I *will* be calling."

As soon as he left, I set up an appointment with the family attorney. Johnnie accompanied me to the offices of Skirving and Thompson, and I filed for divorce. Mr. Thompson said that California was a community property state, and I could have my share of The Crickets' name, appearances, and record royalties, as well as the spouse's portion of Cricket Music Inc. and Zygote Music, which were song and music publishing companies. However, I wanted out of the marriage so badly that, in the negotiations, I gave JI everything he asked for, losing my claim to all of it. That and the restraining order the lawyer filed still didn't keep JI from making harassing phone calls at all times of the night though.

Finally, on August 8, 1967, I received a letter from my attorney stating:

> Re: Allison v. Allison
> The above matter has been set for hearing on August 23,
> (Wednesday) at 9:00 am in Department 6. Your witness
> will have to appear with you at this time.
> Sincerely yours,
> James B. Thompson

The day of court, Mr. Thompson met my sister, who was serving as my witness, and me in the hallway in front of Room 6. He smiled and said, "I've been in the judge's chambers, and he recommends that your case be the last one this morning so there won't be anyone else in the courtroom. He's adding extra security, too, just as a precaution since Mr. Allison has made threats."

Although I expected them to dash through the door at any moment, neither JI nor his attorney showed up to contest the divorce. I was called to the witness stand and sworn in; the judge leaned forward and asked, "Mrs. Allison, are you sure you want this divorce, and can you show cause why this divorce *should* be granted?"

"Yes, Sir," I answered, my chin quivering, my cold hands shaking, and my eyes still glancing toward the door every time I heard the slightest noise.

I guess the judge took pity on me because he didn't ask any details; instead, he said, "I'll have your witness come up at this time." Once Johnnie was sworn in, he asked her if she had seen cause why this divorce should be granted.

Johnnie didn't mince words. "Yes, Sir. She has come home to me at least once a year mentally abused. This time, it was physical, too. She had a concussion and broken tail bone."

"When was the last time you talked to Mr. Allison?" the judge asked.

"A couple of days ago. He said he *wanted* her to get the divorce—that he had things to do, places to go, and people to see. But, he would be back in about a year to get her."

The judge raised his mallet and exclaimed, "Divorce granted."

Johnnie gave me a smile that said it all—it's finished, Peggy Sue. We hugged, and with my arm around Johnnie's waist, Mr. Thompson, Johnnie, and I exited the courtroom. I glanced over my shoulder as I heard the heavy door closing behind us and noticed it didn't completely shut. My body quivered. I knew I hadn't heard the last from Jerry Ivan Allison, and that one day, I'd have to confront my fear of him—but not today. I was happier today than I had been on my wedding day. Today was a day for celebration.

♫

Epilogue

*I*n 1967, the divorce was final, and JI Allison and I verbally agreed that we would stay out of each other's world. He claimed our mutual friends; I was to have nothing to do with any of them. He was to leave "Peggy Sue" as Buddy Holly's hit song, not say The Crickets had anything to do with its creation, and not use my name.

Then, in 1975, JI contacted me about a movie he was producing. He wanted me to sign a contract giving my written permission for him to use my name, one time in one film. When I received the contract from his Hollywood lawyer, the contract was for all rights, personal image, and personality of Peggy Sue—nowhere did it indicate a one time use. As written, JI would have owned and controlled my name, image, and any marketing of my name forever. Along with the contract was a check for one hundred dollars.

Of course, I was extremely shocked by JI's proposal. To validate the way I felt, I called Norman Petty and told him my concerns. Norman told me to ask for a copy of the script, and if it wasn't up to my standards, not to sign it. I did just that, and I didn't sign the contract. The movie was never made.

In 1977, *The Buddy Holly Story* came out and my phone began to ring for interviews. I ignored the offers and continued not to get involved in the politics of Maria Elena Santiago Rodriguez Diaz and JI Allison, even though I was appalled at some of the misinformation that movie spawned. For example, I heard, for the first time, that "Peggy Sue" had originally been titled "Cindy Lou," and that the name was changed so Jerry Allison could use it to gain my favor. How unusual for the story to suddenly appear after twenty years! Kenneth Broad went back to the master tapes and found absolutely nothing with "Cindy Lou" on it. If The Crickets had been recording the song using the words "Cindy Lou" and then changed it, Norman, surely, would have kept it on tape, as he kept everything.

Then, in the middle '80s, Dick Clark Productions called my home and asked me for a favor. Mr. Clark was producing a new TV series, and if I would come on his show and sit in the audience, he would introduce me and show a short clip of Buddy Holly on the *Ed Sullivan Show* in the '50s. I agreed because I believed Buddy Holly deserved to be officially recognized in American music history. Immediately after doing Dick's program, my phone was constantly ringing with requests for interviews—*Rockin' 50s Magazine, Esquire Magazine*, the *Oprah Winfrey Show, Geraldo, People* magazine, and the BBC were among them.

Then, *Buddy - The Buddy Holly Story*, better known by most as "the Buddy play," came out. This time, not only was my name used, but my image, too, and never once did anybody in control ask my permission.

Since the movie and the play, I have continued to get requests to make appearances at special events and do radio and TV interviews. The fans taught me that I could not walk away from who I was and that I had to acknowledge my part in rock 'n' roll history.

I returned to Lubbock to spend quality time with my mother in 1995, and much to my surprise, I found that Lubbock did nothing in honor of Buddy Holly. I began working toward building a Buddy Holly museum and organizing a festival to celebrate his birth.

The Buddy Holly Center is a reality today, but disputes between the City of Lubbock and Maria Elena over how much money she should receive for the use of Buddy's name and image in the festival have killed the event for all his fans.

In 1995, I was asked to write a monthly column in *Lubbock Magazine*, and I have been writing ever since. The only thing this mother of two and grandmother of seven loves better than writing is talk radio.

When I came back to Lubbock, I took out the old journal of 147 entries that I had kept in my youth, put them on the computer, and started this book. Several times during the wee hours of the morning as I was writing, I remembered a sign someone had chalked on an overpass—Buddy Holly lives; I already knew that, but that's another book. Once when Bob Dylan won a big music award, he said, "Thank you, but I wasn't in the studio alone. Buddy Holly was there with me." I truly understand what he meant, and I was never alone writing this book either.

I have enjoyed sharing a short ten years of my life with my readers and feel privileged to have known the people that played a major role in helping Peggy Sue grow up.

♪